GYPSIES AND TRAVELLERS IN HOUSING

The decline of nomadism

David M Smith and Margaret Greenfields

3-17-14
ww
$110.00

First published in Great Britain in 2013 by

Policy Press
University of Bristol
6th Floor
Howard House
Queen's Avenue
Clifton
Bristol BS8 1SD
UK
Tel +44 (0)117 331 4054
Fax +44 (0)117 331 4093
e-mail tpp-info@bristol.ac.uk
www.policypress.co.uk

North American office:
Policy Press
c/o The University of Chicago Press
1427 East 60th Street
Chicago, IL 60637, USA
t: +1 773 702 7700
f: +1 773-702-9756
e:sales@press.uchicago.edu
www.press.uchicago.edu

© Policy Press 2013

British Library Cataloguing in Publication Data
A catalogue record for this book is available from the British Library

Library of Congress Cataloging-in-Publication Data
A catalog record for this book has been requested

ISBN 978 1 84742 873 8 hardcover

The right of David M Smith and Margaret Greenfields to be identified as authors
of this work has been asserted by them in accordance with the 1988 Copyright,
Designs and Patents Act.

Cover design by Policy Press
Front cover: image kindly supplied by www.alamy.com
Printed and bound in Great Britain by Hobbs, Southampton
The Policy Press uses environmentally responsible print partners

FSC
www.fsc.org
MIX
Paper from
responsible sources
FSC® C020438

Contents

List of tables

Acknowledgements

Many people have provided assistance during the research on which this book is based and during the writing of the book itself. First we would like to thank Judith Okely to whom we are extremely grateful for both kindly reading a draft version of the manuscript and for writing the foreword. We are particularly indebted to Joe Jones of the Gypsy Council and Professor Ken Lee formerly of Newcastle University Australia; the staff, volunteers and Committee members of both the Irish Traveller Movement Britain and also Friends, Families and Travellers, our colleagues and friends with whom we worked on several GTAAs which we have data mined to underpin our findings; and Thomas Acton for his support and valuable work with the Gypsy community over many years. We especially want to thank Angie and Charlie Jones for sharing their vital advice and knowledge of the Gypsy and Traveller communities. Without their cooperation and know-how (and community interviewers in other study locales) this research would not have been as complete or complex. We are also grateful to Jackie McPeak for her invaluable practical assistance in formatting and tidying up the draft version of this book and to the librarians at the Gypsy Lore Society archives at the University of Liverpool for their patience with frequent requests to retrieve the archival material that formed the basis of Chapter Three.

Our biggest thanks, however, go to the Gypsies and Travellers in all of the study areas who generously gave their time to share their experiences with us, and without whom there would have been no book, as it is their testimonies that form the most important element of this moving study of a community forcibly sedentarised.

We hope that we have neither missed out anyone from this list who should have been thanked, not misinterpreted any interviewee's words, emotions or experiences in any way. Any errors are ours alone and we greatly welcome comments from Gypsies and Travellers on this text – either to confirm or to challenge our findings.

David adds:

Special thanks are due to John Macnicol for his sound advice and continuing support and also to Lynda Saunders of Canterbury Christ Church University and Allan McNaught Further thanks are due to Ann Marie Ruston for providing my role on the SECC Gypsy health project. I would like to thank my co-author Margaret for completing her portion of the workload in the face of considerable difficulties and to my parents for their recollections of the Gypsy communities in south London and their interesting and informed insights into the issues discussed in this book. I also thank my daughters Anna and Becky for their love and support, but the biggest thanks of all go to Rowena for her patience, tolerance and understanding.

Margaret writes:

First and foremost I want to dedicate this text to, and acknowledge the influence on my life and work of, my greatly loved and missed father Alexander Robert Peter Greenfields (21/6/1919–21/9/2012) and my ever-supportive and hugely admired mother Barbara. I have greatly appreciated, and want to acknowledge the love, tolerance, support and kindness of my children Zack and Madeleine. I want too to thank my hugely supportive line-manager Crystal Oldman – who has repeatedly 'oiled the wheels' to enable me to juggle family and work commitments whilst undertaking this project, and my many kind friends, colleagues, relatives and community members who have supported, cajoled, suggested and proffered contacts or resources, phoned me up, fed me or just 'been there' – you know who you are. Frank Blackmore – extended family by default after all these years, general gofer and person who periodically insists I stop work to listen to a CD, have a coffee or get some sleep – and finally – thank you David, I know at times you really had to struggle to believe we'd get this book completed.

Foreword

This in-depth study of the historic and mainly contemporary circumstances for traditionally nomadic Gypsies and Travellers is timely and deeply shocking. The authors, both social scientists with long-term relevant lived and research experience, combine a broad policy overview with the minutiae of everyday lives from the Gypsy/Traveller perspectives. We are introduced to the cumulative consequences of explicitly negative legislation, alongside deceptively banal micro controls. All of these have the effect of restricting, indeed criminalising, the preferred lifestyles of a people who have survived as nomads hitherto for centuries. Here the late 20th-century history of Gypsies and Travellers in Britain contrasts with the earlier brutally enforced settlement of Gypsies/Roma in communist Europe. A museum near Krakow in Poland documents the seizure from Gypsies of their horses and wagons in 1968, before their compulsory settlement in concrete Soviet-style flats. Is this the fate for British Gypsies who, as the text reveals, are being settled but sometimes by a less visible, seemingly gentle force? Only the multi-million pound eviction of Dale Farm, Essex, in 2011 made a rare media intrusion (Okely, 2011).

While there is welcome increased sensitivity in the UK to racism directed at those of African and Asian descent, the reader of this text is confronted by the casual indifference and arrogant ignorance of any additional racisms towards Gypsies and Travellers. Recent populist internet comments declare it is not racist to lambast fellow 'white Anglo-Saxons'. It is only recently that Traveller groups with no claim to Indian origin have finally gained recognition as ethnic groups, for example the Northern Irish then Scottish Travellers, (cf McVeigh, 1997; Clark, 2008). Thus it is finally accepted that separate ethnic groups need not require exotic orientalisation and non-European origins before rights of autonomy are legally respected (Said, 1978). Smith and Greenfields draw attention to the observations of Trevor Phillips. Supposedly liberal-minded journalists show neither curiosity nor shame concerning entrenched presumptions about so-called 'indigenous drop-outs'.

Thanks partly to policy practitioners, with neither curiosity nor respect for different though interrelated trading histories, Gypsies and Travellers are lumped together with an increasingly fragmented white working-class, themselves the victims of deindustrialisation and economic disaster. Local officials conveniently redefine caravan dwellers denied legal stopping places as homeless, then in seemingly benevolent tradition place them on 'sink estates' where imagined commonalities with the non-Gypsy poor are presumed to minimise conflict. In fact many newly settled residents live in fear of being 'outed' as Gypsies. Such forced co-residence is very different from earlier inter-relations of difference. The ever speeded-up current policies of sedentarisation, so grimly outlined, are very different from the intriguing historical examples of reciprocal social and economic relations between Gypsies and Gorjers (non-Gypsies) – all painstakingly retraced by the authors from local records of both North and South London.

Despite decades of academic scrutiny and intellectual curiosities in extensive publications throughout Europe, it seems that in the hegemonic and media domain there is no such interest in the centuries of Gypsies' nomadic culture and economy. The past is negated where, instead, instant soundbites have media priority. We need to be reminded of the shameless and unrelenting anti-Gypsyism which this detailed study can counter. Here are some examples exposing the context in which serious researchers and anti-racist activists have to work. In 2011 the proposed multi-million pound government-funded eviction of Dale Farm in Essex finally alerted slumbering journalists into knee-jerk panic. It was in any case a deliberate and early political strategy by the Coalition government and the newly appointed Minister for Communities, Eric Pickles, whose policies of site closure replaced those of the former Labour Deputy Prime Minister John Prestcott.

As Smith and Greenfields are fully aware, there are guaranteed political votes in an anti-Gypsy stance. There are no votes in a pro-Gypsy stance whether the politician is representing Labour, Conservative or Liberal Democrat parties. The authors' citation of the former Labour minister Jack Straw's comments are painful evidence. Fortunately for the minister, the most provocative assertions in a local radio station interview are excluded (Straw, 1999). During the 2005 General Election campaign, the then leader of the Conservative party Michael Howard, authorised full-page adverts in national newspapers singling out Travellers as law breakers:

> I BELIEVE IN FAIR PLAY
>
> THE SAME RULES SHOULD APPLY TO EVERYONE
>
> I DON'T BELIEVE IN SPECIAL RULES FOR SPECIAL INTEREST GROUPS.
>
> WE ARE ALL BRITISH. WE ARE ONE NATION

TOO MANY PEOPLE TODAY SEEM TO THINK THEY
DON'T HAVE TO PLAY BY THE RULES-AND THEY'RE
USING SO-CALLED HUMAN RIGHTS TO GET AWAY
WITH DOING THE WRONG THING.

IF YOU WANT TO BUILD A NEW HOME YOU HAVE TO
GET PLANNING PERMISSION FIRST. BUT IF YOU ARE
A TRAVELLER YOU CAN BEND THE PLANNING LAW-
BUILDING WHERE YOU LIKE THANKS TO THE HUMAN
RIGHTS ACT

IT'S NOT FAIR THAT THERE'S ONE RULE FOR
TRAVELLERS AND ANOTHER FOR EVERYONE ELSE

(Howard, 2005)

Yet it was Howard who had steered the 1994 Criminal Justice Act
through Parliament inviting Gypsies and Travellers to buy their own
land. It was predictable that over 90 per cent of such sites purchased
by Gypsies would be refused planning permission. Prescott's attempt
to enforce site provision under the radar was repeatedly vulnerable to
media demonisation. At the 2010 General Election, the Conservative
North Essex MP Bernard Jenkin's official publicity leaflet also highlights
the Gypsy minority, lumping them together with mechanical intrusions:
'This is a precious corner of England. Our countryside is precious....
Pollution, Stanstead Airport expansion, wind farms, traffic, phone
masts, gypsy sites: local people should be able to decide these issues.'
(Jenkin, 2010)

As decades of policies confirm, Gypsy sites are largely accepted
only when provision was a legal obligation imposed by the national
government. Leaving decisions to the local and most vocal electorate
will always privilege the powerful and exclude vulnerable minorities,
especially nomads.

The media ignorance continues even among those presumed
informed. A celebrated presenter on Channel 4 News, respected for in-
depth investigation repeated the tabloid clichés. Interviewing a Traveller
woman he asked why she insisted on that title if she no longer travelled.
Yet, he would be considered racist if this white man asked a woman of
black African descent why she called herself African after years of UK
residence and citizenship. Paradoxically, when I lived on camps in the
1970s the Gypsies, if interrogated by hostile officials, believed it safer to
present themselves as Travellers because they had learned this was then
less stigmatised compared to the iconic Gypsy. It is a commonplace
that the self-selected label a people adopts changes through time. Once

Irish and Scottish Travellers were called Tinkers, or Tinklers, drawing on their skilled tinsmithery (McCormick, 1907). But, with increasing stigmatisation by outsiders, that historic skilled connection was dropped. Shockingly, alleged anti-racist British journalists have no interest in pursuing these concerns when confronted by centuries-established migrants or nomads. The same transformations should be recalled for the US label 'negro', once proudly used by even Martin Luther King and now changed from 'Black' to African–American.

This book's opening chapters document the state's varying policies from the 16th century up to those of the 2010 UK Coalition Government. Alongside the changing but continuing attempts to outlaw nomadism, the authors' dedicated exploration, through varied sources, reveals the brilliant, determined strategies of travelling families. Innovative economic opportunities are, as ever, seized upon. Regrettably, in the mainstream polity, the Gypsies' crucial economic contribution, as geographically mobile self-employed clusters, are rarely recognised. Gypsy/Travellers have adapted to every nuance and change in the dominant sedentarised, once wage labour economy, supplying occasional goods and services exploiting necessary geographical mobility. Crucial documents cited in this text reveal how Gypsies have regularly lived alongside house-dwellers, traded with them and shared agricultural activities such as hop picking in Kent. Much of this vital evidence has been deleted from national memory.

The Gypsies' central role in seasonal fruit and vegetable harvesting was officially recognised in the immediate post-World War Two period. The law decreed that Gypsies were freed from any obligation to send their children to school in the summer term as it was appreciated that they would be accompanying their parents for residence on farms (MHLG, 1967). Conveniently, the Gypsies brought their own accommodation and left when the work was done. All this contrasts with the crumbling sheds and plastic sheeting where foreign, often undocumented, migrants now shelter for the season. They are often under the orders of gang masters who siphon off payment so that even the minimum wage is not paid to the individual worker.

Smith and Greenfields document the tragic consequences of loss of work opportunities among the forcibly housed Gypsies whom we learn are now in the majority. While Conservative Government ministers and the tabloid press might all too soon label such families 'skivers' rather than 'strivers', again there is no awareness of the multiple economic occupations embraced by Gypsies and Travellers through decades, indeed centuries. Long before scrap metal recycling was fashionably green and global demand rocketed, Gypsies played a major role in this. They collected old cars, batteries and so on, subdivided items by category, all in a labour-intensive operation for delivery to specialist yards. The Gypsies' economic niche both in scrap metal and other activities such as seasonal agriculture, building repairs and antique dealing depended on a multiplicity of occupations exploiting self-employment and of course geographical mobility. Thus enforced sedentarisation is a massive impediment for the occupations in which Gypsy/Travellers have been skilled and self-educated through generations.

It is also paradoxical that while the Prime Minister, David Cameron in 2013 has proposed start-up funding for small businesses, the Gypsies have been denigrated for registering as self-employed entrepreneurs allegedly to avoid tax. At the other end of the political spectrum, through decades, some self-defined radicals have insisted that Gypsies should 'join the proletariat', thus denigrating their historic initiative while presuming factory jobs were plentiful and ethnocentrically excluding Gypsies from alternative ambitions as fellow academics. Indeed it has been my joy to supervise the PhD of a Scottish Traveller (Clark, 2001) and a Master's dissertation by a Bulgarian Roma (Okely, 2011, p 25).

Again through multiple poignant examples, Greenfields and Smith challenge the tired myth that Gypsies have for centuries survived in 'primordial' isolation, thus shamelessly ignoring the fact that their economy is interdependent with the dominant society. The Gypsies have always had to 'know the enemy'. The opening shot to every episode of the outrageous Channel 4 '*My Big Fat Gypsy Wedding*' series showed a horse-drawn wagon with an authoritative voice declaring that Gypsies had finally to be 'dragged' into the 21st century. The filmmakers were fully aware that the image was of Gypsies bringing out a 'traditional' wagon just for an annual horse fair. Meanwhile, the Gypsy wagon has been appropriated by the rich and famous, far from these alleged primevals. Multi-millionaires such as the Bee Gees' Robin Gibb and the Rolling Stones' Ronnie Wood each once displayed a highly decorated 'Gypsy wagon' on their extensive country estates. No one would suggest this was proof of primitive isolation.

Simultaneously, the media claims that the 'real Gypsies' with horses and wagons were always welcome. But, as Anthony Howarth has argued (2012), recent New Travellers, self defined as 'Horse Drawns' and with no Gypsy ethnic links, have taken to the road with horses and wagons all decorated with mystical New Age imagery. They recognise all too well that the non-Gypsy public celebrate their roadside presence partly because of the English love of horses. Such animals, unlike humans, cannot be forced to suffer. Horses must be allowed to graze but motorised Gypsies cannot evoke sympathy.

The Gypsy/Travellers have both historic urban and rural connections, as this book's case studies and archival examples vividly reveal. One Gypsy man poignantly describes his rural 'roots'; something he regrets losing now that, against his will, he is settled in urban 'bricks and mortar'. The text reaffirms the Gypsies' major contribution to agriculture before it was run down in the late 20th century. In the 1970s, my site neighbours had regularly picked fruit in Woodbridge. I joined a Gypsy potato-picking gang 10 miles from our camp, north of London.

Again, the media 'experts' show a limited knowledge span. Another celebrity broadcaster, and 'business expert', devoted a one-off documentary in 2012 to the 'puzzling' absence of local East Anglian house-dweller workers for the seasonal fruit and vegetable harvesting. The overwhelming use of individual foreign migrants he explained by individual psychology, namely local residents' 'laziness' and welfare dependency. No awareness was shown of the fact that this work was once mainly done by Gypsies. Through the years the once readily available workers have been compelled to abandon this, thanks to seasonal travel restrictions, enforced without forethought. Gypsy/Travellers learned that any short-term movement away from sites risked losing their regular base on return, again a direct consequence of sedentarist government policy. In the early 1970s, I recall the official presumption well documented by the Ministry report (MHLG, 1967) that Gypsies would 'naturally' be seduced into housing and wage labour jobs. Sites were seen as merely a temporary phase. Inevitably, the restrictions which jeopardised seasonal rural employment opened up the demand for cheap, sometimes trafficked, foreign labour.

Regrettably, such is the power of media celebrities that even when critical information from academics about these issues is sought it is carefully controlled. I was invited to discuss the Dale Farm eviction on the Radio 4 *Today* programme. A chauffeur-driven car would collect me at 7 am. But before ringing off, I naively asked the names of the next day's presenters. One, I learned, had been responsible for the East Anglia documentary which I briefly critiqued. Ten minutes later, I was telephoned back and bluntly informed that my presence would no longer be required. While the shortage of female presenters on *Today* was once justified by a BBC manager because the programme apparently demands 'high testosterone', seemingly a pro-Gypsy female professor is too threatening.

The most devastating chapters by Greenfields and Smith are those based on original empirical research. Here are fully exposed the individual narratives of enforced settlement. The authors draw on impressive focus groups, namely in South West and South East England, where the discussants are willing to express their views and experiences in a rare shared trust. This is thanks to the long-term shared empathetic knowledge of the author researchers. Such qualitative material is complemented and contextualised by quantitative data; all reliably collected and analysed. This pioneering combination is in sharp contrast to earlier policy driven questionnaires conducted by officials invariably perceived by the interviewees as hostile interrogators. The 1960s government Census, for example, naively asked nomadic Gypsies, 'Why do you travel?' (MHLG, 1967), as if the core to a taken-for-granted lifestyle could be given a simplistic one-off answer to outsiders. Proof of this embedded complexity may be understood by non-Gypsy readers if considering the difficulty I faced when the Gypsy children would ask me, 'What's it like living in a house?'. I struggled to answer, with inept descriptions of ceilings, walls and fixed floors. It never occurred to me to attempt to describe staircases and upper floors. All this was later to prove unnerving, indeed hazardous, to the newly housed families in the examples which this text provides years later. It is distressing to learn about children, way beyond toddler age, repeatedly falling and being injured when attempting stairs. They would risk mockery at school.

Given the reliability of Smith and Greenfield's multi-faceted data, it is all the more disturbing to learn that the majority, not a mere minority, of the once nomadic Gypsy/Traveller population are now sedentarised. This is largely *against* their repeatedly stated preference for caravan and shared site residence. There is again a contrast with the empirical data of the 1960s and 1970s when too often the numbers of caravan dwelling Gypsies were undercounted. This was partly a deliberate strategy among local officials with a vested interest in reducing the numbers for which their council would have to provide. Privileged access to the Census returns in my field area confirmed this strategic exclusion. Another contrast with today was the evidence in the 1970s, albeit scattered, that only a minority of Gypsy individuals and families were housed. I would occasionally be shown the houses of frail, aged persons who were regularly visited by kin. Then there were individual persons of Gypsy descent, often women, who had married a gorger. Others sometimes chose housing merely as a temporary measure. In all cases, there were examples of such persons suddenly acquiring a caravan and returning to the road (Okely, 1983).

From this text an accumulated and indisputable depiction of 'culture shock' emerges. We are confronted with the original meaning of a term which has become over familiar, thereby losing its real violence. Nevertheless, social anthropologists, when first embarking on fieldwork beyond their *own* familiar, might be able to empathise with the dramatic change confronted by suddenly housed Gypsies (Okely, 2012). The challenge is for fellow citizens of the same nation and geographical locality to comprehend differences in lifestyles and found in what Malinowski described as 'the imponderabilia of everyday life' (1922, cf Okely, 2012). Ethnocentricity should be confronted within the *same* geographical but potentially culturally alien space.

The dominant sedentary politico-hegemony presumes that moving into 'bricks and mortar' is comforting and privileged rather than total alienation from nomads' alternative lived experience. Preceding the Dale Farm eviction, the Conservative minister Eric Pickles denied any potentially harrowing social consequences of the destruction of the Travellers' mobile homes and paved exteriors by announcing that every Traveller family had been offered housing, all at public expense. Thus their 'rights' were allegedly respected. To the mass media *vox pop,* the Travellers' rejection of this perceived generosity and apparent opportunity for welfare scrounging was incomprehensible. Scant attention was given to the rare Traveller statements leaked to the public that the site residents wished to continue to live alongside their kin and allies rather than in scattered locations, let alone in 'bricks and mortar'.

The chapters giving the Gypsy/Traveller perspectives on highly specific culture shock reveal alienation, unemployment and isolation then leading to depression and ever greater mental health problems (cf Bunnin, 2010). As noted above, the media and other observers show no curiosity as to this culturally specific claustrophobia. Greenfields and Smith offer clear and convincing suggestions as to how both national and local officials could be made sensitive to the risks, indeed the long-term damage, of enforced sedentarisation. The authors give glimpses of Gypsy/Travellers' repeated attempts to preserve and reinvigorate kinship networks and ethnic solidarity – always integral to shared lives on traditional encampments. Decades ago, I noted the preferred circular spacing of Gypsy camps. Children could play in safety under watchful neighbourly, not just parental, gaze. Residents were self-selected, thus enforcing community cooperation. Any random conflict was resolved by the offending family's departure (Okely, 2007). Little of this was then recognised by non-Gypsy officials with power to dictate tenancies on council-run sites, hence the added attraction of owner-occupied land. By contrast today there is even greater confusion and loss when individual families are not only confined to bricks and mortar but also scattered in randomly vacant houses where kinship and other supportive links are officially deemed irrelevant. I recall a council warden even denigrating the Gypsies' classic kinship structures, recognised as crucial around the world by anthropologists, as mere nepotism.

Further insights into the consequences of scattered, now isolated families trapped in alien housing reveal the increasing pressure on married couples. Whereas women had shared living and companionship on sites, whether or not husbands were absent at work, now lone wives may have increased domestic pressures and hitherto unknown expectations. Additionally, I recorded the external hawking and fortune-telling opportunities for women through the 1970s and beyond (Okely, 1996). In this updated study, men with or without self-employment in limited localities, are also facing new pressures, if not despair. Domestic conflict, alcoholism and novel readily available drugs on sink estates open new dark places. The women, now semi-incarcerated, are vulnerable to more surveillance of their children's school attendance.

All this is a harrowing contrast with my experience of living on Gypsy sites in the 1970s, also within the radius of London. Then the threat or indeed enactment of maverick domestic violence was always minimised by the controlling gaze of the surrounding site community. Women had immediate allies just a few yards or caravans away. Ever-present kinship and affinal loyalties provided immediate protection, and often from beyond the specific camp. Nuclear families were not isolates. Tragically, due to increasing marital breakdown, this research suggests the increasing vulnerability of women as newly created single mothers. Yet during my 1970s fieldwork, few if any women, even after marital separation, were abandoned to a lonely fate. In a close knit community with multiple networks, new partnerships were formed. Children accompanied their biological mother and were adopted by the new social father.

A few decades ago, legislation decreed it a *duty* for councils to provide Gypsy sites. Despite the 1968 Caravan Sites Act's many limitations and flaws, that era now seems a lost Utopia. The then Labour government even commissioned an independent report by John Cripps into the progress of the legislation. Cripps generously acknowledged the major influence of our recently published project on Gypsies and government policy (Adams et al, 1975). And the minister Peter Shore endorsed Cripps' findings with the groundbreaking declaration:

> Whatever the previous policies, the Secretaries of State now accept the gypsy's right to a nomadic existence for so long

as he wishes to continue it. There is no intention to put pressure on him to settle or assimilate unless he wishes to do so. (Cripps, 1977, p 1, and Planning Circular 28/1977)

Today, the subsequent yet casual reversal of this ministerial commitment is an utter betrayal. Although Margaret Thatcher was shortly to be elected in 1979, site provision was not reversed until the John Major Government and one stray clause in the 1994 Criminal Justice Act. Nevertheless, as noted above, Gypsies were encouraged to buy their own land. Although the 1997 Labour Government quietly encouraged site provision without explicit reversal of the 1994 Act, all hope was dashed by the 2010 Coalition Government. Here again is a strange reversal of policy by the now Deputy Prime Minister, Nick Clegg. During the 2005 election campaign, as prospective Liberal Democrat parliamentary candidate for Sheffield Hallam, he slated the leader of the Conservative party Michael Howard for his anti-Gypsy electioneering:

> Yesterday I was called by one of the local Sheffield newspapers to comment on Michael Howard's latest tirade against Gypsies and Travellers. Why should we believe anything he has to say on the issue, I asked, given that it was Michael Howard himself, when home secretary, who curtailed the ability of local authorities to deal sensibly with Travellers' sites? How can this be regarded as anything but cheap electioneering when we know that a few months ago Conservative MPs had entered into a cross-party agreement on the issue, only to break that agreement for the sake of a favourable *Daily Mail* headline now?

> This is callous, cowardly politics. When Michael Howard appeared on the TV news inspecting a Travellers' site in Essex earlier this week he stood scowling behind a large metal fence separating him from the Travellers, as if he were dealing with zoo animals rather than human beings. (Clegg, 2005.

One wonders if Clegg, like his broken tuition fees pledge, might also say sorry for his collusion with the government 'curtailing' site provision, and worse.

The authors have convincingly called for great cultural sensitivity among practitioners. I would add the urgent need for a reconsideration of the catastrophic reversal of the original 1977 commitment by the

Secretaries of State. The enforced sedentarisation of Gypsies and Travellers is not only politically unjust but also in these desperate times, economically counter-productive. While we learn from this meticulous study that the vast majority are placed in privately rented or social housing, Gypsies and Travellers have for centuries in England and beyond provided their own accommodation with minimum running costs.

The ever-growing restrictions on movement bring economic loss and in some instances the exploitation of foreign migrants. Smith and Greenfields confirm the massive welfare costs of newly enforced unemployment among the younger generations. Again, in contrast to the multiple skills recorded and celebrated decades ago (Okely, 1983), we read of a disengaged Gypsy youth. While outsiders patronisingly emphasised the Gypsy children's lack of schooling, I was ever impressed by their ingenuity, brilliance and political sophistication. Gypsy children, I have argued, were always *educated*, though not necessarily *schooled* (Okely, 1997). Today we are informed of the Gypsy youths' spatial entrapment, in a cultural vacuum without even those proletarian jobs that were once so arrogantly decreed for them. However, there are moving glimpses of attempts to nurture cultural identity.

Newly created homeless families now become financial 'burdens' for rent and social support where formerly autonomous clusters and mobile family units provided their own shelter. Some Gypsy/Travellers, with the rare good fortune of legally recognised sites, have upgraded to smart chalets with modern facilities. Again these are an obvious alternative to the more costly and unwanted bricks and mortar allotted to them. Such site layout also leaves a flexible boundary between domestic and immediate outside space. There is room for an autonomous zone for external fires, dogs and the beloved horses. Such open-ended spaces were rarely guaranteed in social housing, thereby adding to the loss and cultural confusion. In this era of massive state cuts, it is both racist and financial madness to enforce the sedentarisation of such long-established nomads. This is ethnocentricism, disguised as benign universalism.

In her foreword to an all-embracing study of post-war equality and inequality in the UK, Julia Neuberger declares:

> Of all the categories of discrimination discussed in this volume the one that is the most heart-rending is about Gypsies and Travellers, for whom the picture has barely brightened since 1945, and for whom tolerance is little greater than it was and local authority provision even worse.' (2010, p x)

It is all the more regrettable that in my own foreword to this book I acknowledge that Smith and Greenfields provide even *more* detailed and generalised evidence of discrimination, and explicitly enforced, not accidental, settlement of Gypsies and Travellers. While most states hate nomads, this study also confirms centuries of cohabitation and mutual economic exchange. There is also reciprocity of imagination when a sedentarised majority are confronted by the creativity of difference. Poets such as John Keats and Matthew Arnold, the Oxford professor of poetry, classic novelists, including George Eliot and Jane Austen, and painters such as Alfred Munnings, Augustus John and Laura Knight have all been inspired by Gypsies. John Constable repainted his 1802 *Vale of Dedham* this time foregrounding a Gypsy woman, baby and bender tent (1828). Commentators concede that Gypsies also frequented that now iconicised 'true English landscape'. Simultaneously, Gypsies have been photographed, sketched or painted in the metropolis. As nomads through centuries, they are part of our heritage. Regrettably, the wondrous 2012 Olympic opening ceremony, which celebrated so many variegated histories, excluded the Gypsies. They also are inhabitants of William Blake's 'green and pleasant land' and creative partners co-forging a nation's industrial and technical transformations.

Judith Okely
Emeritus Professor, University of Hull

References

Adams, B., Okely, J., Morgan, D. and Smith, D. (1975) *Gypsies and government policy in England*, London: Heinemann Educational Press.

Bunnin, A. (2010) 'Health and social care needs in Gypsies and Travellers in West Sussex', Report to NHS West Sussex and West Sussex County Council Office for Public Management.

Channel 4 (2012) *My Big Fat Gypsy Wedding*, film series.

Clark, C. (2001) '"Invisible lives": The Gypsies and Travellers of Britain', PhD dissertation, University of Edinburgh.

Clark, C. (2008) Expert Witness Statement (ethnic status of Scottish Gypsy/Travellers), provided in the case of *K. MacLennan v Gypsy Traveller Education and Information Project S/13272/07 f599/132.*

Clegg, N. (2005) 'Boomeranging: The savagely populist campaign designed for Michael Howard by his Australian adviser may backfire', Guardian.co.uk, 24 March.

Constable, J. (1828) The Vale of Dedham, National Gallery of Scotland.

Cripps, J. (1977) *Accommodation for Gypsies: A report on the working of the Caravan Sites Act 1968*, Department of the Environment, HMSO.

Howard, M. (2005) *The Independent on Sunday*, 20 March.

Howarth, A. (2012) 'The Horse Drawns', Dissertation for MA in Social Anthropology, Bristol University.

Jenkin, B. (2010) 'Vote Bernard Jenkin for Harwich & North Essex', East Gores Farm, Salmons Lane, Colchester.

Malinowski, B. (1922) *The Argonauts of the Western Pacific*, London: Routledge and Kegan Paul.

McCormick, A. (1907) *The Tinkler-Gypsies*, Edinburgh: Dumfries.

Ministry of Housing and Local Government (1967) *Gypsies and other Travellers*, London: HMSO.

Neuberger, J. (2010) 'Foreword' in P. Thane (ed), *Unequal Britain: Equalities in Britain since 1945*, London: Continuum.

Okely, J. (1996) 'Fortune tellers: Fakes or therapists' in J. Okely, *Own or other culture*, London: Routledge, pp 94-114.

Okely, J. (1997), 'Non-territorial culture as the rationale for the assimilation of Gypsy children' in *Childhood,* vol 4, no 1, February, pp 63-80.

Okely, J. (2007) 'La justice des Tsiganes contre la loi des Gadje', *Ethnologie francaise* 2 (Avril), pp 313-22.

Okely, J. (2011) 'The Dale Farm eviction', *Anthropology Today*, vol 27, December, pp 24-7.

Okely, J. (2012) *Anthropological practice: Fieldwork and the ethnographic method*, London: Berg, Bloomsbury.

Said, E. (1978) *Orientalism*, New York: Pantheon.

Straw, J. (1999) Local radio interview, *Daily Mail* 20 August, reprinted in J. Okely 'Writing Anthropology in Europe', *Folk*, vol 41, pp 55-75.

.

ONE

Introduction

Conventional and frequently romanticised portrayals of Gypsy and Travellers' lives are often preoccupied by 'paradigm[s] of romanticism and a biological/hereditary nexus' focusing on these aspects of identity until members of those communities are beyond recognition as members of wider civic society (Belton, 2005, p 46). This text seeks to examine the decline of nomadic lifestyles among Britain's Gypsy and Traveller population and 'rehumanise' the debate through exploring the impact of a (largely enforced) sedentary existence on these communities and the collective adaptations that have evolved in response to significant changes to their traditional way of life.

This book explores how these changes have had both generational and gender-based impacts, as over recent decades there has been a steep decline in the ability of Gypsies and Travellers to live a nomadic existence, as residence on permanent caravan sites and in conventional housing has become the norm for most of the estimated 300,000 population (CRE, 2006). The majority of this population, as many as two thirds, are now believed to be living in 'bricks and mortar' housing.[1] The large-scale settlement of travelling communities has been driven by successive policies that have sought to accommodate Gypsies and Travellers (and to some extent recognise their continued cultural preferences for caravan dwelling) whilst engaging with the stubborn and continued issue of unauthorised encampments and the resulting tensions with the settled community (Richardson, 2007b). In practice such policies have often had the unintended consequences of worsening the situation by inflaming conflicts with settled society whilst simultaneously accelerating the settlement of Gypsies and Travellers onto a declining supply of official pitches or, for many more, into social housing where they place additional demands on an already overstretched housing stock. Despite the rate and size of this settlement into 'bricks and mortar' in recent decades and an extensive body of research into the housing 'careers' and residential patterns of other minority groups, this book represents the first detailed study of Gypsies and Travellers in housing to be published in Britain.

The book is thematically organised so as not only to explore the narratives of the individuals in our research sites, but also to include a social history of the interrelationship between Gypsies, Travellers and the working-class communities amongst whom they have traditionally lived, and in close proximity to whom they continue to live, as well as a discussion on the constraints experienced by former caravan dwellers and their routes into housing. We focus too on the changing nature of the Gypsy and Traveller communities in relatively new sedentarised settings, and consider the way in which young members of these ethnic minority groups (often born and raised in 'bricks and mortar' accommodation) retain their distinctive (albeit sometimes hybridised) identities and seek to realise their aspirations for the future.

In this and the following chapter the policy backdrop to increased sedentarisation will be considered. Chapter Three will examine how, despite the popular association of these communities with continual movement, the transfer into housing is not wholly a recent trend, though the scale of settlement is largely a post-World War Two phenomenon. Some nomads have throughout their history opted for a settled life for various reasons, with evidence indicating significant colonies of settled Gypsies and Travellers in urban areas since at least the 19th century and for probably longer. In fact, for nomadic communities Britain's inclement weather and the temporary nature of working patterns meant that the year was often based around seasonal travelling, with the summer spent employed on a regular circuit of fairs and seasonal agricultural work, and winters spent in lodging houses or parked in yards or on sites. So common was this customary practice that for one late-19th-century commentator, the seasonal influx of large numbers of Gypsies and other itinerants into the towns and cities marked the end of summer as surely as migrating birds:

> ... this hastening of a whole people from out the summer heat of the countryside; this reluctant, driven, hurried, human movement from hedge-side home beneath the sun and stars to the miserable makeshifts of city housing, has in it far more impressive revelation of winter's coming than all the autumn flights of birds and wind-whipped beatings of bare branches and bedraggled brown leaves. (*The Leeds Mercury*, 4 November 1896)

Neither is settlement in housing a one-way process: as Brian Belton (2005) points out, just as some nomads have ceased travelling either through choice or circumstance, so others from the 'settled' population have taken to the road for a multitude of reasons, a phenomenon noted and legislated against as far back as the Tudor period (Mayall, 1995) and which continued into the 1970s and 1980s (Earle et al, 1994).

Similarly, it is well documented that housed Gypsies and Travellers will frequently leave conventional housing and return to the road or to residence on a site where such an option exists. A Department of the Environment study conducted in the 1980s revealed that of 523 Gypsy families who entered housing between 1981 and 1985, some 146 families moved back out (Davies, 1987); these findings are borne out by numerous reports of movement into and out of housing from participants in government surveys undertaken as part of Gypsy Traveller Accommodation Assessments (GTAAs). Thus the settlement of Gypsies and Travellers and the extent (and failure of) assimilation into the general population has long been a concern of the state, which has regarded a mobile existence as threatening to, and potentially undermining of, social cohesion.

The two enduring themes in official responses to nomadism have centred on efforts to suppress such mobilities on one hand and to prevent members of the 'settled' population from adopting a travelling life on the other. Under Elizabethan legislation the able-bodied poor were forbidden poor relief if they left their parish, while the 1662 Settlement Acts underlined the centrality of permanent residence and enforced attachment to employment to the maintenance of social stability (Mencher, 1967). Beier (1974) notes that Gypsies and vagrants – both of whom eschewed such conventions and who were therefore often conflated in legislation and in the popular imagination – were subjected to a plethora of attempts to crush them out of existence,

> ... that included refusal of alms, whipping, stocking, imprisonment, branding, ear-boring, forced labour in the galleys, slavery, deportation and hanging. Constructive efforts to solve the problem by setting vagrants to work were small waves in this sea of corporal punishment. (Beier, 1974, p 15)

Robbie McVeigh (1997) argues that while contemporary methods may be less barbaric and are perhaps justified in terms of a 'benevolent assimilationism' the objectives remain the same – the extinction of nomadism and 'sedentarisation' into 'settled' society (Chapter Two). In fact, continues McVeigh, 'sympathetic welfarism' in the form of assimilation may obliterate nomadic identities more successfully than straightforward repression, which more often results in the expulsion of nomadic people from an area with their identity intact and a determination to retain a culture in the face of overt hostility.

> The efforts of well-meaning politicians, social workers and educationalists and health workers who adopt a sedentarist and assimilationist paradigm vis-à-vis Travellers and other nomads is equally genocidal in effect. Forcing nomads into houses is – at a social, cultural and spiritual level – no different from forcing nomads into gas chambers. Whether the rhetoric is couched in terms of kindness to the nomad or sedentary necessity the solution is always the termination of nomadism. (McVeigh, 1997, p 23)

The drive towards sedentarisation has gathered pace in the postwar period alongside an expansion of the four 'institutional clusterings' that characterise modernity: surveillance, capitalistic enterprise, industrial production, and centralisation of the means of violence (Giddens, 1991). The combination of these interrelated forces have intensified industrial, residential and retail development on what were previously accessible scraps of wasteland. In addition zoning of land use has led to stricter regulation over permitted activities and forms of development while an increasing social and spatial segregation of poor and marginalised sections of the population has been enforced through legislation, social policies and ever more sophisticated techniques of surveillance and control. As Giddens (1991) notes:

> Surveillance … is fundamental to all the types of organization associated with the rise of modernity, in particular the nation state, which has historically been intertwined with capitalism in their mutual development. Similarly there are close substantive connections between the surveillance operations of nation states and the altered nature of … power in the modern period. The successful monopoly of the means of violence on the part of the modern state rests upon the secular maintenance of new codes of criminal law, plus the supervisory control of 'deviance'. (Giddens, 1991, p 59)

As we argue throughout this book, legislation, while not the only driver behind the settlement and immobilisation of Gypsies and Travellers, has been the primary factor in this process in recent decades, successfully bringing about the decline in nomadism sought by previous generations of legislators. Hawes and Perez (1995) in their analysis of the evolution of policy affecting Gypsies and Travellers between 1960 and 1993 (see Chapter Two) – primarily relating to the provision of caravan sites and repression of unauthorised camping but also including interlinked education and health initiatives – identify an incremental process emerging through the interaction of various participants including 'local authorities, professionals, gypsy activists and their supporters, ministers and local residents' (1995, p 26).

In the following chapter, the analyses of a number of theorists to sketch the broad contours of policy which has shaped the accommodation options of Gypsies and Travellers in the postwar period are summarised. Detailed analysis of the interrelated development of policy making, note Hawes and Perez, makes it possible to '... pinpoint the way in which the latent hostility and prejudice which surrounds the subject becomes built in to the very legislative structures meant to offer solutions to the issue which generates hostility' (1995, p 26).

Cultural trauma and collective resilience

Our interest in the growing numbers of Gypsies and Travellers occupying conventional housing and the individual and cultural ramifications of this trend is relevant to social scientific interest in 'cultural trauma' and its corollaries – cultural resilience and resistance. The concept of cultural trauma has increasingly been used by anthropologists and educationalists as 'shorthand' for the experiences of individuals and communities from indigenous/First Nation communities who have had to abandon their former way of life as a result of colonialist rule or restructuring of society. Cultural trauma occurs when

> ... members of a collectivity feel they have been subjected to a horrendous event that leaves indelible marks upon their group consciousness, marking their memories forever and changing their future identity in fundamental and irrevocable ways (Alexander, 2004, p 1).

The perception of an event as traumatising is relative, varying between individuals and cultural formations and is dependent on the socio-cultural context of the affected collectivity at the time of the event or situation (Laungani, 2002; Smelser, 2004). To qualify as cultural trauma an event 'must be understood, explained and made coherent through public reflection and discourse' (Eyerman, 2004, p 160) and contains a number of components. Firstly, traumatic change has a particular temporal quality: it is rapid and sudden. Change is also radical and deep in its substance and scope touching the core of the collective order. Secondly, it is interpreted as having particular origins that are exogenous and emanate from outside of the affected group. Finally, it is perceived within a cognitive framework that interprets change as unexpected, detrimental and shocking (Sztompka, 2000, p 452). Proponents of 'cultural trauma' point to similarities among a range of indigenous and nomadic communities – in particular, low educational attainment, high rates of suicide, depression, substance abuse and family breakdown seen amongst peoples who have experienced rapid rates of social and cultural change and, moreover, are widely exposed to racism and discrimination from the economically and socially dominant culture (Tatz, 2004).

Evidence suggests that for many Gypsies and Travellers the transition to housing can be traumatic both psychologically and practically. The alien nature of life in housing and the enclosed physical layout of housing frequently induces feelings of claustrophobia and anxiety, while loss of close-knit community ties, physical isolation, loneliness and hostility from neighbours are common difficulties experienced by housed Gypsies and Travellers (Thomas and Campbell, 1992). In addition practical adjustments such as budgeting for monthly bills and dealing with bureaucracy – particularly for those with limited literacy skills – combined with regulations prohibiting traditional economic and cultural activities add to the strains many face when housed for the first time (see Chapter Six). The accumulation of these circumstances can result in the breakdown of physical and mental health identified by Parry et al (2004) who found that those with long-term illnesses were more likely to be living in a council site or in housing than on a private site or on empty land. The survey also found significantly higher levels of anxiety symptoms among the housed population compared to those residing in caravans (Parry et al, 2004, p 34). The adverse psychological impact of residence in conventional housing has been recognised in law where the concept of a 'cultural aversion' to housing emerged in a planning case. In *Clarke v Secretary of State for the Environment, Transport and the Regions*,[2] the High Court overturned a decision by a planning inspector who had refused planning permission to a Romany Gypsy on the grounds that the relevant authority had made an offer of conventional housing. The judge concluded that if a cultural aversion to housing could be demonstrated, such an offer was inappropriate 'just as would be the offer of a rat-infested barn'. Recognition that a 'psychological aversion' to housing can exist among Gypsies and Travellers has, since the advent of the 2006 Housing Act, been incorporated into guidance and regulations pertaining to assessing accommodation requirement (Fordham Research, 2009). Legal judgments subsequent to the *Clarke* case have indicated that, while local authorities must strive to facilitate a homeless Gypsy or Traveller's customary lifestyle and provide a pitch, if no pitches are available the local authority can offer conventional housing in meeting its duty to accommodate them and their family (Willers, 2010).

The concept of cultural trauma, whilst helpful in illuminating the adverse and dysfunctional effects of social change, only provides a partial analysis of how individuals and groups respond to fundamental restructuring of their social environments. Suedfeld (1997) is critical of the view that people are engulfed by traumatic stress and unable to resist its damaging outcomes at micro or macro levels, arguing that problem solving and maximising individual autonomy in the face of externally imposed constraints are constants throughout history. He notes that individuals and groups have differing capabilities and strategies for dealing with structural changes that may be perceived of as potentially detrimental. These coping mechanisms will affect how people experience adversity in their social environments, while the ability to exert personal control can be a source of self-esteem, pride and improved capabilities to cope with future stressors (1997, p 851).

> Planful problem-solving is a sign of the resilience and indomitability of people and groups, and its presence counteracts the general assumption of social scientists that traumatic events are necessarily and universally destructive to collective and individual psychological functioning. (Suedfeld, 1997, p 853)

As discussed, Gypsies and other nomadic groups have, throughout their history, experienced efforts to eliminate their lifestyle and culture through the use of a variety of strategies. The fact that they have survived these attempts and maintained a sense of group cohesion and collective identity for so long is testament to these communities' resilience. Indeed, as we demonstrate in later chapters, the versatility and adaptability of Gypsies and Traveller culture is often strengthened and reaffirmed through institutional racism and societal prejudice (Chapters Seven and Eight). Hollander and Einwhoner (2004) note that resistance and domination have a cyclical relationship, 'domination leads to resistance, which leads to the further exercise of power, provoking further resistance and so on' (2004, p 548). In the current study, this cyclical process appears to be borne out by our findings, which indicate the sense of embattlement articulated by many respondents. Legislation has been repeatedly introduced to restrict the mobility of Gypsies and Travellers and settle them in houses and permanent sites, and in response those groups have developed innovative strategies to evade or mitigate the impact of the legislation, thus instigating a new phase of policy development. Cultural resilience in this context therefore encompasses active resistance to imposed changes and a determination to preserve cultural values and practices in new situations.

In exploring this phenomenon we are aided by Thomas Acton's (1974) typology of the various adaptive strategies utilised by Gypsies and Travellers. Acton identifies four main strategies, one of which is essentially passive and accords to descriptions of 'cultural trauma', with the remaining three active responses that represent variants of cultural resilience and adaptation. Firstly, Acton identifies cultural disintegration, where Gypsies become demoralised and impoverished while corrosion of their economic base weakens resistance to the dominant ethos of the wider society. Secondly, there are those who adopt a conservative approach by minimising contact with the outside world and resisting changes to their way of life. Yet others may adopt a cultural adaptation approach and accept those influences from external cultures that are advantageous, utilising these as a supplement to, rather than a replacement of, their own culture. Finally, Gypsies may 'pass' and compete with the wider society on equal terms by concealing their cultural identity. The typology is useful in drawing attention to the repertoire of cultural responses that are utilised in different situational contexts and also to the paradox of adaptability identified by O'Nions (1995): namely, that to many outsiders 'true' Gypsies are extinct since they no longer possess a single unifying factor – common language, religion or independently mobile lifestyle – that identifies them as members of a distinctive minority group. However, O'Nions cautions against concluding that Gypsies and Travellers possess no self-awareness or collective identity, citing Nicholls LJ in *CRE v Dutton* (1989), who observed that:

> The fact that some have been absorbed and are indistinguishable from any ordinary member of the public, is not sufficient in itself to establish loss of ... an historically determined social identity in [the group's] own eyes and in the eyes of those outside the group ... despite their long presence in England, gypsies have not merged wholly into the population as have the Saxons and Danes ... They, or many of them, have retained a separateness, a self-awareness, of still being gypsies. (cited by O'Nions, 1995, p 8)

Ann Sutherland (1975) is critical of perspectives that interpret external changes in lifestyle, working patterns and customs as proof of assimilation and the culturally erosive aspects of urbanisation. There are several examples of minority groups that resist enormous pressures to assimilate and manage to live within a wider culture while rejecting its values and social institutions, and Gypsies could be considered an ideal type of such a group. Boundary maintenance between Gypsies and the wider society according to Sutherland is maintained by two factors. Firstly, social relations with 'gaje' (non-Gypsies) are limited to certain types of relationship, primarily those of an economic or political nature. Secondly, a symbolic system and framework of rules exists which place the gaje outside of the group's social and moral boundaries. It is these two factors Sutherland argues, that allow the maintenance of a distinct way of life and sense of separateness under a multitude of situational contexts. As David Sibley comments, 'it is apparent that economic factors have combined to bring Travellers into the city without altering the essential elements of their world-structure' (1981, p 76).

Such rigid boundaries were not observed in the research locales on which this book is based and examples of intermarriage and friendships outside the Gypsy and Traveller community were frequently reported. Such intercommunity relations, however, were generally with people who had grown up in close physical and social proximity to Gypsies and Travellers and who had acquired a close knowledge of their community free from the prejudices and stereotypes of the wider society (Chapters Seven and Nine). Notwithstanding the presence of positive social relations with non-Gypsy neighbours and associates, in almost all cases there was a marked preference for social relations with fellow Travellers with a tendency towards frequent in-group interaction and only minimal relations with 'outsiders'. McVeigh (1997, p 12) notes that despite the pervasiveness of anti-Gypsy prejudice and racist stereotypes many Gypsies and Travellers still believe in their own superiority *vis-à-vis* settled society. Their marginal status and negative public profile is continually resisted and contested through emphasising the inferiority of the non-Gypsy world. Rena Gropper's (1975) study of Gypsies in New York argues that such attitudes are an important component in maintaining solidarity and resisting assimilation.

> Gypsy culture perpetually is bombarded by outside influences and periodically besieged by strong coercive attempts to assimilate. Only those individuals who are unshakeable in the superiority of Rom-ness and only those units that can safeguard Gypsyhood by a judicious

strategy of fission-and-fusion, bend-and-resist, cooperate-and disband are capable of passing the Romany way onto the next generation. (1975, p 189)

In spite of the heterogeneity of Gypsy, Traveller and Roma groups worldwide, two features have been identified as common to all groups, which together ensure a constant process of re-adaptation and versatility. 'Economic adaption combined with inflexibility of certain basic rules is the Gypsy's forte and the consequence of flexibility is often change' (Sutherland, 1975, p 3). Gmelch (1977) in his study of the economic and social adaptations made by Irish Travellers following urban migration argues that they have managed to avoid assimilation by remaining outside of the wage labour system. Retaining family based self-employment characterised by a diversity and flexibility of occupations in urban environments allows them to occupy a similar economic niche to the one they had occupied in rural contexts prior to settlement. The content of their work has changed but the structural prerequisites have not (Gmelch, 1977, p 89; Smith and Greenfields, 2012). Kornblum and Lichter (1972), while rejecting a 'culture of poverty' perspective argue that Gypsies represent a group whose historical experience of prejudice and scarcity allows them to survive and even flourish in relatively deprived environments. Adaptation and collective survival is therefore a dynamic process that requires negotiation of cultural and ethnic boundaries rendering those boundaries more elastic.

> The survival strategies that actors invoke ... reflect culturally appropriate understandings of the boundaries. Thus there exists a dialectical relationship between boundaries and survival strategies: each shapes the other, so that newly designed boundaries influence possible strategies, while the performance of these strategies reinforces these boundaries. (Konstantinov et al, 1998, p 734)

The issue of boundaries and their permeability or otherwise is also pertinent to the current study. While there is an abundance of literature addressing the marginalisation of Gypsies and Travellers as a consequence of wider sociopolitical forces there is very little on the micro-level expression of these forces (Powell, 2007; Powell, 2008). This book represents one of very few attempts to explore everyday relations between Gypsies and Travellers and the generally working-class populace they live amongst, necessitating a simultaneous exploration of boundary maintenance and the penetrability or otherwise of those boundaries. Accordingly, following Sztompka (2004, p 451) the perspective we employ regards culture both as a context of change comprising the pool of cultural resources and engaged by individuals in 'labeling, defining, (and) interpreting certain events' and as an object of change affected by 'agential praxis and particularly by major social upheavals'. Within this text we apply this model to an analysis of how Gypsies and Travellers have experienced and responded to life in conventional housing, creating a culture of dynamic resistance within a rapidly changing environment.

Notes

[1] Between 2002 and 2012 the total number of Gypsy caravans increased by 24 per cent and in January 2012 there were an estimated 18,750 Gypsy and Traveller caravans in England. Of these approximately 36 per cent (6,800 caravans) were located on local authority or socially rented sites, representing a decline from 46 per cent of the total in January 2002. Conversely, 49 per cent (9,100 caravans) were situated on private sites, which is an increase of 15 per cent over the same period. Around 15 per cent (2,850 caravans) were situated on unauthorised sites. This figure is comprised of 10 per cent on unauthorised developments (1,800 caravans) where the land is owned by the Gypsy/Travellers but planning permission has not been granted and 5 per cent (900 caravans) situated on unauthorised encampments. This compares to over 19 per cent of the total (2,687 caravans) which were stopping on unauthorised sites in January 2002 (DCLG, 2012).

[2] *Clarke v Secretary of State for the Environment Transport and Regions* [2002] JPL 552.

TWO

Space, surveillance and modernity

In this and the following chapter, the empirical sections of the book will be situated in their broader theoretical, historical and contemporary contexts and an attempt will be made to tease out the interconnections between these dimensions. For example, historical and comparative studies show that racism and persecution have been constant features of the relationship between Gypsies, Travellers and the wider society, albeit the degree and virulence has varied at different periods according to wider social, political and economic conditions (Kenrick and Puxon, 1972; Fraser, 1995). However, the prejudice and marginalisation experienced by nomadic communities today, while displaying much historical continuity, is also related to factors specific to contemporary socioeconomic and political processes such as a general increase in inequality and polarisation of life chances as well as a growing social and political intolerance towards disadvantaged groups over the past three decades (McGhee, 2005). As Wacquant (2008) observes, these processes have unleashed massive 'structural violence from above' on large sections of the unskilled labour force in the 'advanced' economies of the western world, consigning many to economic redundancy and social marginality (2008, p 24). At the same time as traditional 'blue collar' jobs have been decimated through deindustrialisation and globalisation, so the (former) manual working classes have had to contend with large-scale immigration that is generally championed most vocally by those social groups who benefit directly or indirectly from a cheap and flexible immigrant labour force (Hanley, 2011). Consequently many immigrants are channelled into the same decaying and spatially segregated neighbourhoods as economically redundant sections of the native population. These marginalised segments of the native and immigrant populations are socially and spatially segregated from the rest of society, where 'territorial stigma' with its attendant class and ethnic dimensions is a reality of their daily lives. As Wacquant notes:

> Any comparative sociology of the novel forms of urban poverty crystallizing in advanced societies at century's turn must begin with the *powerful stigma attached to residence in the*

> *bounded and segregated spaces*, the 'neighbourhoods of exile'
> to which the populations marginalized or condemned
> to redundancy by the post-Fordist reorganization of the
> economy and the post-Keynesian reconstruction of the
> welfare state are increasingly consigned. (Wacquant, 2008,
> p 169, italics in original)

The decline of nomadism, and the corralling of those who once pursued such lifestyles onto permanent caravan sites or into predominantly poor quality, stigmatised areas of social housing where they reside with other marginalised and disenfranchised sections of the population is but one small aspect of the more general social and spatial polarisation of society that Wacquant examines. Nevertheless it is core to this study. This book explores how the stigma attached to such spaces of marginalisation manifests itself daily in media, political and popular discourse: in contemporary 'offence averse' Britain, Travellers and the economically redundant sections of the white working class represent probably the only two groups who it is still acceptable to ridicule publicly or to describe in offensive terms (Nayak, 2006; Webster, 2008). Indeed, it is no coincidence that the term 'pikey', which has long been a derogatory term for Gypsies and Travellers, has increasingly been applied to young white residents of social housing in recent years while 'chav' (from the Romany word 'chavi' for child) has become a byword for 'poor white trash' (Harris, 2007) as the two groups have merged in the public consciousness into one criminally inclined, welfare dependent and spatially segregated, incorrigible 'underclass' (Rooke and Gidley, 2010).

In terms of legislation and policy both nomads and the 'rough' (in contrast to the 'respectable') elements of the working classes have long been the recipients of policies aimed at behavioural change and conversion 'from above'. Efforts to assimilate Gypsies and other itinerant groups have a long history though according to Mayall (1988, p 3) they became more prominent in the early 19th century for three main reasons. Firstly, the massive social upheavals caused by industrialisation and the transition from a rural to an urban society meant that commercial nomadism lost much of its previous importance. While some managed to adapt to urbanisation, for others declining work opportunities led to increasing marginalisation and a growing recognition of Gypsies and itinerants as a 'social problem' requiring state attention. Secondly, the increasingly zealous attempts by religious institutions and individuals to convert Gypsies to conventional Christianity. Thirdly, the rising social importance of the middle classes and dominance of a bourgeois ideology that emphasised those traits necessary for economic growth and material advancement: time discipline, individualism, rationality and self-help. This ideology was the driving force behind efforts not just to reform Gypsies and other peripatetic groups, but was part of a much wider process of middle-class evangelism that set out, and largely failed, to recreate the 'lower orders' in its own image (Stedman Jones, 1974). Gypsies, by rejecting two of the main pillars essential for the smooth functioning of an urban industrial society – regular waged employment and permanency of residence – symbolised a visible opposition and challenge to middle-class notions of an ordered and civilised society (Khazanov 1994). Consequently they were, along with other members of the 'residuum' who either would not or could not assimilate into the urban proletariat, considered as requiring corrective treatment (Powell, 2007).

> They (Gypsies) stand apart from the majority of the population both culturally and economically with their resistance to incorporation into the wage-labour market and persistent reliance on the family as the key economic unit serving to isolate them as a distinctive fringe group in any society which stresses permanency and settlement. (Mayall, 1988, p 1)

The most common response of officials towards Gypsies has been to enact strategies of spatial control and restriction of movement. This has taken a variety of forms throughout history, such as the 1530 Egyptians Act, which sought to halt the migration of 'Egyptians' into the country and banish those already present. The Act was amended in 1554 to exclude those who settled and gave up their 'naughty, idle and ungodly life and company' (Mayall, 1995, p 21). The expulsion of migrant Roma populations from EU countries such as France and Italy in recent years and increased monitoring of nomadic populations even in traditionally 'liberal' countries such as the Netherlands marks a revival of such policies (Van Bochove and Burgers, 2010). The main trend, however, in keeping with the assimilationist logic of state policies since the 19th century, has been concerned primarily with settlement. Again this has manifested itself in different ways in different contexts from removing the wheels of caravans and shooting the horses of Polish Gypsies in 'The Great Halt' of the 1950s (Bancroft, 2005, p 28) to settlement into ghettoised areas of poor quality housing across much of Central and Eastern Europe under communism. As discussed below, in the UK the main objective of postwar policy has been to make nomadism progressively difficult to sustain. McVeigh (1997) argues that antipathy towards nomadism is based on an ideology of 'sedentarism' which he equates to a particular form of oppression like racism or sexism that represents a 'system of ideas and practices which serve to normalise and reproduce sedentary modes of existence and pathologies and repress nomadic modes of existence' (1997, p 9). Modernity and the rise of the nation state surrounded by borders represented the triumph of sedentarism, suggests McVeigh, and was driven by a desire for order and control which, to implement, required political action and social reform:

> ... with the arrival of the nation state and the notion of the border, space began to be occupied in a totalised way – there were fewer and fewer places for nomads to move on to. They were increasingly problematised and controlled and repressed within nation-states intent on the centralisation and consolidation of power and surveillance. (1997, pp 17–18)

The current period, he continues, represents the triumph of 'sedentarist hegemony' which, while not reducible to either racial or class based explanations is shaped by both, a theme explored by Mulcahy (2012) in his study of the governance of nomadic Travellers in Ireland and the impact of public hostility on policing practices. In the case of principles of 'public and national order', increasingly this takes the form of a categorisation and racialised treatment of English Gypsies, Irish Travellers and more recently of East and Central European Roma. Class is also relevant to sedentarist ideology since nomadism, with its intermittent demand for land usage, calls into question capitalist notions of legal 'ownership' of land and private property (Greenfields and Home, 2008). The relationship between sedentary populations and particular places conflicts with the nomad's relationship with, and use of, land and the environment, particularly when they share social space. The resistance to assimilation and wage labour and rejection of the notions of order and control that individual property rights and settlement entail means that the existence of nomadic communities symbolise rejection of, and alternatives to, that system. Thus writes McVeigh, 'the political and cultural resistance of nomads continues to subvert deep-seated beliefs about the normalcy of settlement and wage labour that pervades the whole of sedentary society' (McVeigh, 1997, p 22).

Despite the fact that the policy approach may have shifted over time from expulsion and extermination towards settlement and assimilation, this seemingly benign and paternalistic approach has done little to reverse the deprivation and inequalities experienced by Gypsies and Travellers and in many cases has exacerbated social problems through eroding traditional community structures, hierarchies and social control systems (Greenfields and Smith, 2011). Processes of spatial exclusion and boundary maintenance which have always served to keep lower status groups separated from those more affluent and powerful continue but in a different form: the contemporary function of such processes represents one aspect of a more generalised social and spatial concentration of the poorest and most disadvantaged social groups into areas of social and public housing where they are removed not just from middle-class society but increasingly from the core working class (Byrne, 2005; Webster, 2008). The following section outlines the policies devised by (often well-meaning) Parliamentarians and agents of the state in the post-war period that have led to a large-scale movement away from nomadism largely into these marginalised neighbourhoods, with the ultimate outcomes of these phased and segmented processes on the lives of those affected by them addressed in later chapters.

Policy and settlement

The general direction of policy post World War Two has been to make a nomadic existence progressively more difficult to sustain. The 1959 Highways Act prohibited camping on highways while social security Acts have isolated casual labour, restricting an itinerant existence and encouraging permanency of residence (O'Nions, 1995; Belton, 2005). The issue of site provision in the postwar era that would so profoundly impact on Gypsies and Travellers was devised in the context of reconstruction, economic regeneration and homelessness, which fuelled the rise in caravan dwelling and unlicensed site development. Taylor (2008, p 118) notes that despite official distaste such developments formed an important stop-gap measure in meeting housing shortages and there was certainly some acceptance by central government that they would need to remain until housing demand could be met. Ward (2002) stresses the sheer scale of squatting in post-war Britain and the linkages between 'self-help' accommodation, residence in shacks and old vehicles and the co-existence of bombed out (typically poorer working class) urban people and Gypsies and Travellers who had the skills to subsist in temporary and makeshift accommodation. Subsequently Government policy moved towards tacit encouragement of local authority housing, residential caravans and Gypsy site provision – all developments which were generally opposed at the local level as contrary to an ideal of smart residential housing. In practice post-war housing developments were, as Young and Wilmott (1957) found, often regarded as less than ideal by the new residents who frequently valued tight-knit community bonds and the ability to live life in public spaces, over highly regulated access to facilities. The opposition to the development of caravan sites (both for Travellers and other homeless people), argues Taylor, highlights a more general and recurrent tension in relations between central government, local authorities and 'outsiders' marked by an ideology of impartiality at the central governmental level and the desire to expel Travellers from an area at the local level (Taylor, 2008, p 53).

The Caravan Sites and Control of Development Act 1960 did not explicitly refer to Gypsies and Travellers but was aimed at controlling the continuing widespread use of unofficial caravan sites by postwar homeless families, prohibiting the setting up of unlicensed camps and allowing district councils to act against those camping on common land. This legislation was to have a major impact on Gypsies and Travellers as many stopping places were placed out of bounds while those who had purchased their own land were unable to obtain a licence without planning consent and faced eviction, most notoriously in Kent on sites which had a long tradition as stopping places, and which in some cases had been willed or given in good faith in perpetuity to Traveller families to provide them with a home (Greenfields, 2006). The Act also gave discretionary powers for local authorities to develop sites and by 1967 14 sites had been opened as a sop to both outraged Traveller families and local residents troubled by the sight of nomadic families evicted from their own land onto the roadside (Hawes and Perez, 1995, pp 20–1). An inevitable consequence of the 1960 Act was to increase the visibility of Gypsies and Travellers heightening tensions with the settled community and focusing public and political attention on the 'Gypsy problem'.

Norman Dodds who became an MP in 1945 and whose constituencies of Dartford and later of Erith and Crayford contained some of the sprawling 'van towns' discussed in Chapter Three, had campaigned and lobbied for a more humane treatment towards Gypsies ever since his election to Parliament. The increasingly negative impact of the 1960 Act on his constituents did not pass unremarked by this campaigning politician, with Dodds repeatedly arguing that granting discretionary powers to local authorities to build sites was insufficient to meet the shortfall caused by the Act. Thus he argued there was a clear need for a national strategy to ensure that Gypsies and Travellers' traditional way of life was not destroyed. Planning Circular (6/1962), largely implemented as a result of the persistence of Dodds and a few other socially conscious politicians, called on authorities to undertake surveys of Gypsies and Travellers in their locality and to devise plans for appropriate provision. This guidance utilised the example of a pioneering local authority site set up in Ashford, Kent in 1960 as an example of best practice. However, the Circular also made it clear that it regarded public sites merely as an intermediate stage towards the assimilation of Gypsies into housing, not as a permanent solution (Porter and Taylor, 2010).

In response to the public visibility of evicted Gypsy and Traveller families being pushed from pillar to post, the first national census of the Gypsy population was undertaken in 1965 (by police officers, who were expected to know where to find most of Traveller encampments in their areas). The census findings were published as *Gypsies and other Travellers* in 1967 and proved important as 'it was upon the findings of this report that all subsequent legislation and action at the time ensued' (Hawes and Perez, 1995, p 21). The calculation of 3,400 travelling families in England and Wales comprising of 15,000 individuals was certainly an under-estimate, as the report acknowledged, due in part to local authorities driving Gypsies and Travellers out of their areas prior to the survey to enable the authorities to claim that no demand for sites existed in their locality (Kenrick and Clark, 1999; Kabachnik, 2007, p 42). The 1967 report revealed that only one third of the country's nomadic population had access to water and refuse disposal, and that around one half lived on sites without any amenities, providing compelling evidence of the necessity for a coordinated national approach to the issue of site provision.

The 1967 report had highlighted the shortcomings of assuming that adequate site provision would occur through humanistic 'persuasion', government Circulars and reliance on the private sector. Thus in 1967 the Liberal MP Eric Lubbock (now Lord Avebury and still a stalwart of Gypsy and Traveller politics) put forward a Private Member's Bill requiring local authorities to provide sites in their area. After significant amendments, including awarding authorities the right to be awarded 'designation' status (exchanging limited site provision for the power to penalise individuals camping in unauthorised locations), the 1968 Caravan Sites Act was passed (Home, 2006; Richardson, 2007). This Act, as Belton notes (2005, p 115), was the only Caravans Act to apply specifically to Gypsies and 'remained for 25 years, the foundation upon which all subsequent interaction between Gypsies and the state has been posited' (Hawes and Perez, 1995, p 22). The Act avoided an ethnic definition of Gypsies and referred to persons of nomadic habit regardless of race or origin. The Court of Appeal subsequently extended this definition to encompass purposeful travel, economic independence and a tradition of travelling, effectively excluding New Travellers from the terms of the Act (Clements and Campbell, 1999). However subsequent amendments to legislation and case law have more recently afforded such nomadic groups the opportunity to apply for authorised Gypsy sites (Johnson and Willars, 2007).

Hawes and Perez (1995, pp 28–9) identify three areas in which the 1968 Act was defective. Firstly, the size of the Gypsy population was severely under-estimated while exemptions allowed authorities to make no provision if they could prove (based on their self-administered 'caravan count') that they had insufficient nomadic populations to make such provision worthwhile. London Boroughs were afforded a particular exemption, enabling them to achieve designation if they provided 15 pitches, effectively excluding most Gypsies from residing or resorting to the capital. This forced them to move into housing, orbit in caravans around the edges of the metropolis or risk unauthorised encampments on waste land or in semi-industrial peri-urban areas. Secondly, the Act focused wholly on site provision and neglected issues of social provision, meaning that site residents' access to education, medical care, public transport and even hygienic, safely located sites were ignored when local authorities simply made the minimal provision necessary to comply with legislation or local pressure. Indeed, a number of local authority sites were cynically provided on land which was not passed as fit for housing, frequently on former sewage works or contaminated land which have thereafter been the subject of numerous claims of health impacts on residents (Greenfields, 2006; Richardson, 2007a). Thirdly, Hawes and Perez (1995) note, the Act set no time scale to provide sites and there was little political will to direct authorities to comply with the Act, an issue which is common to this day even under newer legislation (Richardson, 2007a). Indeed it was not until 1985 that Section 9 of the Act allowing recalcitrant authorities to be directed to comply was invoked, and from then onwards a series of judicial reviews occurred meaning that implementation was, in effect, court led (Waterson, 1997, p 131).

Belton (2005) argues that the 1968 Act hastened the settlement of the country's nomadic population. In the short term, the Act pressurised nomadic families to settle into housing, through providing authorities with a means of legal harassment to deal with recalcitrant mobile families, bringing Gypsies and Travellers into contact with conventional housing market norms (albeit of the low-level municipal type that was a feature of the interwar landscape). In the longer term, the Act increased competition for site vacancies, ensuring that those who were allocated an official pitch tended to stay there, and also limited travelling patterns through regulations stating that if someone left a public site for more than a few weeks in a year their pitch would be lost (Greenfields, 2006). At the same time, legal harassment of itinerants made nomadism increasingly unattractive, meaning that those who could escape from the cycle of harassment and eviction did so (2005, pp 116–18). Some years after the Act's implementation the government initiated a policy review in the light of the slow progress on site provision. The review led to the report in late 1976 by Sir John Cripps, *Accommodation for Gypsies*, which noted that by that year only 133 sites had been provided, offering 2,131 pitches in total (20 per cent of which had been in existence prior to the implementation of the 1968 Act) and accommodating a mere one quarter of formerly nomadic Gypsy families in England (Obadina, 1998, p 245). Cripps argued that consistent undercounting of the Gypsy population by local authorities meant that the government's estimate of a demand for 200 new sites would probably need to increase by an additional 300 sites. The report made a series of recommendations to increase site provision including Exchequer funding of the capital cost of sites; assistance to those who wished to buy their own land; and adoption of a more permissive attitude to unauthorised camping while the site development programme was in process.

As a result of Cripps' recommendations Planning Circular 28/77 was passed, urging a more 'flexible and sympathetic approach' to accommodating Gypsies and Travellers. To boost the process further the 1980 Local Government, Planning and Land Act made 100 per cent grants available to local authorities for the provision of public rented sites and where this provision was made enabled them to strengthen designation provisions all of which did result in a rise in site provision. By the start of 1983 around 42 per cent of the Gypsy and Traveller population was accommodated on local authority sites (Hawes and Perez, 2005, p 34). However, tensions between policies devised by central Government and its implementation at the local level amidst frequent and vehement local opposition to site provision remained the major barrier to the Act's success. Designation which provided an incentive to boost local site provision came at the cost of criminalising Gypsies and Travellers who sought to pursue their traditional way of life. Although Government Circulars and statements of the period emphasised the validity of Gypsy culture there was also an assumption that over time they would enter housing and assimilate into the general population. Since many areas which achieved designation status did so by providing the minimum number of pitches, the Act would ultimately make such traditional lifestyles untenable.

> The ethical point to stress is that this element of the legislation, in the interests of the settled majority, restricts the rights of a minority culture, to the extent that it threatens not only a way of life but the very existence of the Travellers altogether. It is of no consolation to Gypsy families that authorities are exhorted to a 'passionate' approach to action under designation powers, nor does it mitigate the discriminatory nature of the Act. (Hawes and Perez, 1995, p 36)

Despite the system of 'reward' for provision of sites, the slow pace at which such accommodation became available is clear when one considers that between 1981 and 1994 only 38 per cent of local authorities obtained designation status and a further 38 per cent made no site provision at all (Obadina, 1998, pp 245–6). In response, and following a period of consultation where interested parties forwarded proposals for improving policy outcomes, Dr Gerald Wibberley was commissioned in 1986 by the then Conservative government to assess the responses and to draw up a series of proposals to increase site development. The possibility of settlement into housing was a frequent theme of interest, as indicated by the subsequent DoE report *Gypsies and Housing* (Davies, 1987), which hinted at the ultimate aim of the emergent accommodation policy:

> The Wibberley report had suggested that ... the contribution which this possibility [housing] offers is small but significant. However, in order to analyse this trend the DoE's own research division undertook a survey which argued that conventional housing might make an increasing contribution to the Gypsy accommodation problem. (Hawes and Perez, 1995, p 43)

A 1991 debate in the House of Commons indicated widespread support for sedenterisation policies though the subsequent change of direction was ideological and represented a 'radical departure' from previous approaches which had taken more of a 'tolerant' approach to nomadic lifestyles, assuming that as the benefits of housing became clear to them, Gypsies and Travellers would willingly become accommodated in conventional bricks and mortar premises (Hawes and Perez, 1995, p 117). However, the policy shift was framed by a drive to reduce public expenditure, a conflation of traditional Gypsy and Traveller lifestyles with incipient moral panics over 'New Age Travellers' and outdoor 'raves', imminent elections and a desire to trump Labour as the party of 'law and order'. Such was the context within which the far-reaching and draconian 1994 Criminal Justice and Public Order Act was formulated. This wide-ranging Act restricted many existing civil liberties and rights and adopted a significantly tougher approach towards certain forms of anti-social behaviour, particularly those associated with 'alternative' lifestyles (Gilbert, 1999). Gypsies and Travellers were once more highlighted and perceived of as anti-social by dint of their refusal to sedentarise and join the house-owning democracy envisaged by the hard-line Tory Government of the time (O'Nions, 1995).

In terms of site provision the Conservative Government favoured private over collective provision emphasising 'value for money' and equity by arguing that the best solution was to encourage Gypsies and Travellers to provide their own sites (Kenrick and Clark, 1999). Supporters of this stance were critical of the 1968 Act for its failure to provide sufficient sites and argued that the 'market' would provide greater impetus to deliver sites than local authority duties. Moreover they argued that the 1968 Act had exacerbated problems of illegal encampments resulting from designation and lack of incentive for Travellers to self-provide and for giving Gypsies a separate (and frequently presented as overly favourable) status in planning terms (O'Nions, 1995). The proposals were argued to be fairer as they placed Gypsies and Travellers and the general public on the same footing (Bancroft, 2000). The 1994 Act was introduced in the face of a broad coalition opposed to the proposals (of which in excess of 40,000 people turned out to demonstrate at each of two large protest marches) including, among others, local authorities, Gypsy and Traveller organisations, the National Farmers Union and Landowners' Association many of whom noted that the aims of the Act were clearly to settle Britain's nomadic population albeit in a more coercive manner than previously. Kendall (1997, p 81) moreover, notes that early drafts of the Act stated that Travellers would be 'encouraged' to enter conventional housing if they 'wished' to, whilst others pointed out that the terms of the Act meant that in practice many would enter housing whether they 'wished' to or not as

> Gypsy families and those others who choose to follow a similar [nomadic] mode of living will be forced to choose between assimilation by living in housing and illegality

> and criminalization if they continue caravan living. Such
> a choice hits at the heart of traditional Gypsy culture and
> justifies ... concerns ... about respect for minority rights.
> (Hawes and Perez, 1995, p 126).

Part II of Act repealed the duty on local authorities to provide sites
and scrapped the government grant for site development resulting
in the closure of many council sites and exacerbating the growing
shortage of pitches on authorised sites (Home, 2006). The Act also
increased the powers of local authorities to evict Travellers stopping
on unauthorised sites, removing the right to stop anywhere but on an
official site. Refusal to leave an unauthorised camp or returning to the
same site within three months was made a criminal offence and powers
given to the police to impound and confiscate vehicles. In response
to convoys of New Travellers travelling en masse, the Act also specifies
that six or more vehicles travelling together constitute a convoy and
can be dispersed. These provisions severely restricted the viability of
nomadism, as Bancroft notes:

> Since Gypsy-Traveller families can easily own three trailers,
> two or three families travelling together can be enough to
> constitute a convoy and cause an offence under the Act.
> Making it harder to travel together has meant that networks
> of family and friends which are central to the organisation
> of Gypsy-Traveller society have been made more difficult
> to sustain. (Bancroft, 2000, p 10)

Despite the criminalisation of unauthorised camping and increased
powers to break up travelling convoys, caravan counts throughout
the late 1990s and early 2000s indicate that the 1994 Act failed to
produce a discernible decline in unauthorised encampments. This
was largely a consequence of young Gypsies and Travellers marrying
and forming new households whilst being unable to access pitches
and thus going 'on the road', combined with an increased number of
families made homeless following the closure of public sites (Crawley,
2004). Among New Travellers, who were, many assumed, the primary
targets of such anti-nomadic legislation, a relatively rapid exodus to
live in Europe or return to houses was noted, to the extent that this
population became significantly less visible (Dearling, 1998). While the
apparently contradictory statistical finding on numbers of unauthorised
encampments would appear to be in opposition to the main theme
of the book, which concerns the decline of nomadism and increasing

settlement among traditional travelling groups (English Romanichals and Irish Travellers), we argue that the policy backdrop is key to understanding the drive to sedentarisation and the continuing problems of unauthorised encampments post 1994. Indeed when presenting the empirical findings on routes into housing, it was the sharp reduction in local authority provision and slow progress in expanding private site capacity, which forced many onto the road and from thence into 'bricks and mortar'.[1] A further element is the fact that caravan-dwelling populations represent a flow of people rather than a static community. As many former nomads have entered housing so others are in transit between travelling and settled lifestyles and formerly 'settled' people have been absorbed into the ranks of caravan dwellers, making it difficult to assess the size and duration of caravan-dwelling populations over time with any degree of reliability (Belton, 2005, p 122). As the population changed, swelled and contracted, the increasing legal harassment and a speedier eviction process made it increasingly difficult for 'roadside' Gypsies and Travellers to access health, education and other services, which provided a further stimulus for many families to settle in housing (Chapter Five). Moreover, the sheer 'churning' of transient and homeless Gypsies and Travellers as rapid eviction followed rapid eviction led to the situation where, as one police officer noted in a Home Office study, Travellers were 'being chased from one bit of land to another bit of land to another bit of land … you just chase them around'. In response many joined together in larger groups on fewer sites, increasing public anxiety and instigating fresh cycles of evictions (Home and Greenfields, 2006, p 9).

With the emergence of a new policy consensus that the 1994 Act had failed to deal with the growing tensions around roadside sites and unauthorised developments (self-owned land turned into sites by Gypsies and Travellers) and the election of the New Labour administration in 1997, it had become clear that a new direction was required and a far-ranging policy review of Gypsy and Traveller accommodation, education and health matters was undertaken (Greenfields, 2007a). The 2004 Housing Act was updated and amended to require local authorities to assess the accommodation needs of Gypsies and Travellers in their area (as they already did for the wider community under Local Housing Needs Assessments). The mechanism for assessing accommodation need for Gypsies and Travellers was the Gypsy and Traveller Accommodation Assessment (GTAA). GTAAs required that both housed and sited families should be consulted over their current and future preferences for sites or alternative forms of accommodation. In a drive to reduce unauthorised encampments,

Planning Circular 01/2006 *Planning for Gypsy and Traveller Sites* created mechanisms and duties for local authorities to identify land in their area suitable for site development, and the centrally funded Gypsy and Traveller Sites Grant made £56 million available to fund new sites and refurbish existing ones at no cost to local authorities. It was envisaged that GTAAs would moreover, provide the evidence base from which authorities would develop their local accommodation strategy with pitch requirements within a wide-spread area fed into Regional Spatial Strategies and allocated between Local Planning Authorities (DCLG, 2007). With the advent of these policy drivers, and a relatively well-resourced and experienced Government civil service team overseeing developments, it finally appeared that a concerted effort was finally being made to meet the accommodation needs of Gypsies and Travellers and tackle the issue of unauthorised camping.

The advent of the newly elected Coalition government in 2010, however, brought a return to 'older' style policies of repression. Within a month of gaining power, the government reversed most of the incentives for councils to identify land for sites and cancelled local authority bids to build or refurbish sites (Hill, 2010). In December 2010 the newly minted Localism Bill included provisions for abolishing regional spatial strategies and 'top down' targets for the provision of Gypsy sites in favour of a decentralised system, governed by local authorities and designed in consultation with local people – creating a climate where unpopular plans (such as the delivery of local authority sites) were likely to be overturned in the face of local opposition (Ryder et al, 2011). Whilst, on the face of it, the Localism Bill was not overtly 'anti-Gypsy' and contained provisions for incentives to authorities to provide sites through payment of the New Homes Bonus, an allocation of £60 million for new site provision and the promotion of Community Land Trusts, a review of provisions by a series of policy experts led to unanimous calls for a rethink on policy and claims that the new regime could have disastrous impacts given that the most fervent opposition to Gypsy and Traveller sites is found at the local level in parish councils and neighbourhood forums (Ryder et al, 2011).

Supporters of localism claim that it engages marginalised sections of society who have become detached from the top-down nature of the political process. On the other hand, it has been argued that devolving power to local communities may also deepen and perpetuate inequalities. Parvin (2011) for example, notes a growing polarisation in political engagement based on social class and between deprived and affluent areas. It is unskilled, low-paid and economically marginal social groups who display much lower levels of engagement regardless of ethnicity meaning that they have little influence over political decisions that affect their lives. Localism, argues Parvin, could thus

> … merely replace one form of tyranny with another, by giving engaged, articulate, advantaged members of local communities the power to dominate and marginalise disengaged, disaffected disadvantaged members of that same local community. (Parvin, 2011, p 48)

Indeed evidence from reviews of the 1968 and 2004 Acts strongly suggests that local authorities would not make adequate provision for site delivery without central Government directives or regional targets. The scrapping of Circular 01/2006, combined with the localism agenda, therefore has created a climate which may give free rein to local prejudice and be reflected in a rise in planning refusals and enhanced rates of eviction, pushing more Gypsies and Travellers onto the roadside where they face hostility from the wider community, cycles of enforced movement and reduced access to health, education and welfare services. In such circumstances many Gypsies and Travellers will have little choice but to enter housing with the attendant social and cultural dislocation that often accompanies such a move.

Having outlined the main policy drivers behind the settlement and immobilisation of the UK's travelling communities, the remainder of this chapter outlines theoretical accounts that position the processes of spatial management to which itinerant communities have been subjected with intensifying rapidity in the postwar period, within an analytic framework. Despite the differences of emphasis in the various texts considered, the common thread is that of spatial boundaries between Gypsy/Travellers and the majority society, and the way in which sedentarisation of the former has largely been imposed from the outside, predominantly as a result of the state policies described in this chapter.

Outsiders in urban society

David Sibley's *Outsiders in Urban Society* (1981) is one of few attempts to theorise the urbanisation of Gypsies and proceeds from two general propositions: firstly, that all societies will adopt policies that aim to either exclude or incorporate outsider groups into the mainstream. Secondly, that industrialised societies – capitalist or socialist – are characterised by centralised power, hierarchically organised institutions and, as economies develop, by a progressive segregation and classification of land use that eliminates activities that either do not contribute to, or undermine, the productive process (1981, p 37). In his account, Sibley takes issue with both imperialist and Marxist perspectives on the social position of peripheral groups such as Gypsies and Travellers. The first, emphasises cultural and physical distinctiveness, and is associated with 19th-century imperialist anthropology. It was also present in the writings of the Gypsy Lore Society in the late 19th and early 20th centuries through its preoccupation with the Indian origins and ancestry of Britain's Gypsies which, it was argued, was being diluted through intermarriage and urbanisation leading to cultural decline and assimilation into the urban poor (Mayall, 2004). This perspective leads to romantic ethnic stereotypes which, when Travellers are experienced as a group at first hand and the romantic stereotype is accordingly dispelled, contribute to the attribution of deviancy:

> Where outsiders come into close physical association with the larger society, particularly in cities, the romantic image, the pervasive myth about minority culture, is retained as a yardstick against which outsiders are measured … The myth can be retained because failure to meet mythical expectations is attributed to deviancy or to social pathologies that are somehow the product of urban living. (Sibley, 1981, p 6)

Marxist perspectives, meanwhile, view capitalist domination and integration into the class structure as omnipotent forces; with the peripheral status of minority groups representing a transitional stage between cultural autonomy and incorporation into the capitalist system (Schopflin, 2000, p 26). The spatial expansion of capitalism and exploitation of industrial resources requires the removal of competing claims to land from indigenous populations and state-led efforts to assimilate them into the urban working classes. This argument, notes Sibley, rests on the assumption of complicity between capital and the state, which he argues is often difficult to demonstrate empirically, particularly at the local level. Nevertheless, government policy towards Gypsies generally reveals 'an ideology of control that does not vary with the political complexion of the local authority but is generally in harmony with the interests of capital' (1981, p 11). Another problem with Marxist perspectives concerns the relation between the working class and peripheral groups: there are, Sibley maintains, cultural and economic features of peripheral groups that differentiate their interests from those of the working class. These differences represent real divisions that cannot be explained as false consciousness on either the part of the working class or peripheral groups.

Finally, similar processes of exploitation and incorporation are found in societies not based on a capitalist mode of production such as in the former socialist states of Eastern and Central Europe, these parallel responses both representing a more general modernist orientation underpinned by 'a belief in progress or an inevitable change to a mature state where the path of change is clearly mapped out and is inherent in the political system' (Sibley, 1981, p 12). Conflict between dominant and peripheral groups therefore is a consequence of cleavages in cultural and economic interests rather than an opposition of interests between capital and the working class of which peripheral groups form one element. Thus while the labelling of minority groups as 'deviant' has important consequences for that group it is also necessary to address the factors 'that make some social groups different from the rest, that is, the structural forces that lead to some groups being identified as outsiders' (1981, p 24).

Sibley locates the fundamental difference between the dominant society and Gypsies in John Berger's (1979) distinction between 'cultures of progress' (founded on an ideology of progressive accumulation) and the 'cultures of survival' (based on tradition, continuity and adaption to external change) that characterise peripheral groups. It is the world-structure of such groups that sets them apart from the urban majority. This world-structure is maintained and reproduced by the 'existence of a cultural boundary that serves to absorb or deflect pressure exerted by the larger society'. Gypsies represent a 'case of a culture that is within but outside the dominant system' with economic independence and the barrier between themselves and the gorjer (non-Gypsy) forming the basis of collective resistance to assimilation into the dominant society (1981, p 15). Developing the argument that peripheral and outsider groups are differentiated from the urban majority by their world structure, Sibley argues that Gypsies represent a 'muted group' meaning they are detached from the mainstream due to the existence of a communication barrier, with part of their culture remaining 'muted' or hidden from the outside. Since that part which is visible fails to accord with 'exotic' stereotypes, manifestations of Gypsy culture in an urban setting and the squalid urban camping grounds on which many lived until relatively recently, reinforced the deviant label 'since to have appeared to have abandoned a noble existence in harmony with nature, for one that conflicts with mainstream conceptions of order and harmony is an indication of degeneracy' (Sibley, 1981, p 19)

For Sibley, deviancy and deprivation represent two sides of the same coin. While the former involves the breaking of societal norms and the latter implies a lack of resources, the assumption is commonly made that deprivation results from fecklessness and social inadequacy (Geremek, 1991). This connection is frequently made with respect to Gypsies and Travellers: poor health and education is the fault of their nomadic habits instead of the inability of bureaucratic state agencies to respond adequately to minority lifestyles. This line of argument then justifies policies aimed at resocialisation and remedying of the perceived cultural pathology, as recommended for Irish Travellers by the Itinerant Settlement Committee movement in the 1960s for example (Noonan, 1998). More recently the Dale Farm Travellers refusal to accept Basildon Council's offer of 'alternative accommodation' in conventional housing was met with bewilderment in the media. Basildon's offer, argues Sedgemore (2011), displayed a 'typically bourgeois British racism against Gypsies and Travellers' based on socially engineering the group out of existence. Both deprivation and deviancy therefore are labels derived from the norms of mainstream society, their aim being to justify a policy of regulation and control. However, the appeal to equality and social justice means that

> The discriminatory nature of these policies is masked ... by the emphasis on the higher standards that will enable the minority to enjoy the lifestyle of the majority, and it is easy to appeal to a sense of social justice in providing a deprived ethnic group with bathrooms or electric lighting. (Sibley, 1981, p 182)

Sibley refutes the modernisation thesis, that the presence of peripheral and indigenous groups in cities is a recent process driven by the pervasive influences of modernity and urbanisation that destroys traditional cultural mores and lifestyles. Instead he argues that urbanisation of nomadic groups occurred in a similar fashion, and at a similar rate, to the rest of the population as the economic activities of such groups depend on interaction with the wider society. Traditional economic practices of family-based self-employment, flexibility and adaptability were refashioned allowing the group to retain its economic independence and cultural autonomy in an urban environment. In explaining why Gypsies constitute an increasingly visible outsider group, Sibley attaches more significance to symbolic forms of social control and spatial order than to the internal social structure of the group, arguing that the nature of the urban environment is of vital importance in explaining their social status. The 19th-century city contained an abundance of enclaves and marginal spaces beyond state control and surveillance that were congenial for settlement by nomadic communities (see further Chapter Three). Changes in the structure of the housing market, legislation strengthening local government control over land usage and the imposition of spatial order through single use zoning and residential segregation eliminated the marginal spaces previously occupied by Gypsies and other itinerants (Mayall, 1995). These processes in turn strengthened the boundaries both between social groups and, by increasing their visibility, between Gypsies and mainstream society, intensifying the hostility directed towards them since 'the margin occupied by British Travellers is progressively narrowed as land is incorporated into those categories that are considered economically and socially acceptable, making it more difficult for the minority to retain its autonomy' (Sibley, 1981, p 182).

Accordingly, over the long term the autonomy of peripheral groups is likely to be weakened and dependence on the wider society increased, argues Sibley. He notes that conflict between the state and minority groups are particularly acute when three related conditions pertain: when services such as accommodation are subject to state control and allocation; where the culture of the minority group is widely perceived as deviant; and where integration as an aim of policy, has not been achieved (1981, p 90). These findings have been borne out more recently in studies on working-class responses to in-migration from diverse countries with visible cultural differences from the receiving nations (Hudson et al, 2007; Philips and Harrison, 2010). Indeed, in the case of Gypsies and Travellers, state-provided accommodation reveals that strong classification in the form of spatial boundaries and a minimum of social mixing is an integral element of society's approach to peripheral groups (Richardson, 2007b). The failure of the 1968 Caravan Sites Act to deliver sufficient site capacity and remove the problem of illegal camping was largely a result of vociferous organised opposition to local site development and a lack of political will, which resulted in many sites being located in residual, polluted and undesirable areas so as to minimise conflict with the settled community. Efforts to impose dominant forms of social and spatial order on local authority caravan sites are evident in site design, with economic activities prohibited and restrictions on fires and the keeping of dogs. In addition, sites are designed according to clearly demarked boundaries between residential and recreational areas, which are antithetical to the economic and social organisation of Gypsy settlements and violate the group's own sense of spatial order (Sibley, 1981, p 107). Similar restrictions on parking caravans outside housing or on the lighting of fires in gardens are similarly in conflict with the group's cultural norms and use of domestic and public space in social housing (see Chapter Six). Myths about Gypsies therefore – both romantic and deviant – help to define the boundaries of the dominant system with state policy towards minority groups concerned primarily with their integration and control. In practice, however, this desire to purify and classify social space 'reinforces the boundaries of the system ... so what is on the outside becomes more conspicuously different' (Sibley, 1981, p 196).

Building on Sibley's general theoretical insight that the structural and ideological forces that construct minority groups as different (and therefore deviant) should be the starting point for analysis, Angus Bancroft (2005) develops Sibley's emphasis on the relation between spatial control and social exclusion. Like Sibley, Bancroft adopts a historical and comparative perspective but in exploration of the position of Gypsies, Travellers and Roma in Europe, focuses his analysis on the relationship between European modernity; globalisation, changes in European society and in particular the enlargement of the EU, which has brought those nations with the largest Roma populations inside the EU boundaries.

Modernity, space and exclusion

Bancroft's starting point is that the social order is also a spatial order, since the construction of space reflects power structures that fix the position of marginalised and excluded groups as outsiders both socially and spatially (Bancroft, 2005, p 51). He examines the exclusion and regulation of Roma and Gypsy Travellers in Europe in terms of spatial regulation and explores how the social position of those groups is intrinsically related to the changing spatial orders and formations that accompanied the rise of modernity. The exclusion of, and prejudice towards, Roma and Gypsy Travellers has been a constant theme in European history and regardless of debates surrounding the alleged origins of the various groups one element in particular, unites their diversity:

> There are many different groups of Roma and Gypsy-Travellers in Europe and the rest of the world, many of whom do not recognize any commonality between each other. Yet their experience, of being accorded the lowest social status, of enduring persecution and exclusion,

spans the differences between the separate groups and the
countries they live in. (2005, p 33)

Despite this historic continuity and the revival of anti-Gypsy actions
such as emergent pogroms in Central and Eastern Europe (Sigona and
Trehan, 2009), the regulative patterns that these groups are subject to
gives rise to new forms of exclusions. In adopting a pan-European and
historical perspective Bancroft explores how governance, regulation,
the monitoring and control of space and the development of status,
ethnic and national identities that accompanied European modernity,
contributed towards spatial segregation and restrictions on the
movement of Roma and Gypsy Travellers at a continental level and
spatial cleansing and ghettoisation at a local level (2005, p 146). From the
perspective of the European nation state Gypsies represent a 'backward'
element of society thus symbolising a counterpart to modernity and
the creation of national identity. Bancroft draws on Simmel's (1971)
concept of the 'Stranger' to understand how the majority society erects
boundaries between itself and Gypsies. The Stranger represents both
closeness and distance, freedom, a refusal to assimilate and a lack of
commitment to the majority society which means that he/she is always
viewed with wariness and suspicion. Thus the 'internal enemy, the
resident outsider has had a central function in defining and affirming
a European identity' (2005, pp 168–9).

For Bancroft the focus on 'backwardness' is an important element of
political and policy discourse and partly explains why Roma and other
nomadic communities have been subject to so much state legislation
and attention since 'for the nation state to have an internal population
which rejects some of the key principles of modernity shows up the
mismatch between the universalizing principles of modernity and the
inequalities which it creates and sustains' (2005, p 24). The advance of
bureaucratic rationalism during the 18th and 19th centuries has led
to the replacement of exoticised stereotypes of Gypsies with one that
borrows more from the 'culture of poverty' and emphasises cultural
decline, degeneracy and criminality. Romantic stereotypes of 'backward'
Gypsies living a 'pre-modern' existence. however. still play an important
role in the collective consciousness particularly when it coexists with
the demonisation and criminalisation of contemporary Travellers and
'the image of the true Gypsy recedes quickly in the minds of the local
gauje population whenever some real life Gypsy-Travellers are present
but unwanted' (Bancroft, 2005, p 40). On a larger scale, notes Bancroft,
treatment of Roma and Gypsy Travellers across Europe reveals as
much about national stereotyping and political hypocrisy as about the

citizenship rights of, minority populations (Sigona and Trehan, 2009). Thus, in Western Europe politicians bemoan the treatment of Roma in Central and Eastern Europe, viewing it as evidence of those nations' barbarity and political immaturity, while overlooking the position of Gypsies and Travellers or the treatment of incoming Roma populations in their own countries (2005, p 3), a point which did not pass unnoticed by commentators during the 2011 evictions from the Dale Farm site in the UK (Goodall, 2011; Home, 2012).

The universalising drive behind modernity combined with the rise of state bureaucracies meant that policies to assimilate their Gypsy populations through various measures were adopted across Europe from the 18th century onwards. The other official solution to the 'Gypsy problem' was associated with the rise of racial science in the 19th century and would reach its zenith in the mid 20th century with the Nazi genocide of Roma and Gypsy Traveller populations (Kenrick and Puxon, 1972). The response of contemporary European states towards Roma and Gypsy Travellers meanwhile displays much continuity with 19th- and early 20th-century policies, comprising policies of control and regulation and spatial exclusion policies such as the forced closures and vigilante attacks on Gypsy and Roma camps in Italy during 2008, French President Sarkozy's decision in 2010 to clear Roma camps and deport over 10,000 Romanian and Bulgarian Roma, and Basildon Council's decision to evict and clear the Travellers on the Dale Farm site in Essex in October 2011 (Home, 2012). These processes of spatial cleansing, control and regulation combine to segregate Roma and Gypsy Travellers into frequently overcrowded and poorly serviced caravan sites or into areas of low quality housing constituting 'hyperghettos' that are devoid of institutional structures and social amenities and generally subject to surveillance technology (Richardson, 2006; 2007b). In advanced industrial societies this represents one aspect of a more general process whereby discourse surrounding crime and disorder leads to the exponential increase in 'gated communities' designed to the keep the hazardous and disorderly sub-classes at bay, and increasingly sophisticated forms of surveillance technology create 'safe zones' for the powerful and affluent and 'dark zones' where the police contain the poor, marginalised and economically superfluous elements of society (Davis, 1990). Despite the obvious parallels, this does not represent the implementation of a Panopticon regime of surveillance, discipline and correction, argues Bancoft, but:

> Rather it is the segregation of irreducible subjects, incorrigible others. It matters not what they do, as long as

> it is done somewhere else. It is a kind of reverse Panopticon,
> with the safe zones under constant watch, and the unsafe
> zones walled off and largely ignored except on the occasions
> when they erupt into hot zones as in the Los Angeles riots
> of 1992. (2005, pp 73–4)

As considered previously, treatment of their Roma and Gypsy populations reveals much about national stereotypes and misunderstandings. It is easy, Bancroft observes, to point to extreme historical examples such as the Holocaust or the brutal treatment of Roma in contemporary Central and Eastern Europe, as a measuring rod against which Britain's enlightened and humane treatment of Gypsies and other minorities may be compared, and to neglect the more mundane outcomes of state policy and regulation on the daily lives of those communities. Increasing bureaucratic control and spatial regulation limits their movement while weakening their family structures, economic practices and forms of social organisation (Bancroft, 2005, p 170). However, while the operation of the modern state and society combine to restrict the choice facing Gypsy Travellers to one between forced movement and forced settlement, the spatial structures of modernity also provide spaces of resistance and survival.

Conflict over the control of space have become more intense in recent years as the activities of the nation state have turned increasingly towards the creation and management of 'safe zones' for global capital and its beneficiaries (Garland, 2001). A core aspect of this process has been an intensification of spatial regulation and cleansing, which takes a variety of forms from 'defensive architecture' to the privatisation and regeneration of urban centres around the lifestyles and consumption practices of the advanced service class 'whose cultural practices and values, their local ideologies have articulated a useful dominant ideological and cultural paradigm for this stage of capital' (Jameson, 1989, p 40). In Britain the countryside was rapidly transformed in the post-war period, becoming strongly designated for either residential or agricultural purposes. Rural Gypsies and Travellers have found themselves between these two zoning principles while residual and marginal land on wasteland and on roadside verges have decreased in number and been progressively enclosed, thus closing off many traditional camping grounds (Home, 2006; Greenfields, 2006). Despite lip service being paid to diversity, tolerance and equality, in reality this only extends to certain minority groups, generally those championed by an urban liberal elite and/or those groups who are numerically significant and politically vocal and active enough to warrant courting from politicians, a recognition which led Trevor Phillips (the then Chair of the Commission for Racial Equality) to state in 2004 that prejudice against Gypsies and Travellers was the 'last acceptable form of racism' (CRE, 2004). For others, especially 'those minorities who are perceived as violating the neat social and spatial ordering of modernity', exclusion and rejection continues, argues Bancroft (2005, p 171). As detailed in Chapter One, the 1994 Criminal Justice Act revealed these exclusionary processes in stark form and represented a legislative attempt to purify space through removing and excluding those groups who were deemed to have violated spatial boundaries – 'new age' Travellers, hunt saboteurs, environmental protestors as well as 'traditional' Gypsies and Travellers. In this respect the 1994 Act can be seen as reaffirming spatial boundaries or, as Bancroft puts it, 'a way of symbolically re-establishing the boundaries of decency' (2005, p 66). Similarly, Sibley notes that such legislation acts to establish who is deemed to 'belong' and who it is legitimate to exclude from certain spaces (1995, p 14).

> The countryside it seems belongs to the middle class, to landowners and to people who engage in blood sports. A rigid stereotype of place – the English countryside – throws up discrepant others. The presence of these discrepant groups reflects the anxieties of those in dominant positions who see their material interests threatened. (Sibley, 1995, p 57)

Nevertheless agency will always reassert itself, both in influencing the place of marginal groups in the city and country and in the ways that place and space is used. Bancroft highlights an ongoing and cyclical relationship between the state and Gypsy/Travellers as the former introduces ever more repressive methods of spatial control and the latter find strategies to circumvent them (2005, p 65). While the 1994 Act could have represented the death knell for Gypsies and Travellers, as will be shown in later chapters, various adaptive strategies such as the maintenance of traditional uses of domestic space in conventional housing, utilising formal and informal exchange mechanisms in order to continue semi-nomadic lifestyles within housing, and the conscious reformulation of spatially concentrated ethnic enclaves on public housing estates, have allowed many Gypsies and Travellers to refashion traditional practices, strategies and collective forms of adaptation to assert agency and a modicum of free choice in the face of increasing bureaucratic control and structural constraints (Greenfields and Smith,

2010, 2011). The community and micro-level outcomes of these more general and long-term trends that Bancroft highlights are therefore examined through detailed empirical investigation from Chapter Five onwards.

Ethnicity, social closure and legislation

While the accounts by Sibley and Bancroft emphasise the separateness of Gypsies and Travellers (albeit enforced through discrimination and legislation), Brian Belton develops an alternative perspective. This model stresses the permeability of the social and spatial boundaries that Sibley and Bancroft identify, as well as the extent of movement between caravan and house dwelling in response to wider social forces. Belton starts from the position that much research on Gypsies and Travellers has erroneously prioritised the role of genealogy and/or heritage as the basis for collective identity, and he is critical of the tendency among scholars to posit an underlying unity connecting the diversity of travelling groups. Such accounts, he suggests, place too much stress on the distinctiveness of Gypsies and Travellers by focusing on similarities between different nomadic groups and downplaying differences:

> This position is problematical; it suggests a tenuous connection of Gypsyness, grouping people together around fragmented similarities of language, ritual or tradition often with little correlation between these considerations. (Belton, 2005, p 10)

Consequently, the fluidity between house and caravan dwelling and the possibility of recruitment to caravan dwelling from non-Gypsy sources is neglected, meaning that the significance of hybridised and non-ethnic travelling groups, some of which have existed in Britain for centuries, (Beier, 1985) is overlooked. Belton, by contrast, while not denying the Gypsy/Romany element and influence on Britain's nomadic population, views the caravan-dwelling population as a more mixed and heterogeneous group. He argues for a wider perspective on the creation of the nomadic population, regarding a sense of group identity as more a product of social and economic policies (in particular housing and planning policy) than of ethnic or racial origins, thus directing attention to the social pressures to adopt nomadism on members of the 'settled' population, a theme identified in relation to the growth of 'new Travellers' in the 1980s (Dearling, 1998; Greenfields, 1999). Just as legislation has forced many Travellers to move into housing, so caravan dwelling has long been an option for homeless individuals and families with restricted accommodation options. Historical and contemporary evidence suggests considerable intermingling between the travelling and 'settled' populations with long established travelling groups displaying significant 'cross pollination' with people moving in and out of caravan dwelling as a result of intermarriage, work opportunities and personal circumstances (see further Chapter Three). Indeed many of the rituals, practices and customs identified as 'Gypsy traits' such as attendance at annual fairs, the keeping of bone china, gender roles and the emphasis placed on family and community were also common among the working classes, though today many of these traits have been considerably more diluted than among many Gypsy/Travellers. It was previously noted that there has been a long association between 'urban Gypsies' and low-income urban areas suggesting that nomads and other itinerants have long lived in close social and spatial proximity to the urban working classes with a considerable level of acculturation occurring between the groups over time.

The implication is, therefore, that any clear dichotomy between Gypsies and 'gorjers' based either on race or ethnicity is extremely problematic. Similarly caravan dwelling is not necessarily an indication of Romany/Gypsy origins, as identity can be socially ascribed or culturally adopted while the desire to travel and live nomadically 'is not confined to one ethnic or cultural niche' but has long attracted members of the 'settled' population (Belton, 2005, p 72). Many people identified as Gypsies and Travellers by lieu of their lifestyle display no ethnic or familial connections to long-established travelling families, though Belton does concede that hereditary factors may play a role in the continuation of a travelling lifestyle over successive generations (2005, p 59), a finding also noted by Greenfields (1999) in her study of the origins of 'new Travellers'.

For Belton, legislation is the key causal factor in the evolution of ethnic identity due to the cumulative impact of internal migration following industrialisation, housing shortages and legislative pressures on the travelling population to cease their nomadism. Accordingly, he widens the scope of analysis beyond the 'one-dimensional focus' on the effects of legislation on Travellers which follows the racial/ethnic preoccupation of many scholars and which, he suggests, obscures the wider purpose of legislation as a tool of 'far reaching social discipline' by limiting analysis of the impact of legislation to an 'incursion on minority lifestyles' (2005, p 20). Post-war legislation had a much wider purpose than control and regulation of a relatively small minority group and sought to enforce housing market norms and conventional family structures on those who sought alternatives outside of that market by adopting cheaper and more communal ways of living (Ward, 2002). The failure of the public and private sectors to supply adequate amounts of low-income housing in the post-war period provided the conditions where alternatives to conventional housing and homelessness were developed, which the state was then obliged to legislate against:

> the post-war legislation affecting Travellers is collectively an extension of State control in the interests of capital that addresses certain contradictions arising out of the housing market and those that the market produces who are obliged to seek alternatives outside that market. (Belton, 2005, pp 120–1)

Belton highlights a consistent link between caravan dwelling and homelessness from the municipal 'caravan colonies' that grew up on the edges of many towns in the interwar period – a low-cost solution to high demand for affordable housing – through to the post-war period where severe housing shortages fuelled the number of caravan dwellers. Between the late 1950s and early 1960s there was a growing national awareness that the country faced a severe housing crisis and it was in this period that the caravan-dwelling population became a topic of national debate. The 1961 national housing census revealed 75,373 households comprised of 183,688 people resident in caravans (2005, p 62). Legislation relating to caravan dwelling and caravan sites in the 1960s was underpinned by a desire to reform and control this population but also by a degree of tolerance of nomadic lifestyles (2005, p 109). As discussed in the previous section, the flawed nature of the 1960 Caravan Sites and Control of Development Act gave rise to public and political concern over the 'Gypsy problem' as increased numbers were pushed onto the road and, since camping on commons was outlawed in the Act, onto patches of land closer to the settled community. The Act's defects eventually led to the statutory duties (along with designation status and enhanced powers to expel nomads) in the 1968 Act. These provisions, argues Belton, allowed local authorities to control the caravan dwellers through minimum site provision and in the longer term reinforced the spatial exclusion of Gypsies and Travellers:

> Poor implementation of the 1968 Act made the option of trailer living unattractive. Sites were rarely if anything more than poorly serviced, often vandalized and the focus

of local prejudice, discrimination and police surveillance. In effect many sites could be likened to Bantustans, sometimes surrounded with deep ditches, corrugated iron and/or barbed wire. (Belton, 2005, 119)

Comparative analysis of biannual caravan counts and homelessness statistics over a 20-year period from the mid 1970s until the introduction of the 1994 Criminal Justice Act reveals that a gradual rise in homelessness from the late 1970s until the mid 1990s followed by a slight decline from the mid 1990s was mirrored in 70 per cent of caravan counts, which demonstrated similar trends over the same period. Peaks in homelessness coincided with peaks in caravan counts throughout the mid 1980s with the nomadic population composed of fewer 'traditional' travelling groups suggesting that many were recruited from among house dwellers (such as New Age Travellers) and from the growing ranks of the homeless, representing a contemporary manifestation of a historical process of 'affiliation as well as instances of recruitment/conscription from one group to another' (2005, p 105). The 1994 Act followed the same logic of post-war policy, although in a more coercive manner, by making nomadism increasingly harder and forcing the travelling population into housing while promoting private site development. Belton's central argument, therefore, is that the impact of legislation, which has progressively segregated and marginalised all of the varied nomadic groups, has led to an increasing political consciousness between different travelling communities. This has been accompanied by a process of social closure which 'constitutes a defensive closing of ranks rather than an ethnic homogeneity' (2005, p 96).

Firstly, repressive legislation has made nomadic caravan dwelling unattractive to all but a small hardcore living on the margins of society who become identified by cultural and ethnic symbols. Secondly, this excluded group then use their marginalised ethnic identity as a form of defence and a platform from which to achieve rights and recognition. It is more often the political community that generates the belief in common ethnicity, argues Belton, thus demonstrating that ethnicity is simultaneously a divisive force in terms of the wider population and a unifying force in that it connects previously heterogeneous groups. In the case of Gypsies and Travellers, this solidarity 'coagulates and arises out of political pressures' (2005, p 10).

A position of this type allows such writers to theoretically champion an oppressed ethnic group, and fight the cause of minority rights but it obscures other possible forms of group generation arising out of the relationship between the Travelling population and social phenomena affecting a much wider constituency. (Belton, 2005, p 15)

The wider and more practical consequences of Belton's analysis concerns appropriate policy interventions. The policy response is ultimately shaped by whether hereditary factors and ethnicity are the crucial variables in explaining the inequalities and the marginal social status of Gypsies and Travellers or whether the status of the travelling population is viewed as a result of social conditions such as homelessness arising out of dysfunctions in the housing market. In the case of the former this will require a network of decent-quality, well-maintained caravan sites ,or for the latter ,massive investment in social housing and accompanying reforms of the housing market (2005, p 146).

All three of the accounts discussed above examine the urbanisation and settlement of Gypsies and Travellers through an analytic framework that encompass wider issues – social, political and economic and the role of state action within that theoretical model. From different starting points, Sibley and Bancroft both focus on the intensification of modernist techniques of production and the increasingly encompassing surveillance technology and regulative apparatus of the state which are employed to spatially control and regulate those minorities who do not adhere to conventional notions of land usage or of regular waged labour as a result of having developed alternative ways of living. As Bancroft puts it, 'Those minorities who are perceived as violating the neat social and spatial ordering of modernity are subject to rejection and exclusion' (Bancroft, 2005, p 171), while for Sibley, the need to integrate and assimilate non-conformists is undermined by relegating them to marginal space which paradoxically reinforces social boundaries and the minority group's 'otherness'. These important insights form the implicit assumptions underpinning the empirical chapters, which provide a 'grass-roots' perspective on the broad theoretical analysis provided by the two authors.

Belton's analysis, by contrast, is concerned more with the nomadic and caravan-dwelling population than with Gypsies/Travellers per se. By highlighting the non-Gypsy origins of many of Britain's contemporary travelling population and shifting the analysis from hereditary factors to legislation as a generator of ethnic identity, Belton could be accused of 'de-legitimising' Gypsies and Travellers, though Belton's contribution assists our arguments in relation to the similarities and variables which cross-cut the relations between housed

Gypsies, Travellers and the working classes among whom they reside. Bancroft acknowledges the ethical and methodological dilemma that researchers can face when the research process involves critique and re-evaluation of existing categories and constructs, yet to do so in the case of Gypsies and Travellers can be taken as affirming settled identity and undermining the former's identity (Bancroft, 2005, p 42). However, Belton's main concern is not with the origins and identity of Gypsies and Travellers but how the various heterogeneous and assorted nomadic communities that have been a constant though marginal feature of British society, have developed a common identity in relation to threats to their lifestyles from the state and political actors (Vermeesch, 2007).

In accounting for the number of caravan dwellers over successive decades, Belton does not account for the rising number of Irish Travellers who comprised a growing element of the nomadic population in Britain between the 1950s and 1980s as increasing numbers moved between Ireland, Scotland and England. Trends also ran in opposite directions with significant numbers moving back to Ireland in the early 1980s in response to rising hostility in England (McLaughlin, 1999). No accurate figures exist for these populations, although in the late 1990s O'Dwyer (1997) estimated that there were 15,000 Irish Travellers 'on the road' in Britain, which is probably an underestimate and also excludes those who are semi-nomadic, residing in conventional housing for part of the year (Power, 2004). GTAA evidence from various parts of Britain certainly seems to suggest that Irish Travellers are less likely to be residing on local authority (LA) provided sites, and more frequently found on the 'roadside' or on 'private rented' pitches. Power (2004, pp 16–17) highlights how many Irish Travellers have been excluded from LA sites, with this exclusion becoming more entrenched over time as many families settled permanently on official sites restricting access for other families. Moreover, with a young age profile, early marriage and an average of eight children per family the Irish Traveller population is growing fast and now forms a major element of the country's Traveller population (Power, 2004, p 6).

The policy relevance of Belton's work is extremely pertinent in the current context. Despite Mayor Boris Johnson's promise that there would be no 'Kosovo style social cleansing' of the poor 'on his watch', several London councils have been attempting to house families in parts of the country where rents are cheaper as a result of the Coalition government's cuts to Housing Benefit (Taylor, 2012). Capping the Local Housing Allowance (LHA) at 30 per cent of average local rents with future rises tied to the Consumer Price Index could result in 134,000 households being unable to afford their rents and facing eviction or movement to cheaper accommodation (Fenton, 2010). Given Belton's central argument concerning the close correlation between homelessness and caravan dwelling, the coming years may well provide credence to his thesis if people resort to nomadism in preference to homelessness or resettlement in already deprived areas where rental prices are affordable precisely because of poor employment options and out-migration (Tilly, 2005; Clapham et al, 2012). Moreover, Belton's emphasis on the fluidity between housing and caravan dwelling and on mixing between the 'settled' and travelling populations is of central relevance to the current text. Later chapters of this book examine the extent of interaction between the two groups and the conditions under which those interactions and processes of mixing occur. Despite the current chapter's engagement with recent analyses of the impact of modernity and state policy, such discussions have a long historical lineage. In the following chapter we turn our attention to the growing urban presence of Gypsies and Travellers from the 19th century onwards and the processes that influenced earlier phases of settlement into housing.

Note

[1] Private sites only exceeded 40 per cent of pitch provision from January 2008 while socially rented provision declined from a peak of 49.4 per cent in January 1997 and fell beneath 40 per cent of caravans in January 2007 where it has displayed a gradual decline since (DCLG, 2012). Private site development was spurred significantly following Circular 01/2006. Prior to the Circular, 68 per cent of appeals relating to Gypsy and Traveller sites were rejected. In the two years following the Circular, 65 per cent of appeals were granted planning permission (Ryder et al, 2011).

THREE

Gypsies, nomads and urbanisation: a social history

Since the mid 19th century questions surrounding the urbanisation of Gypsies, the consequences of increasing contact with 'gaje'/'gorjer' (non-Gypsy) society and the qualitatively different nature of such interactions in urban contexts, have been central to scholarly debates concerning the origins and destiny of this group. According to Mayall (2004), the most basic distinction in this debate is between two paradigms. The first provides racial, linguistic and ancestral explanations highlighting the Indian origins of the various diasporic Romani groups that are today scattered around the world (Hancock, 2002; Kenrick, 2004). This model was initially promoted in the journal of the Gypsy Lore Society (GLS), which was founded in 1888 by scholars and others interested in the culture and language of the Gypsies. At that point in its history, the GLS favoured a model based on scientific racism, which was strongly opposed to the 'mixing' of cultures and sought only to legitimise those Gypsies deemed to be of 'pure-blooded' ancestry (Hancock, 2007). Whilst the stigmatisation of 'half-breed Gypsies' and the insistence on the purity of bloodline is now widely discredited as a product of its time, the early work undertaken by members of the GLS into linguistic and socio-cultural patterns remains critical to the recognition of Gypsies as a people with Indic origins and an admixture of diverse European heritages as they made their way from the Balkans (where they were first recorded in around 1300 CE) towards the British Isles.

In contrast, the second model of Gypsy and Traveller origins offers a socio-historical explanation pointing to the many indigenous nomadic groups that emerged in Europe in the early modern period. This perspective highlights nomadism, economic and cultural practices and collective stigmatisation as the primary criterion for inclusion (Gmelch, 1986; Lucassen et al, 1998). Despite the overlap between these positions and an acknowledgement of intermixing between Romani and indigenous travelling groups, the political and legal ramifications of this dichotomy means that such nuances have often been ignored. Classification of different nomadic groups along racial lines and the construction of status hierarchies to classify those groups has long been of concern to state officials and other commentators. Historically, argues Mayall (2004, p 4), official efforts to label different nomadic groups for legislative and policy purposes symbolise the perennial failure of state responses to nomadism and provide 'the clearest instances of how responses and category definitions are inextricably linked'. As Sibley (1981) (discussed in Chapter Two) notes, the romantic portrayal of 'true' Gypsies living a rural existence in horse-drawn wagons provides a template from which to denigrate Travellers who fail to accord to this image. These historical stereotypes persist and are frequently invoked by the media and politicians. In 1999, for example, then Home Secretary Jack Straw argued during a radio interview that

> "There are relatively few real Romany Gypsies left, who seem to mind their own business and don't cause trouble to other people, and then there are a lot more people who masquerade as Travellers or Gypsies, who trade on the sentiment of people, but who seem to think because they label themselves as Travellers that therefore they've got a licence to commit crimes and act in an unlawful way that other people don't have." (Jack Straw, Home Secretary, in an interview with Annie Oathen on Radio West Midlands, 22 July 1999)

This notion of an inauthentic itinerant underclass has infiltrated policy making to the extent that local authorities have utilised the idea of 'full blooded' Gypsies to denounce the majority of Travellers in their localities as well as (prior to the enactment of the 2004 Housing Act when the 'planning definition' of a Gypsy or Traveller emphasised nomadic habit rather than culture and ethnicity) to justify non-compliance with legal requirements to provide sites (Okely, 1983, pp 16–17; Power, 2004). The tendency to consider the move towards urban environments as either a manifestation of cultural decline and the imminent demise of 'traditional' lifestyles or else as the contemporary expression of an ongoing process of adaptation and cross-fertilisation between different marginalised groups, is accordingly largely dependent on the stance taken in relation to this debate. If Gypsies are regarded as once comprising of a 'pure blooded' race characterised by a rurally based, isolated culture and possessing innate tendencies to 'wanderlust' then their urbanisation and settlement will be regarded as detrimental and a potential cause of 'cultural trauma', a model utilised to a large extent by informants in our study. Indeed, there is certainly a wealth of evidence which points to the often devastating psychological and cultural effects that state-led attempts at settlement have had on members of Gypsy and other travelling communities (O'Nions, 1995; Greenfields and Smith, 2010, 2011).

Nevertheless, as discussed in Chapter One, over-emphasising the culturally corrosive aspects of large-scale socioeconomic changes and the policy drive to immobilise travelling groups overlooks the resilience of such groups and their ability to actively resist external forces through refashioning traditional cultural practices and values to changing circumstances (Fortier, 2009). An increasingly town-based and stationary existence has not necessarily led to assimilation and a dilution of collective identity, nor removed the collective stigma and structural exclusion that many continue to experience regardless of place and type of residence. Ethnic identities have inevitably evolved due to spatial proximity and cross-group interaction and a process of acculturation in the sense of a 'dual cultural outlook' has been identified in many younger community members (see further Chapter Nine). However, the tendency for assimilation to lag behind acculturation is reinforced by residential segregation and hostility from the dominant society, meaning that ethnic boundaries persist and continue to have important consequences for in-group members (Sanders, 2002).

Social historical studies indicate that Gypsies and Travellers have a long presence in urban locales with residence in conventional housing being neither a recent trend nor one driven exclusively by external pressures to settle. Their growing presence in towns from the 19th century and their proclivity to establish themselves in low-income areas means that the working-class residents of those areas have probably had the most sustained history of social and economic relations with Gypsies (as with most minority ethnic groups) in recent times. Relatively early census data (from both 1881 and 1891) provides evidence of 'tented' Gypsies sharing surnames with, and living in close proximity to, 'Gipsey [sic] pedlars' or 'Gipsey hawkers' enumerated as resident in houses in locales across the country (albeit predominantly in urban areas) indicating that the preference for close coexistence noted amongst the research sample for this study has deep historical and cultural roots.

However, despite the cultural and social affinities that have evolved over time the relationship between Gypsies and the urban working class, in either its historical or contemporary guises, has received scant attention both in the literature on Gypsies and in historical accounts of the working classes (Hobbes, 1989; Stedman Jones, 2002). As discussed in Chapter Seven, the preoccupation with social divisions and the boundaries between groups has often blinded social scientists to the relations that exist between these groups and the socioeconomic contexts under which those boundaries are breached. Belton's (2005) analysis, discussed at length in Chapter Two, is an obvious exception, as is Evans' (2004) historical account of Gypsies and Travellers in Kent and South London in which the author explores the relations that existed between Travellers and inner city Londoners, with close personal contacts forged in the hop gardens of Kent and Surrey:

> In Kent, the East Enders and Travellers spent a month every year working and living alongside each other in the hop gardens. The cockneys learnt about the outdoor Gypsy life, cooking on open fires and living simply in huts, barns or cowsheds; the Travellers got to know something of working-class inner-city ways from these unpretentious gorjers. (2004, p 7)

This image of mutual conviviality does not intend to minimise the long history of mutual prejudice and conflict that has existed between 'settled' Gypsy/Travellers and the (generally) working-class populace they live amongst (Chapters Seven and Eight) but is provided to illustrate that social relations at a micro-level are generally too complex, contradictory and multifaceted for generalisation. Accordingly, a comprehensive analysis of inter-group relations needs to account for the socio-cultural formations of the specific locales where those interactions take place as well as the particular historical trajectories of those areas. With these preliminary observations in mind, the remainder of this chapter continues the settlement theme commenced in the previous chapter and locates the theoretical and analytic perspectives discussed previously in a more detailed and historically grounded analysis.

Gypsies have long-standing connections to most urban conurbations in Britain particularly in the Midlands and the North West, while Kirk Yetholm in Scotland and the New Forest in Hampshire were two of the earliest recorded examples of large-scale settlements of Gypsies into housing. The focus in this chapter however is predominantly on London and its environs, with reference where applicable to the settlements in the Hampshire/New Forest areas, reflecting linkages between housed Gypsies and Travellers in the South Western study region and the large groupings of housed families in the Southampton area. The first reason for this geographic specificity is that several research fields in which the empirical sections of the book are based were either conducted in various parts of Inner or Greater London or else in locations in Southern and Western England. Linkages between London and the Home Counties were therefore repeatedly reflected in the fieldwork, with many participants in the South East having networks of relatives and connections with other Traveller families in the capital, and some participants in the South West referring to relatives living in Greater London as well as around the New Forest. Moreover, the metropolitan theme provides evidence of historical usage of important sources of economic opportunity where ethnic identities can be concealed and work secured more easily than in the smaller locations from where many Gypsies and Travellers originated. Historical evidence indicates significant movements of Gypsies, vagrants and other itinerants between the southern counties and London in the 19th century and particularly between the four counties surrounding the capital – Essex, Middlesex, Kent and Surrey – and London (Collins, 1976; Evans, 2004).

Secondly, by the middle of the 19th century London was the centre for the southern travelling population, many of whom entered the city for trade opportunities, en route to annual events such as the Epsom Derby or to participate in the traditional horse fairs and weekly auctions which ringed the city in peri-urban locales such as Barnet, Southall, Mitcham and Croydon. Evidence, too, from the proceedings of the Old Bailey criminal court indicates established Gypsy and Traveller communities in housing as well as campsites across London and the surrounding areas from the 17th century onwards.[1] Accordingly, Mayall (1988) tells us that London contained the largest population of Gypsies and other itinerants in the country. Thus in terms of exploring the historical association of Gypsies and Travellers with urban areas (still attested to by the variety of London street or area names containing reference to their presence such as Gipsy Hill, Barnet Common; Gypsy Corner, Acton; Romany Road in West Norwood) and their residence in conventional housing, London provides a logical starting point.

Settlement in the 19th and 20th centuries

Whilst it would be a mistaken assumption that the presence of city-dwelling Gypsies and Travellers is solely a product of modernity and industrialisation, several factors combined to increase the presence of these communities in towns and cities throughout the 19th and 20th centuries. Winstedt (1916) proposes that the earliest historical records pertaining to the presence of Gypsies in England refer to their presence at Lambeth, then a growing suburb of the city with something of a reputation for lawlessness, and now a densely built up part of the city just south of the Thames. He notes that Gypsies had been recorded in the area as early as 1514 (less than a decade after they were first recorded in Scotland) with references concerning the death of a 'gentleman' leading to enquiries being made of an 'Egypcian' woman who lodged at Lambeth and told fortunes in the area. The presence and distinguishing apparel of Romany migrants were familiar enough to courtiers by 1517, that we are told by Vesey-Fitzgerald that several memoirs and letters refer to court ladies dressed in finery and 'attired like to the Egyptians, very richly' by that date (1973, p 28). By 1621, Ben Jonson was able to present a court masque entitled the 'The Gypsies Metamorphosed' pertaining to stereotypes of subversive vagrants and the linkages between Romany wanderers and border-crossing migrants who change allegiances and appearances to suit their current need, while on 11 August 1668 Samuel Pepys recorded his wife, her friend and their servant going to visit the Gypsies at Lambeth to have their fortunes told (Netzloff, 2001). Thus relatively early in their recorded history, Gypsies and Travellers were familiar figures in London and its environments.

In the early 18th century in the (then) rural area of Norwood (now incorporated into South London) a long-established community of Gypsies resided in the area now known as Gypsy Hill, within easy reach of both the City and Croydon in Surrey (an area still with a relatively large population of Gypsies and Travellers). So great was their fame that a pantomime called 'The Norwood Gypsies' was staged in Covent Garden in 1777. Norwood was also the home of Margaret Finch the 'Queen of the Gypsies', who was born in Sutton in 1740 and reputedly lived till she was 108, achieving considerable fame as a fortune teller during her life. By the mid 19th century, however, the Enclosure Acts and raids by the authorities had dislodged the long-established camps around Norwood, with many Gypsies subsequently settling into housing in the immediate area. Somewhat surprisingly, however, the place of Gypsies in London folklore has generally been neglected by folklorists and local historians alike despite the not insignificant role they play in the social topography of the city. Warwick (1972) notes the enduring legacy of Gypsies not just in local place names around the Norwood area in particular (Gypsy Hill, the Gypsy Tavern pub) but also in local folklore, utilising a saying stating that 'if you look into the eyes of a Norwood local you look into the eyes of a gypsy' (1972, p 28). Samuel (1973) in his turn, identified the 'ancient haunts' of the travelling community as being in St Giles, Tothill Fields, The Mint, Deptford, Southwark and Penge, with others accompanying the massive growth of the city in the Victorian era as Travellers were progressively pushed out of the city centre. White (1986) makes several references to Gypsies and Travellers residing amongst the urban poor in North London, with some enterprising individuals (one woman in particular) hiring out wagons to costermongers, shares of squalid rented rooms to the even more indigent and even lending money made on horse trading at Barnet Fair as late as the 1930s.

Thus it is self-evident that Gypsies and those vagrants amongst whom they moved, and from whom they sometimes gathered new recruits, had a significant presence in the city prior to the onset of industrialisation. Beier's (1985) historical analysis of vagrancy reveals that the South East was at the crossroads for the countries' vagrants and Travellers, with the multifactorial opportunities afforded by London being the main pull factor. The city was also a major source of the itinerant population, with the capital's inability to assimilate its migrants an important factor in the growth of vagrancy between the 1500 and 1700s (Beier, 1985, p 41).

Although Gypsies were subject to a separate body of legislation in Tudor England they were often classed as vagrants for legislative purposes. The state's response ranged from attempts at 're-socialising' vagrants into employment through to more draconian approaches such as flogging, imprisonment and deportation with 'the multiplicity and occasional ferocity of the means employed in the battle underlin[ing] the seriousness which they [authorities] viewed the seriousness of the problem and its fundamental intractability' (Beier, 1985, p 152). The scope of legislation to deal with vagrancy, beggars, Gypsies and other itinerant groups was continually revised between the 1500s and the 1800s until repeal of the Egyptians Acts in 1783. However this did not end official discrimination, with the 1822 Vagrancy Act consolidating previous laws, while the 1824 Vagrancy Act has been described as 'the most pernicious piece of legislation against Gypsies and Travellers in the nineteenth century' (Mayall, 1995, p 29). The 1824 Act took a broad definition of vagrancy allowing magistrates to bypass trial by jury and dispense discretionary justice against vagrants and Gypsies, and also gave the police additional powers to move them on. The Turnpikes Act of 1822 levied fines on Gypsies camping on the roadside, and a series of Hawkers and Pedlars Acts passed between 1810 and 1888 which required registration and possession of a licence to undertake such work were repeatedly used to instigate prosecutions against vagrancy. Indeed between 1760 and 1914 when the Enclosure Acts were terminated approximately 6.5 million acres of land were enclosed by parliamentary means accounting for some 20 per cent of England's surface area and placing many camping grounds off limits (Wordie, 1983). In turn, the Commons and Enclosures Act of 1899 allowed local authorities to issue by-laws regulating use of their Commons, thus stimulating a series of by-laws in the late 19th and early 20th centuries that closed off more traditional camping grounds, making traditional nomadism and residence in caravans and tents ever more difficult within the Greater London area (Mayall, 1995).

Moreover, a combination of enclosures and a concerted attack against Gypsies and vagrants by a better-organised rural police force following the Country Police Acts of 1839 and 1856 pushed Gypsies and Travellers closer to the towns and cities. Increasing demand for industrial and residential land meant that land was progressively tamed and regulated with the advance of a modern industrialised society as 'along with the intervention of state into society went increased regulation of open space and the creation of 'governable spaces' (Bancroft, 2000, p 44). State intervention to tackle some of the most pressing problems facing the urban poor of the era (such as the condemnation of sub-standard housing) also had implications for Gypsies and Travellers. Section Nine of the Housing of the Working Classes Act 1884 included the power to inspect moveable dwellings and permitted prosecution where overcrowding occurred or conditions were considered as injurious to health. This inevitably impacted on families living in caravans, wagons and tents, a situation thrown into stark relief in the records of the Gypsy Lore Society (which published a regular roundup of reports of Gypsies involved in court proceedings) where families and individuals were frequently fined or had their wagons or tents destroyed as 'unfit for habitation'.[2]

Further, despite the good intentions behind Forster's Elementary Education Act of 1870 and later Acts of 1876 and 1880 which resulted in compulsory education for children between the ages of five and ten, the Acts were designed for sedentary society and created considerable difficulties when applied to nomadic groups.

In recognition of the hardship afforded to travelling families of ensuring that their children received schooling when they were dependent upon mobility for their livelihood, section 118 of the 1908 Children Act contained relevant provisions for bona fide Travellers by requiring only a minimum of 200 attendances at school between October and March while allowing the child to travel with their parent or guardian between April and September (when most harvest work occurred) albeit issuing fines to parents who failed to comply (Bowen, 2004). While such legislation was couched in universalistic paternalistic terms, clearly a potential existed for policies to mesh with a plethora of pressures for sedentarisation, and risk eradicating nomadic practices amongst semi-urbanised families in particular. Writing with regard to the 1910 Education Act for example, one school governess noted its anomalies which meant that a Gypsy child might potentially (in conforming with the legislation) attend five different schools in a week with a separate entry made onto a register in each case. She also observed approvingly that 'the tendency of the Act must be to benefit the community at large because the ultimate aim would be the extinction of gipsyhood [sic.], which in itself in the 20th century was an extraordinary anomaly' (*School Government Chronicle*, 10 June 1910). Unsurprisingly, the cumulative impact of such legislation, along with changing working patterns, was a key factor in the changing balance between periods of time spent travelling and settlement into housing, with this disjointedness becoming more pronounced throughout the course of the century until even in the 21st century many families living in housing or on caravan sites feel unable to travel other than in the school holiday periods (Clark and Greenfields, 2006).

Aside from legislative pressures to settle, changes in the nature of society and industry had a profound impact on the economic basis of Gypsies' daily life and culture. Until the early 19th century, the itinerant labour force played an important role in the provision of goods, services and entertainment to remote rural communities (Mayall, 1988; Ryder and Greenfields, 2010). However, within a relatively short time frame, the shift towards an urban-based society, mass manufacture of cheap goods, new forms of entertainment and improved transportation rendered many traditional means of livelihood redundant, resulting in a drift towards new economic opportunities in the towns and the emergence of more seasonal travelling patterns. Despite this rapid shift towards settlement in this period, distinctions between nomadism and settlement were less clear cut than today with Gypsies merely one element of a wide range of peripatetic groups that included 'navvies', itinerant artisans, tramps and (after the failure of the potato crop in the 1840s) large numbers of destitute Irish. In addition to the above groups could be found the travelling 'brush and basket makers, horse dealers, tinkers, cheapjacks, miscellaneous hawkers, travelling potters, fairground people and the like' (Fraser, 1995, p 216). Thus the general pattern for Gypsies (as for a significant segment of the semi-itinerant working classes), involved spending the winter months lodging in towns and cities followed by a spring migration to the suburbs for employment in market gardens and the summer months spent in Sussex, Surrey and Kent for the harvests. The movement between town and country was dictated largely by fluctuations in labour demand and by synchronisation in peaks and troughs of demand in urban industries and agriculture (Collins, 1976). Samuel (1973) notes that:

> The distinction between the nomadic life and the settled one was by no means hard and fast. Tramping was not the

prerogative of the social outcast as it is today; it was a normal phase in the life of entirely respectable classes of working men; it was a frequent resort of the out-of-works; and it was a very principle of existence for those who followed the itinerant callings and trades. (Samuel, 1973: 152)

However, in the cities Gypsies continued to occupy a distinctive peripatetics' niche retaining the basic economic traits of occupational flexibility: family based self-employment and exploitation of an area's social resources. Adapting these traits to an urban environment, they moved into salvage, hawking goods, and street and market trading 'buying cheap, selling dear and gambling fiercely' (Thompson and Smith, 1877, p 2). Gypsies and other pedlars were therefore a familiar sight in the streets of London until relatively recently, where they played an important function in the provision of cheap goods to poor urban dwellers (Weston, 2002). Mayall's (1988, p 54) more general point that such trading relationships suggests a relationship of mutual symbiosis may thus be correct. Nevertheless, the numbers and persistence of these pedlars on London's streets are revealed in complaints in newspapers of continual door knocking in working-class areas by 'gipsy cadgers'. In one letter, the writer argued that this practice required outlawing, observing that while residents of Upper Edmonton had to suffer constant disturbances, if this practice had been occurring in wealthier districts it would quickly lead to legislation to combat it (*Daily Chronicle*, 19 January 1909).

Seasonal agricultural work also remained an important source of employment for Gypsies and for the urban working classes until the mid 20th century. Mechanisation of agriculture did not reduce demand for operations that required hand tools such as hop and fruit picking until after World War Two. Indeed by the late 1800s, improved cultivation methods and shorter harvests increased labour demand, with the shortfall in workers drawn largely from Gypsies, itinerant Irish and Welsh labourers and urban dwellers particularly from the Black Country and London (Collins, 1976). Mayhew estimated that in the mid 19th century one third of London's street traders spent the summer months 'tramping' the countryside working in market gardens, farms and following the country fairs (Mayhew, 1985, pp 149–50), while Stedman Jones (1974) calculates that in the 1870s 35,000 Londoners left the city for the hop-picking season and Samuel (1973) records that in 1891 there was a 'grand exodus' from Poplar as over 800 largely Irish residents attended the harvests in Kent and Surrey. Unsurprisingly, social interaction and linguistic borrowings between these different groups is apparent in Mayhew's description of London costermongers, 'part of the Nomades of England' and their language, which he noted was

> ... peculiar in its construction: it consists of an odd medley of cockneyfied English, rude provincialisms, and a large proportion of the slang commonly used by gipsies and other travelers [sic.], in conveying their ideas to those whom they wish to purchase their commodities. (1985, p 184)

Use of Romani-based slang has also been documented in various social groups as a group lexicon arises from increasing interaction between different marginalised groups experiencing both social and legal exclusion.[3] Such use of an exclusionary 'hidden' language can be said to be 'symbolic of commercial nomads' constant struggle to escape the control of settled society' (Matras, 2010, p 21) operating as a means of discussing matters best unheard by 'outsiders' whilst conveying group membership on the speakers.

Alongside the blurring of language, interpersonal relations occurred between those in close proximity, with Mayall (1988) noting that marriage between Gypsies and 'gorjers' was not uncommon in the 18th and 19th centuries and became more frequent with the increasing urban presence of the former. Rejecting ancestral and racial explanations for the origin of Britain's nomadic population, he argues that while Gypsy/Travellers formed a relatively cohesive group, identifiable and distinct both from 'settled' society and the large heterogeneous body of itinerants, the basis of this group does not reside merely in biological or homogenous ancestry. Instead, Mayall highlights the intergenerational transmission of cultural patterns which include a particular lifestyle and employment habits and are an outcome of itinerant descent, thus encompassing significant ancestral diversity.

> There are records of intermixing between the Egyptians and native 'loyterers', outcasts, highway men, smugglers, vagabonds, tinkers, pot-hawkers and umbrella makers from 1612 on and by the 19th century the group of Gypsy-Travellers would have been able to trace their origins to each of these groups and others besides. (1988, p 88)

Similarly, while observing that London's Gypsies formed a 'distinct class', Thomson and Smith (1877) note that many of the various nomadic tribes in the city were allied either through kinship or similarity of lifestyle and '... form a section of urban and suburban street folks, so divided and subdivided and yet so mingled into one confused whole, as to render abortive any attempt at systematic classification' (p 1).

The presence of a persistent 'residuum' of the urban poor who lived in a manner not dissimilar to Gypsies is apparent in press coverage from the era. One such report described the 'London gipsies' who rarely strayed far from the city, living in tents on Hackney Downs, at Stratford and at Plaistow (all areas which in the 21st century still have identifiable Gypsy and Traveller populations) earning a living hawking goods in the winter, and spending the summer in Epping Forest basket making and caning chairs (*Little Folks*, 1 November 1888). The more general visibility of Gypsies in towns and their camps, which were found all over the capital and were becoming larger and more permanent through the course of the 19th century, also received considerable press attention. In 1879 *The Echo* argued that the enclosure acts and tighter regulation of land use was succeeding where the penal laws of the Middle Ages had failed and regretfully concluded:

> Hence the gipsie is haunting the vicinity of towns, losing his characteristic habits and though not decreasing in number, is to some degree getting merged among the drifting population that hang on the outskirts of civilization. (21 February 1879)

In urban contexts, fraternisation between Gypsies and the urban poor disturbed the scholars who studied Gypsy customs, lore and language and who were keen to preserve their lifestyle and language from contamination by the working classes on one hand, and those who were concerned at the latter's potential for absorption into the vagrant and wandering classes on the other (Behlmer, 1985). The Gypsy Lore Society in the 1890s reported concern at the seeming increase of beggars, thieves and degenerates among the 'wandering classes', justifying and supporting the persecution of non-Romani itinerants as they attributed cultural contamination and decline of their chosen group to increasing social interaction with these inferior nomads. Gypsy Lore Society members disdainfully noted the increase in half-breed 'diddikais' and other 'pretenders' to Gypsydom whilst supporting the right of 'pure' Romanies to pursue their 'traditional' way of life (Mayall, 1988, p 131). These racialised concerns remained current throughout the 20th century where the structural forces propelling nomadic groups closer to the cities and merging with the native population were said to symbolise a 'new stage in the ingestion of the Gypsies' that could potentially create 'amorphous masses of so called asocials' (Arnold, 1970, p 63).

The notion of a hierarchical and racialised classification of travelling communities is also relevant when considering the position of Britain's Irish Travellers, who have experienced prejudice and discrimination as both Irish *and* as nomads. From the perspective of the Gypsiologists, Irish 'tinkers' occupied an intermediate position below the Romany Gypsies but above the half-breed 'diddikais' and vagrants (Helleiner, 2001, p 39). Today Irish Travellers comprise a major component of the UK's nomadic peoples while over 16 per cent of the participants of the studies cited in this text were of Irish origins (Chapter Four). Moreover historical and contemporary evidence indicates the presence of these nomads in urban areas and in housing particularly during the past two decades. The following section will therefore consider the factors behind the presence of Irish Travellers in the UK before considering the settlement patterns of nomadic communities in urban areas.

Irish nomads in Britain

While Irish Travellers (also known as 'Minceir' or 'Pavees') have a distinct origin from the Romani/Gypsy populations and have travelled and resided in Ireland and mainland Britain for centuries, the precise origins of this population remains controversial and a matter of considerable scholarly debate (McCann et al, 1994; Helleiner, 2001; Bhreatnach and Bhreatnach, 2006). Explanations range from the fanciful (remnants of pre-Celtic populations related to the early Kings of Ireland), to the mundane (beggars who have adopted a nomadic way of life). A recent study by the Royal College of Surgeons in Dublin for example, suggests that there was an ancient separation between Irish Travellers and the wider Irish population (at least 1,000 years ago) citing evidence of a distinct genetic marker, found amongst many Travellers and strengthened as a result of inter-communal marriage (Hough, 2011). Such findings support Gmelch and Gmelch's (1976) supposition that not all Traveller families had ancient origins, with some adopting a nomadic lifestyle at a later period, often due to poverty or war. Nevertheless, they also argue that a substantial minority of Travellers were descended from communities with a long-standing tradition of nomadism associated with highly skilled artisan trades such as being a 'tinker' (or metal-worker) practising their craft in both Ireland and mainland Britain.

Ni Shuinear (1994), however, presents socio-biological evidence to refute the widely held belief that nomadic communities in Ireland represented a 'culture of poverty' formed of landless peasants forced into nomadism and casual land labour initially as a consequence of Cromwellian encroachment into Eire. Later this landless and disposed peasantry increased substantially through homelessness and hardship during the potato famines of the mid 19th century. Ni Shuinear bases her argument that Irish Travellers comprise a distinctive ethnic group through applying Barth's (1969) criteria of ethnicity, which includes shared cultural values and forms and a population which identifies itself, and is identified by others, as constituting a distinguishable category. She also presents perhaps slightly less substantial evidence of a distinct genome found amongst Irish Travellers and a supposed 'physical distinctiveness'. Norris and Winston (2005) identify a series of specific 'Traveller community characteristics' which they argue supports the view of Travellers as distinctive from the wider Irish population both in England and Ireland. These include endogamy (a tendency for intra-community marriage), adherence to core cultural values (such as a close identification with and commitment to nomadism) and culturally distinct rituals such as those surrounding courtship and funeral practices. Other characteristics include use of a shared language (the two dialects of Gammon/Shelta or Cant), intensive immersion in extended family networks and importantly a belief (shared by both 'settled' Irish populations and Travellers themselves) that they are a separate people. In essence these characteristics are broadly similar to the requirements for fulfilling the grounds for recognition as an ethnic community under British law (the 'Mandla and Dowell Lee Criteria', see further Clark and Greenfields, 2006). In a study of Irish Travellers on a local authority site in England, Griffin (2002a; 2002b) highlights certain hybridised practices which incorporate Roman Catholicism (as practised by the majority of Irish people) with distinctive Traveller 'adaptations', while hygiene boundary maintenance practices bore close resemblance to those utilised by other nomadic populations demonstrating both cultural distinctiveness and commonality of experience between Travellers, Gypsies and other nomads, and suggesting a probable blurring or cultural interchange between these populations.

Despite disputes over the origins of Irish nomads, which parallel long-running debates over the genesis of English Gypsies discussed earlier in the chapter, it is clear that since at least the 18th century and perhaps earlier, Irish Travellers were acknowledged as a separate population amongst the large number of itinerant workers traversing Ireland and England. Tens of thousands arrived in the mid 19th century escaping from starvation and disease. By 1841 there were over 400,000

Irish-born residents in Great Britain, largely comprised of low-paid labourers and mainly residing in the major urban areas (Thompson, 1968, p 469). Between January and June 1847, 300,000 Irish were added to Liverpool's population of 250,000 (Griffin, 2008, p 41) while some 73,000 of London's population – around 4 per cent – were Irish born (White, 2008, p 131). As discussed previously, just as with Gypsies and large swathes of the English poor, there was a significant seasonal migration among the Irish in the 19th century, as described by White:

> So the great market gardens around London brought in thousands during the summer months: Irish potato pullers in Poplar and West Ham, hop and fruit pickers in Kentish London, vegetable and flower cultivators from Acton to Barking and Mortlake to Woolwich. They shipped to Bristol or London in the spring, tramped to the fields, made do in crude huts or under canvas. (White, 2008, p 131)

Irish Travellers were undoubtedly part of this huge movement of people although evidence indicates that Irish nomads have had a presence in mainland Britain over a number of centuries indicating a long-standing tradition of migrating from Ireland to Britain (and back again) for employment purposes, with larger (and longer-term) migrations occurring in the 19th century and again in the 1930s and 1950s alongside larger waves of Irish movement to Britain for employment purposes. Each phase of Traveller migration has maintained close-knit ties with relatives resident in Ireland (often with core groupings of Travellers in County Cavan, Donegal and Galway) and a constant flow of visitors and migrants from the UK to Ireland for courtship, marriage and funerals. McKinley's (2011) memoir comprehensively details Traveller family migration to join relatives for varying lengths of time at locations in Northern and Southern Ireland as well as travel and temporary settlement in a number of English regions. McKinley refers to cultural variations between families living in different countries and to distinctive practices such as dowry payments and arranged marriages among certain families, with other practices such as early marriage and returning deceased family members to Ireland for burial remaining common to the Traveller population as a whole.

The virulence and persistence of anti-Traveller racism has been a core theme in the writing of many scholars and Traveller activists (such as ni Shuinear, 1994; Helleiner, 2001; Hayes, 2006; McVeigh, 2008). The extent of such racism in Ireland may be a further factor in the increasing presence of Irish nomads in mainland Britain from the 19th century.

Scholars have suggested for example, that the intense denigration of nomadism in Ireland is of relatively recent origin and is grounded in the rise of privatised property, colonialism and capitalism, all of which have led to increased stigmatisation of communities which rejected the dominant models of sedentarism, 'social progress' and statutory control of colonised peoples (MacLaughlin, 1998; McVeigh, 2008). McKinley's (2011) personal testimony of her family and community in Belfast discusses experiences of fire-bombings and regular beatings carried out by both 'sides' in the Northern Irish 'Troubles', indicative of the depth of marginalisation and hatred experienced by Travellers in both North and Southern Ireland. As in Britain, racism and opposition to having Travellers settled in 'their' locales has frequently thwarted government attempts to settle Travellers from the 1950s onwards (Norris and Winston, 2005; Hayes, 2006; Bhreatnach and Bhreatnach, 2006). The 'Report of the Commission on Itinerancy' in 1963 had highlighted the poverty and squalid living conditions of many nomadic families and concluded that the only available solution was 'to a positive drive to housing itinerants, if a permanent solution based on absorption and integration is to be achieved' (cited by Noonan, 1998, p 159). In response, over 70 voluntary 'Itinerant Settlement Committees' were formed across Ireland with the explicit aim of integrating Travellers into mainstream society through settling them on caravan sites and into housing, though the latter was often opposed by organised residents of the proposed recipient neighbourhoods (Gmelch and Gmelch, 1974).

Gmelch and Gmelch (1985) in noting the history of cross-channel migration of Travellers to mainland Britain link the growth in such migration to increased urbanisation and industrial changes in Ireland during the 20th century and conscious survival and adaptation strategies practised within the communities. More recent strongly anti-nomadic changes in policy and legislation in Ireland in the late 1990s led to a marked increase in the number of Irish Travellers migrating to the UK and seeking to settle on a more permanent basis. The consistent refusal of the Irish Government to recognise Travellers as an ethnic minority, referring to them instead as a 'social group' (in contrast to Britain where Travellers were recognised in law as a minority ethnic community in 2000), means that Travellers are (at least theoretically) subject to greater protection from racism and enforced sedentarisation in Britain (including Northern Ireland) than in Southern Ireland where they are subject to chronic undersupply of sites, high rates of unemployment, and widespread discrimination in access to services, with resultant education and health exclusion (Irish Traveller Movement Britain, 2010).

As discussed in Chapter Two, there are no clear statistics on the number of Irish Travellers in Britain. Pavee Point estimated in 1997 that there were at least 15,000 Irish Travellers living in the UK (O'Riain, 1997). However, findings from GTAAs have found an average family size of eight children amongst Irish Travellers and an annual population growth rate of 3 per cent per annum, suggesting that the population is significantly larger than this baseline figure. The relatively recent history of settlement of Irish Travellers onto authorised sites in both the UK and Ireland has led to intense pressures over access to pitches in both countries, while in Britain, authorised local authority sites have largely been populated by longer-settled Romany Gypsies. Accordingly, there has been a noticeable increase in residence on unauthorised sites amongst Irish Travellers in Britain and a corresponding shift into housing for these populations in Ireland. The 2011 Irish Census data found a sharp decline in caravan-dwelling Travellers since the 2006 census – potentially caused by a combination of a large (32 per cent) reported increase in the population since the last census, a shortage of sites and criminalisation of nomadism. Subsequently reports have estimated that Travellers resident in housing increased from 65 to 84 per cent of the population within a five-year time frame (*The Irish Times*, 2012).

In the UK, Irish Travellers (regardless of their form of accommodation) are likely to be subjected to both anti-Irish and anti-Traveller discrimination (Power, 2004). They also experience exclusion and prejudice from the 'settled' Irish communities that they often live amongst in English cities (Walter, 2001, p 271). A study of Irish Traveller prisoners in the UK (MacGabhann, 2011) found that they comprise up to one per cent of the prison population, frequently being fast-tracked into custodial sentences for relatively minor offences amid concerns that they would abscond to Ireland if subject to community orders. Once in custody they are frequently disadvantaged in access to training or pre-/post-release support as a result of poor literacy skills, discrimination by staff and other prisoners and the inability to remain in contact with family members who are facing eviction or who remain nomadic. Traveller prisoners were significantly more likely to remain in custody for longer than their peers or to commit suicide or self-harm in prison, adding to the notable health inequities and premature morbidity already experienced by both men and women from these communities. It is estimated from the limited available evidence (and see further Clark and Greenfields, 2006) that the majority of housed Irish Travellers in

Britain are resident in major urban conurbations associated with high levels of Irish migration between the mid-19th and 20th centuries, notably London, Liverpool, Manchester and Birmingham.

The 'Metropolitan Gypsyries'

As suggested above, the association of Gypsies with certain places results from such communities travelling a regular circuit for employment-related purposes, typically covering a relatively small area and returning to the same camping grounds over successive generations (Greenfields, 2006). Rickard (1995), for example, indicates that some of the largest Gypsy families in East Kent have been there for several centuries with little alteration in travelling patterns between the early 19th and late 20th centuries. In urban contexts this finds its equivalent in the propensity to retain a neighbourhood base generally, as in the cases of Norwood, Hackney Marshes, Barnet and Southampton, where there were once long-established camping grounds prior to clearance and dispersal resulting in local settlement of Gypsy families familiar with the area. Perhaps because of this long-term association with certain locales, unlike other minority groups who commonly struggle to gain access to the social and economic rewards of assimilation and escape often deprived ethnic localities, urban anthropologists have noted the tendency for Gypsies to remain in low-income urban neighbourhoods over successive generations (Kornblum, 1975). Interestingly, as illustrated by references in White (1986) and O'Neill (1990) following the transition to conventional housing, the general trend appears to be a continuation of semi-nomadic lifestyles and (at least for initial generations of settlers) the replication and reformulation of traditional living patterns and domestic arrangements.

Early references to house-dwelling Gypsies described their homes as 'presenting the same empty appearances as is seen in the houses of Gypsies in the East. The whole household will be found squatting on the floor and dispensing with all unaccustomed articles of furniture' (Bath et al, 1875, p xiv) whilst Winstedt (1913) found among the Galician Gypsy coppersmiths who arrived in England between 1911 and 1913 that 'When they become house dwellers they, like most English Gypsies under the same circumstances, simply camped in one room of the house and left the others untenanted' (1913, p 277). More recently, Sutherland's (1975) anthropological account of American Roma in California observed the tendency for related families to live closely together in the same neighbourhoods and inside their homes to prefer open spaces to privacy, which often meant removing internal walls to create communal living spaces (pp 59–61). In Britain, among the Battersea Gypsies studied in the 1970s, it was observed that most houses 'retain many of the exotic features of a caravan' (Sandford, 2000, p 81). We found similar spatial and domestic arrangements as well as decorative adornments when undertaking the present study.

Sibley (1981), in contemplating the use of urban space by Gypsies and Travellers, notes that the social geography of urban areas in the 19th century and the existence of enclaves outside the control of authorities made those locales suitable for the camps that were generally a precursor to residential settlement in those spaces of social exclusion. In 1864 George Borrow, who popularised the 'romantic' and exotic image of Gypsies in his series of books purporting to detail travel with, and the language of, the communities, visited the three grand 'Metropolitan Gypsyries' the largest of which was located on the borders of Battersea and Wandsworth, and two other camps: one at 'The Potteries' in Notting Dale and the other at the Mount in Shoreditch. Borrow described the inhabitants of the camps and their accommodation, which consisted of an assortment of tents and caravans. The caravans, unlike the romantic imagery of the horse-drawn caravan were described as 'dirty, squalid places, quite as much as or perhaps more than the tents, which seem to be the proper and congenial homes of the Gypsies' (Borrow, 2001, p 77). He also described their working patterns which for the men largely consisted of skewer and peg making, the weaving of baskets and tinkering while the women wandered the streets dukkering [fortune-telling] and swindling unwary town dwellers.

In addition to the Romany inhabitants of the Wandsworth camp he also identified other 'strange, wild guests ... who, without being Gypsies, have much of Gypsyism in their habits, and who far exceed the Gypsies in number'. These he classified hierarchically, setting the tone for much of the later writings on Gypsies and other travelling groups, in the manner of the Gypsy Lore Society who were, in their early days, much influenced by his work. Those he identified included the 'Chorodies' or indigenous travellers who were 'the legitimate descendants of the rogues and outcasts who roamed about England long before its soil was trodden by a Gypsy foot' (p 79). In addition were the 'Kora-mengre', the lowest of hawkers 'who go about the country villages and the streets of London, with caravans hung about with various common articles, such as mats, brooms, mops, tin pans and kettles' (p 80). Despite their many similarities the latter two groups had 'none of the comforts and elegancies of the Gypsies'. They were of 'low swinish Saxon' origin and described by Borrow as 'detestable', 'brutal' and 'repulsive'. Finally he identified the vagrant Irish the 'Hindity-mengre' (filthy people) whose principal trades he stated were 'tinkering' and making fake gold rings from brass, at which they were particularly adept.

During Borrow's visit to the Mount in the East End he noted a colony of housed Gypsies in one of the area's streets 'who are in the habit of receiving and lodging their brethren passing through London to and from Essex and other counties east of the metropolis' (p 81), a situation attested to by our study of census records across London. Borrow, moreover, observed the (unspecified) 'peculiar aspect' of the street that was familiar from his experience with housed Gypsy communities in Spain. Camps were still present in the East End in the 1930s with reports of yards sandwiched between the slums of Aldgate, Limehouse and off the East India Dock Road, with many residents of Bethnal Green able to claim Gypsy origins (*The Spectator*, 29 March 1935). White (1986) interviewed residents of Finsbury Park, North London who had memories of Gypsy families living locally in the 1920s and 1930s who had, in the 1890s, been required to move from traditional stopping places in the vicinity, after an elegant crescent and small park was laid out over a traditional local halting place. The entire Notting Dale (now Notting Hill) neighbourhood of West London was classed by Borrow as a Gypsy region 'where Gypsies, or gentry whose habits very much resemble those of Gypsies, may at any time be found' (p 82). In the mid 1800s it was recorded that between 40 and 50 Gypsy families regularly camped between the Kennington Potteries and Wormwood Scrubs on grounds described as a 'Slough of Despond in the winter, all puddle, swamp and quagmire and in a moral aspect not more inviting' (*The Missing Link Magazine*, 1856, p 125). The area was at that time in a state of flux, lacking in organisation, inhabited by a displaced and transient population, neglected by the authorities and untouched by redevelopment making it ideal for Gypsies and itinerants to go about their business.

> ... it is in fact a mere chaos, where there is no order and no regularity; where there is nothing durable ... it is quite the kind of place to please the Gypsies and wandering people, who find many places within its bounds where they can squat and settle, or take up their quarters for a night or two without much risk of being interfered with. Here their tents, cars, and caravans may be seen amidst ruins, half-raised walls, and on patches of unenclosed ground. (Borrow, 2001, p 82)

Booth (1902, pp 151–2) in the notebooks of his study of working-class districts of London reported that in the (then) slum area of Notting

Hill 'gypsy [sic.] blood is very evident amongst the children in the schools and noticeable even in the street'. More recently, Griffin's (2008) study examines the continuing presence of Gypsies and Irish Travellers in the Notting Hill area and the lingering cultural influence of these historical connections by drawing on James Clifford's (1992) critique of community as temporally and spatially bounded. Clifford extends notions of community to include 'sites of travel', arguing that anthropological efforts to study autonomous cultural formations neglect the constant interactions between cultures, the hybrid cosmopolitan experiences that emerge and the 'world of intercultural import–export in which the ethnographic encounter is always already enmeshed' (1992, p 100). For Griffin, Gypsies and itinerant traders therefore form an intrinsic element of the social fabric of west London whose influence is felt not merely in their physical presence but in shaping the aesthetic element of certain neighbourhoods (a conceit shared by O'Neill (1990) who refers to the complex mixtures of people resident in her East End childhood streets). In documenting how the Notting Hill area of London has been infused by its nomadic heritage Griffin observes that many locals in the vicinity of the Westway Traveller site under the A40 flyover and around the Latimer Road area are of Gypsy descent, noting that a number of terraced houses in the area 'sported lucky horseshoes, horse-head doorknockers and front window displays of horse figurines; all minor testaments to the past importance of this animal locally' (2008, p 296). The 'little communities' found in the vicinity of Latimer Road, argues Griffin, represent 'sites of travel' as much as sites of residence and their representation in the form of horse symbols and adornments a reflection of the area's historically grounded 'migratory tendencies' (2008, p 72). Similarly, Greenfields (2006) notes displays of cultural identity among housed Gypsies in Southampton. Her observations from a 'Gypsy area' of the town close to a number of former 'aitchin tans' (stopping places) reveal

> … neat rows of bungalows, many with caravans parked outside, some with stables and sheds and the majority of such bungalows displaying gleaming crystal and china in the front windows. Another characteristic sign of Gypsy or Traveller occupancy is the presence of low stone walls with wagon wheels or models of horses' heads adorning the brickwork or gate posts. (Greenfields, 2006, p 121)

Not only the western reaches of the city but also South London underwent enormous expansion during the 19th century, with the population south of the Thames growing from under 500,000 to almost 2 million between 1841 and 1901 (Draper, 2004). Growth of the southern part of the city drew in many Gypsies and destitute rural poor, particularly from Kent, Surrey and Sussex, who would have a discernible influence in the formative cultural and social make-up of working-class South London. Both Wandsworth and Battersea contained a noticeable Gypsy presence by the mid-19th century, with members of these communities resident both in housing and on encampments near the Southwestern railway viaduct where they were known to present for about six months of the year, while yet others camped under the area's many railway arches around the area of Clapham Junction station (Sibley, 1981, p 79). The 1911 census reveals substantial housed colonies of Gypsies in Fairfield Street, Wandsworth, many of whom originated from Kent, Hampshire and Surrey and who were occupied as hawkers, dealers or blacksmiths. Booth identified Gypsies in Wardley Street and Lydden Grove the poorest neighbourhoods of Wandsworth where he described a yard full of caravans with the wheels removed and each inhabited by a family (Booth, 1902, cited by Sibley, 1981, p 80). That entire area contained several such yards: one in Clapham Junction was occupied by over a dozen caravans and had been there 'for as long as locals could remember' (*Birmingham Post*, 9 September 1919) with others located in the Sheepcote Lane and York Road areas of Battersea. Besant (1912) observed that:

> In York Road among busy shops is a large music hall and behind it a winter encampment of Gipsies with their caravans closely parked together in a large yard all living in their vans as if they were on the road. (Besant, 1912, p 165).

Battersea and Wandsworth were also visited by the tribes of Galician Gypsy coppersmiths discussed earlier, who stopped in South London en route to South America and initially received sensationalist press coverage in Edwardian England with reporters enchanted by 'the display of priceless silks, and bizarre colours and heavy gold and Oriental luxury' (*People's Journal*, 2 September 1911). The exoticism quickly evaporated, however, as the 150 Galicians who had rented large houses in Garrett Lane, Earlsfield and in nearby Southfields and pitched tents in the gardens were evicted on sanitary grounds whereupon they decamped to a field in Beddington Lane, Mitcham (Winstedt, 1913). The entire Garrett Lane area which runs from Tooting to Wandsworth was described as a 'miserable and squalid district' populated principally by hawkers and regarded as one which had long been inhabited by

Gypsies (Besant, 1912, p 234). In 1879 two local landlords, William Penfold and Thomas Mills, were summonsed for renting land in Wardley Street and Garrett Lane to Gypsies who camped on the land. Following a sanitary inspection the camps was deemed injurious to health and the inhabitants evicted (*The Local Government Chronicle*, 4 January 1879). And the evidence goes on – as far down as one wishes to excavate, the entwined nature of Gypsy, Traveller and urban working-class communities seems irremediably complex.

As we have noted, certain locales appear to lend themselves to housing a transient population: Mitcham on the borders of South London and Surrey was one such place. By the late 19th century Surrey was a main centre for Gypsies, itinerants and vagrants with an estimated (though probably exaggerated) 10,000 in the county alone, many of whom had been expelled from London through a combination of 'the Metropolitan Police, land agents, sanitary authorities and building developments' (Mayall, 1988, pp 158–9). The seriousness of the 'Gypsy problem' was thus a frequent topic of discussion within Surrey County Council (SCC) meetings and a sub committee was formed in 1906 to identify appropriate solutions for dealing with the high proportions of nomads and itinerants in the area. The sub committee favoured national legislation to register all caravan and tent dwellers and as a result sponsored the failed Moveable Dwellings Bill in 1908 which would have placed considerable pressures on nomadic communities (Bowen, 2004).

Mitcham had long been one of the poorest parishes in Surrey and records of Gypsies camping in the area date back to the 1700s. Between the mid-19th and early 20th centuries the area declined in respectability as several landowning families departed and its population grew significantly as outward migration from London increased the population of poor and displaced residents (Smith, 2005, p 67). Of these, Gypsies and itinerants formed a significant minority: the 1881 census records 230 Gypsies and vagrants camping on Mitcham Common. Mitcham Fair held (and still held) annually in mid-August was a huge event, attracting tens of thousands of Londoners, and despite its reputation for unruliness, survived repeated attempts to have it closed, thanks to its Royal Charter granted by Queen Elizabeth I in 1512 (East, 1980). The fair was thus a core annual event on the Travellers' calendar and provided ample opportunities for trading, horse-dealing and working the fairground stalls. Mitcham provided other attractions for Travellers also – the area contained an abundance of market gardens which provided regular seasonal employment with the locality becoming an important site for industry in the early to mid-20th century, particularly the 'dirty industries' such as paint making, chemical works and bone boiling, which had been expelled from inner London by the 1845 Health Act. The importance of Gypsy labour to the area's industry in this period is revealed by Montague, who notes that

> ... when Purdom's [paint and varnish] factory was originally established production had been seasonal, taking place mainly in the winter months when Gypsy and other casual labour employed on the physic gardens during the rest of the year was available at very low rates. (Montague, 2006, p 79)

Despite a series of by-laws being passed against Travellers in Surrey during the 1890s including the Mitcham Common Act of 1891 and the subsequent establishment of a Board of Conservators to regulate its use, by 1909 there were over 190 vans camping more or less permanently on the common. In addition, many more were stopped on patches of vacant land and in the town's many caravan yards, while other Gypsies had moved into the small terraced houses that were known locally as 'Redskin Village' (in reference to the dark colouring of its inhabitants) by the 1920s.[4] According to Montague, by the 1930s the area had become one of the most disreputable and notorious in the district and was 'associated in the public mind with some of the worst slums in the emerging township' (Montague, 2006, p 113). The area remains firmly embedded in local folklore and even today many long-established Mitcham residents can trace their family ancestry to Redskin Village. The area's association with Gypsies and Travellers continued in the post-war period as slum clearance and development of vacant wasteland resulted in many being housed in the new estates (Acton, 1974, p 168). The town was also regularly visited by nomadic Gypsies in the post-war era and development of one such housing development (on the former Wandgas site) was delayed for some time in the mid 1970s as the proposed site was occupied by several dozen caravans forcing Merton Council into a long legal process to have them evicted. As recently as 2009, Travellers have been reported stopping on Mitcham Common and regularly resort to camping in the town's industrial estates and car-parks, as areas of once marginal wasteland, which provided stopping places, have been used for housing developments (Burnett, 2009).

These examples (and particularly the case study of Mitcham) reveal how certain narratives of place remain submerged and invisible, meaning that our knowledge of the past and how it shapes our present urban environments frequently remains incomplete (Burgess, 2000).

As Britain has become more diverse ethnically, attention has tended to focus on patterns of ethnic inequalities and segregation in urban areas (McCulloch, 2007) as well as the contribution that different minority groups have played in local urban environments and processes of identity formation (Deutsch, 2008). However certain trajectories of minority settlement and of local ethnic and cultural formation, which may play an important role in shaping what Griffin (2008, p xix) terms the 'historical and geo-spatial contexts' through which people identify with particular localities, have been neglected. It has been estimated that up to one third of Mitcham's population may be of Gypsy and Traveller heritage (Merton Council, 2010). In spite of the estimated size of this population, a recent report into Merton's ethnic minority communities gave no mention of the Borough's longest established minority group or of their historical role in the area, while devoting only one page to housing and social exclusion issues amongst the Borough's Irish Travellers (London Borough of Merton, 2004). The history of Gypsies and Travellers in Mitcham, and in urban locations more generally, thus remains a 'hidden history' of how these communities have resisted official state-sponsored planning and control, through defining and creating their own spaces in urban locations. As Burgess observes:

> By reshaping urban space—that is, planning—those in authority sought to eliminate the threatening chaos and disorder. In doing so, they subjugated the others and reasserted or solidified their own position. Then, when they prepared the official record of what they had done (i.e., their history), they not only explained or justified their actions in abstract terms—claiming as their goal, for example, efficiency, better sanitation, or some other social good—they also made no mention of the other they had subjugated. The others were thus doubly harmed: first by being subjugated and second by having their very existence denied in the official history. (Burgess, 2000, p 647)

Between nomadism and settlement: the interwar 'van towns'

The two World Wars and the massive social upheaval and extension of state powers that total warfare entailed proved to be another impetus to sedentarisation. The Defence of the Realm Act originally introduced in 1914 prohibited camping in certain areas and this downward pressure was an important factor in driving Gypsies and Travellers closer to the towns in this period (Taylor, 2008, p 32). Simultaneously, nomadic families experienced a squeeze from the opposite (upwards) direction, as intense development, population growth and suburbanisation altered the location and nature of urban settlements and many of their earlier inner-city enclaves were erased. It was on the margins of the city where police supervision was lighter that many of the 'van towns' that peppered the outer ring of London and other urban conurbations in the early to mid 20th century became located. The growing size and prominence of the 'van towns' should also be seen against the backdrop of serious housing shortages post-1918 and again after World War Two (Burnett, 1986). Shortages of affordable housing led to a proliferation of makeshift 'shanty towns' by homeless urban dwellers, while the division into plots and sale of derelict and abandoned agricultural or other barren land resulted in a growth of self-built 'plotland' developments in the interwar period (Ward, 2002). These improvised developments were found all over the country, though largely occurred in the South East, with the largest concentrations in South Essex, within easy reach of employment in London (Hardy and Ward, 1984). Sibley (1995, p 59) notes how, as working-class creations, plotland developments were considered to be abhorrent eyesores by many influential commentators while the residents of such sites – in common with Gypsies and Travellers – were viewed as 'squatters' (Shoard, 1987; Ward, 2002). Such discourse, continues Sibley, had an important bearing on practice and in shaping conceptions of who were the rightful heirs to the English countryside, a theme which has been continued in subsequent analyses of 'othered' communities' use of rural space (Richardson, 2006; Cloke and Little, 1997; Milbourne, 1997).

A further surge in improvised accommodation occurred in the immediate post-World War Two years driven by bombed-out city dwellers and returning soldiers frustrated by slow progress in the provision of new housing. Such encampments often grew up on decommissioned military camps although they were rapidly quashed by the Town and Country Planning Act of 1948 under the power given to local authorities to control 'disorderly development', thus leading to the exclusion of working-class people from rural middle-class spaces and the control of where and how homeless people could (and should) live (Shoard, 1987). The new town of Basildon in Essex was designated as a housing provision area in 1949, designed to provide tidy (though isolating and soulless – see Young and Wilmott, 1957) accommodation for the homeless East Londoners and army camp squatters resident on the sites at Pitsea and Laindon where by 1945 approximately 25,000 people lived without any proper water supply or surfaced roads (Dabbler, 2011).

For Gypsies and Travellers, however, less keen to move into new build housing estates, the no-man's land of rural Essex where new towns sprang up, had provided easy access to both city and country, land to graze horses and a convenient base for seasonal travelling patterns. In addition, the borders of London and Kent contained many such camps, with sites such as Corkes Meadow at St Mary Cray in Orpington being legendary for their rough and ready ways and conviviality, mixing Gypsies and locals. The area had long received large numbers of seasonal Gypsies and other itinerant workers to work on the area's hop and fruit farms. As demand for such work declined, combined with the increasing difficulty of finding stopping places, the van towns grew in size and permanency, forming an intermediary stage in the transition to large-scale settlement in housing, a pattern noted also in rural Hampshire around Southampton (Greenfields, 2006). In 1951 it was estimated that around 250 people lived constantly on Corkes Meadow in Kent, with numbers growing in the winter. Despite repeated local authority attempts to evict the residents, numbers rose to 600 by 1957 (Evans, 2004, p 67). Clearance of the site (subsequently developed for housing in the 1960s), at around the same time as other large-scale evictions in the South East, led to widespread enforced local settlement. Today the Borough of Bromley (within which St Mary Cray is located) has the largest settled community of Gypsies and Travellers in the country with between 1,000 and 1,500 families resident in the borough (London Borough of Bromley, 2008).

The largest of these peri-urban camps was on Belvedere Marshes near Erith on the borders of South East London and Kent. The camp was first established in the 1890s after nine plots of land were purchased by a Gypsy and rented or sold to other Travellers. The camp grew through the early decades of the 20th century until it accommodated a fluctuating population of 2,000 people living in approximately 400 caravans, sheds and huts (Stanley, 2002). In 1935 a reporter from the *Evening Standard* was dispatched to the camp where he reported that 'it would be hard to believe, without seeing it, that a community so primitive could exist within a dozen miles of Charing Cross' (*Evening Standard*, 3 January 1935). Erith Council launched a long and protracted battle to evict the 'marsh people'. Eventually, it was not the authorities that moved the inhabitants but the North Sea floods of 1953 that engulfed the camp, dislodging many residents, while the remaining 700 people were finally evicted in 1956. Many of those displaced from the marsh remained in the area, entering housing or moving onto the area's authorised sites, including the huge Thistlebrook site in nearby Abbey Wood. The marsh camp still remains strongly embedded in the local consciousness, however, and it is reported that the local travelling community still refer to those who originally moved from the marshes as a 'family' (*Local Dialogue*, 2009). In 2011 a six-metre-high galvanised steel statue of a Gypsy cob horse was installed on a roundabout in Belvedere – a testament to the area's Gypsy legacy and to the dozens of cob horses still found grazing on wasteland surrounding the area's industrial sites (*Bexley News Shopper*, 16 February 2011) as well as marking the longevity and persistence of urban Travellers' attachment to their locale.

In conclusion, this chapter has sought to supplement the theoretical perspectives outlined in the previous chapter and frame the empirical findings which will be presented later, through offering a historical account of Gypsies and Travellers' presence in urban environments and conventional housing. In this chapter, we have highlighted the unacknowledged legacy of nomadic cultures in the social and cultural fabric of many urban locales and the lasting influence that those cultures have played in the formation of a distinctively working-class environment particularly (though not exclusively) in London. Whilst such an account can at best only provide a partial analysis, it has described how social, economic and legislative factors as well as changes in the use of land and regulations governing its use have combined to produce a more urban and town-based existence for many Gypsies and Travellers whilst simultaneously increasing the extent and intensity of contact with non-Gypsy populations. Although it is important not to overstate the structural pressures to sedentarisation, it is also valuable to recognise that the capacity for choice is situated within a wider framework of structural determinants (see further Chapters Five and Six). The long-term outcome of the processes described in this and other chapters has been to severely circumscribe the alternatives facing many Gypsies and Travellers, to the extent that an estimated half of every generation of Romany Gypsies has entered housing throughout the 20th century (Kenrick and Clark, 1999). The clearance of the van towns described above and other large settlements (such as the 300 Gypsies evicted from Darenth Woods, Dartford in 1962) marked an important stage in the transition from traditional nomadic (or semi-nomadic) lifestyles towards permanent settlement on sites or in housing.

The post-war trend of the clash of cultures between classes, and house and former van dwellers was captured (albeit presenting the Gypsy protagonists somewhat grotesquely) by John Arden's play Live Like Pigs

(1958) about a Gypsy family unwillingly living on a housing estate. The play highlighted the social ramifications of the settlement of Britain's nomadic communities, the problems of adapting to life in housing and the neighbourhood prejudices that the family endured, themes which still remain relevant to many housed Gypsies and Travellers. In subsequent sections we address these concerns, after describing the sample of participants and the research locales in the following chapter.

Notes

[1] A searchable archive of cases detailing defendants, crimes, victims and witness statements between the years 1674 and 1913 is available online at http://www.oldbaileyonline.org/. Search notes on exploring evidence of Gypsy and Traveller participation in cases can be accessed at http://www.oldbaileyonline.org/static/Gypsy-traveller.jsp.

[2] See the website http://www.romanygenes.webeden.co.uk/#/affairs-of-egypt/4531852436 (accessed 30 August 2012) for examples from the Annals of the Gypsy Lore Society 'notes and queries' detailing various cases, including the occurrence in 1909 of a prosecution against one 70-year-old Nathan Buckley for failing to provide for his family: (1) a tent in a reasonable watertight condition; (2) sufficient privy accommodation; (3) a sufficient water-supply; (4) a sufficient covered ash-pit and dust-bin; (5) a suitable dry floor to a tent.

[3] *Polari*, for example – used traditionally by actors, sailors and gay men – being based on a curious admixture of 16th-century 'thieves' cant', Romani, London backslang, Yiddish and Italian (see further, Mayhew, 1985, p 47; Baker, 2002).

[4] One improbable but intriguing piece of local folklore offers an alternative explanation of how the area acquired its name. That is, during one of Buffalo Bill Cody's visits to England with his Wild West show in the early 1900s a few of his Red Indian travelling entourage, on passing through the town, were attracted to the Gypsy life and, recognising the similarities with their own lifestyles, decided to remain camping with the Mitcham Gypsies, eventually marrying local Gypsy women and settling in the area.

FOUR

The research sites and population sample

Introduction

In this chapter we set out the sites of the various research studies and introduce existing data which we have drawn upon to support our findings, for example Gypsy Traveller Accommodation Assessments (GTAAs). In addition we discuss how we developed the follow-up qualitative studies into the experiences of housed Gypsies and Travellers which form the core of this text.

As noted previously, GTAAs arose in response to New Labour's in-depth policy review of Gypsy and Traveller circumstances which commenced in 2003 (Greenfields, 2007a). The findings from the review and consideration of representations from activists, academics and Gypsy and Traveller community groups led to specific requirements being inserted into the detailed policy guidance (implemented as Circular 01/06). These specified how local authorities should respond to planning applications and identify land for new sites. The Planning Circular was inextricably linked into the 2004 Housing Act which placed a duty on local authorities to review the current and future accommodation needs of all local residents. Guidance on undertaking GTAAs was subsequently produced, which provided detailed advice on the assessment of need for Gypsy and Traveller communities (CLG, 2007). Importantly, in response to an accumulation of anecdotal evidence from community groups and academics that large numbers of local authority housing placements broke down and lobbying for their inclusion in GTAA surveys, the needs of Gypsies and Travellers residing in 'bricks and mortar' were for the first time incorporated into the reviews. The inclusion of 'housed' Gypsies and Travellers marked recognition of the fact that aspirations to live in a culturally 'appropriate' or traditional way were not necessarily extinguished once a family had become 'settled'.

Once completed, the results of GTAAs surveys were to be considered and built into Local Development Frameworks and Regional Spatial Strategies (Richardson, 2007a; Greenfields, 2008). For the first time therefore researchers were able to draw on evidence relating to the household situation of Gypsies and Travellers in 'bricks and mortar', a community who were previously invisible in administrative statistics once they were no longer living in caravans and hence subject to the bi-annual 'caravan count' (Niner, 2004). As considered below there are significant methodological difficulties in attempting to accurately assess the numbers of housed Gypsies and Travellers in any area. In a number of areas, consultants who have undertaken GTAAs (whilst in other ways seeking to comply with the Guidance issued by the CLG (2007)) have largely ignored these housed populations. Research teams have often claimed either that it is too difficult to access these 'hard to reach' groups as a result of the lack of clear recording of their ethnicity in existing data sets, or have merely interviewed a small number of housed respondents and failed to even calculate the size of the housed community in a particular locality.

Whilst the challenges inherent in assessing numbers are indeed great, we realised that the richness of data which could be obtained from analysing GTAA responses from these previously 'voiceless' groups provided a unique opportunity to consider their well-being and circumstances which went beyond the identified purpose of the survey, which was to discover how much need existed for caravan sites amongst housed Gypsies and Travellers. Thus whilst the initial data on which our research is based is drawn from two study areas in which we had worked both individually and as members of separate (and the same) GTAA teams, we realised that there was clear scope for further in-depth studies into the accommodation 'careers' of housed respondents.

In one area in which one of the present authors undertook a GTAA, on reviewing the findings the local authority were as surprised as the research team to discover that there was a large housed population living predominantly in one or two housing estates. Indeed, it was a result of interviewees 'snowballing' contacts that the initial GTAA team were able to discover that a rich network of interconnected families lived in close proximity on those estates. Little institutional knowledge or memory existed in that local authority area pertaining to the closure of some sites a few years earlier and the rehousing of a number of families on a fairly run-down housing estate. As a direct result of the findings from that initial GTAA survey and the intervention of a local Romany activist who was also aware of the large networks of housed families in several locations in the county, the local authority commissioned a follow-up study. The aim of this study was to explore other accommodation and support needs of housed families on those estates as the initial GTAA survey had indicated high levels of social exclusion. This subsequent study, which included in-depth focus groups with housed families, thus formed the basis of the data set that we have developed, as well providing us with the core questionnaire which was then replicated (with occasional localised variations) in the three other study locales.

Within a year of this study of housed Gypsies and Travellers, the author involved in that project was offered the opportunity to work on a further GTAA in an adjoining local authority area, providing the opportunity to access further information on housed Gypsies and Travellers. At the same time, both authors were invited to participate (led by a colleague from another institution) in a GTAA in another area of the country which was historically known to have a large housed community. Once more, the data set grew. When one of the present authors thereafter undertook a commissioned project on behalf of a housing association (discussed in more detail later) we realised that we had plentiful comparative data to explore the circumstances of housed families in distinct parts of the country. To ensure some parity of data and allow us to explore certain topics in greater detail we sought in-house university funding and obtained support to allow us to carry out a series of targeted qualitative interviews with housed families in the second study area which mirrored our initial GTAA 'follow-up project'. Finally, to counter-balance the wealth of data (predominantly on Romany Gypsies) which we had drawn from the targeted studies in peri-urban areas and data mined from our series of GTAAs, we conducted interviews with Irish Travellers living in London to enable us to compare and contrast experiences, attitudes and housing histories across regions and ethnic groups and also undertook in-depth interviews with a sample of 'long-term' housed Romany Gypsies in an area of south London with a long historical association as a 'Gypsy area', who were known to one of the present authors. Finally, where during the lengthy course of this data-collection process we were offered the opportunity to undertake an additional interview or focus group (for example, a focus group was carried out in one of our study areas on behalf of a Government agency to explore community cohesion and inter-ethnic relations in the area), we have also incorporated relevant findings into the data interrogated in this text.

In the succeeding chapters the results of these findings from diverse sources will be presented. These sets of information cannot be analysed on a 'like-for-like' basis since they comprise survey data, individual interviews and focus group interviews and the purposes for which the data was gathered varied. Despite this, we were struck by the overwhelming similarities revealed by thematic analysis (see further Appendix A: Methodologies).

The population data

In introducing the local areas in which the studies were undertaken it is apposite to consider the 'best information' available on the size of the housed Gypsy and Traveller populations in the broader locality in which the studies were carried out. Whilst the present authors worked on some GTAAs in the broader region, given that no set rules of commissioning exist and local authorities commission individual consultants who all have their own set of practices, the quality of data, methodologies utilised and assessments carried out may vary significantly between GTAAs. Thus whilst the CLG guidance (2007) provided a list of required subjects to be included in GTAAs and gave a strong 'steer' on methodologies, there is still considerable scope for variation between studies which may or may not always be attributable to population differences within a study locale.

As discussed, GTAA teams who have conducted studies in the broader geographical areas within which our research was conducted have acknowledged that figures for the housed population are notoriously difficult to estimate. As a result of methodological difficulties in 'guestimating' housed populations even the best estimates given within each of the GTAAs are accepted as a probable underestimate of the true figure of Gypsies and Travellers residing in conventional accommodation in their respective localities.[1] Of the four GTAA's summarised in Table 1, one did not even provide any estimate of the housed population, citing methodological difficulties in estimating numbers. The main difficulty in calculating numbers of housed Gypsies and Travellers is the extremely limited administrative data for these populations which contrasts sharply to the relative ease with which numbers of Gypsies and Travellers residing on both authorised and unauthorised caravan sites (estimated by dividing an 'average' household size by the numbers of caravans enumerated on a biannual basis by each local authority) can be assessed. For housed families, only limited data is available from Traveller Education Services statistics (and then only for families who are relatively recently settled in housing and known to the service) although this information source only identifies households with children and, moreover, only where there is self-identification of ethnicity.

Attribution of ethnicity meanwhile, remains notoriously low given many Gypsy and Traveller households' preference to 'pass' as part of the mainstream population and their reluctance to state their ethnic identity on official forms for fear of experiencing discrimination (Cemlyn et al, 2009). Furthermore, health records had not until recently begun

Table 1: Estimated population of housed Gypsies/Travellers by study area and tenure type (from GTAAs)

Area	Estimated number of households	Social housing[1]	Private rented	Owner-occupiers	Other (eg B&B, staying with relatives)
London	3,223	68%	20%	5%	7%
South West	162	61%	11%	28%	0%
South East[2]	116	77%	6%	17%	0%
Total	3,463	68%	12.6%	17%	2.4%

Notes

[1] Council and Registered Social Landlord property.

[2] The South East study location covered two GTAA areas. The figures cited here for estimated number of households represent estimated figures from one GTAA combined with the actual number of interviews (39) conducted in the other GTAA, as the latter gave no estimate of the housed population.

to utilise an 'ethnic code' for members of these communities, and even where some individual health practices have opted to provide this facility (see for example Leach, 2009) the shortfall in use of the code resulting from reliance on 'self-identification' pertains as it does in educational settings. At a wider NHS level, to date there is still no central policy on inserting an ethnicity code into documents to identify Gypsy and Traveller patients, a subject of considerable frustration to those practitioners and researchers engaged in exploring the anecdotal (and verified in small-scale localised studies) over-representation of these communities in terms of certain health conditions. Thus records pertaining to housed populations are often sparse and to further limit the effectiveness of the data sets, there is no consistent practice for recording ethnicity of tenants (let alone owner-occupiers) across the UK. Although the 2011 census data for the first (and last) time will provide some evidence on Gypsy and Traveller numbers in Britain, these data sets are not yet available at the time of writing and in any event are dependent upon self-identification by household members.

Accordingly, the estimates of overall housed populations reproduced in Table 1 may be more or less accurate depending upon the quality of locally available data and the methodologies utilised by different research teams. The limited value of these statistics (and the reason for presenting them here) therefore lies in providing rough population estimates and in triangulating official figures with alternative methodological approaches. Smith (2008), for example, found 103 households in 'bricks and mortar' in just one much smaller locale than constituted a GTAA area (total population 38,000) in the South East through employing community interviewers who were able to utilise their own social ties and knowledge of the local Gypsy and Traveller community. Similarly, across all areas in which we have worked, anecdotal reports provided by local Gypsy and Traveller residents and housing officers generally indicate significantly larger housed populations than those provided by GTAAs, suggesting that in all the study areas a significant proportion of housed Gypsies and Travellers are 'hidden' from public bodies and officialdom.

In the area that we have designated the 'South East Region', only one of the two GTAAs which overlap the research sites attempts to estimate the housed population of Gypsies and Travellers and, based upon Traveller Education Service data and local authority statistics, arrived at a figure of 78 households. However, another GTAA area in the South East study area adjoins London, for which we have been able to identify estimated figures for housed populations from the relevant GTAA report (DCA, 2006). The pan-London GTAA (Fordham Research, 2008) indicates that the housed population in the area adjoining our study locale contains relatively high numbers of housed (mainly Romany Gypsy) families, estimated by David Couttie Associates (2006) at approximately 1,300 families. Accordingly, it would appear self-evident that there is overlap and likely propinquity between the locales, allowing us (particularly when triangulated against data from a neighbouring area discussed in Chapter Three) to calculate with some degree of confidence that several hundred families, at least, reside in housing in our chosen study area. Hence whilst precise figures for housed Gypsies and Travellers for a region, GTAA area or smaller area cannot be collated with any confidence from GTAA reports, in the absence of more accurate data sources, Table 1 provides a rough approximation of the likely distribution of housing tenure in the respective area.

As noted earlier, the findings reported in this text also draw, where relevant, on a survey commissioned by a housing association conducted by one of the present authors (Smith, 2008). Key data findings from this study (which sought to collect statistical data on the Gypsy and Traveller population in the locality with the view of ensuring that newly devised policies were sensitive to the needs of these populations) are shown in Table 2. Whilst it was well known that there was a large population of predominantly English Romany Gypsies in that study area and that they constituted the largest minority ethnic group in the area, prior to the specialist survey little data existed to support public authorities in taking their needs into account. In total, Smith's team undertook a total of 158 household surveys, comprising a population of 460 people living in a variety of circumstances (housing, official and unofficial sites). Those living in conventional housing accounted for 65 per cent of the total. The findings revealed important data relating to the characteristics of housed Gypsies in the area and to patterns of residential clustering. Of the 103 households surveyed in conventional housing, nearly three quarters were concentrated in just five neighbourhoods, providing evidence that Gypsies and Travellers are consciously recreating social structures and patterns of life analogous to those found on sites (Chapter Eight).

Table 2: Social landlord commissioned survey conducted in a borough within South East area: by housing tenure and length of residence in current accommodation

Housing tenure					Length of residence in current accommodation			
Number of households	Social housing	Owner-occupier	Private rental	Other/B&B/ temporary accommodation	0–1 year	1–5 years	6–10 years	10 years+
103	91%	0%	5%	4%	12%	24%	20%	44%

The survey also revealed important data in regards to respondents' attitudes towards living in conventional housing. When questioned as to whether they would remain in housing if the opportunity arose to live on a site, 53 per cent replied that they would stay in a house with 47 per cent expressing a preference to move onto a site. However, cross-referencing the responses by the length of time respondents had lived in housing revealed marked differences: 44 per cent of those expressing a preference for remaining in housing had been housed for 20 years or more and considered themselves either too old or too used to living in 'bricks and mortar' to return to a site; 83 per cent of those housed for over 20 years said that they would stay in housing given the choice; and 17 per cent stated they would return to a site. Conversely, of those who had lived in housing for between 1 and 10 years only 34 per cent would remain in housing while 66 per cent would move to a site (Smith, 2008, p 30). These findings indicate the extent of 'cultural aversion' to conventional housing that exists, whilst we discuss the qualitative evidence pertaining to the often devastating impacts of such 'enforced settlement' in Chapter Six. The quantitative findings from this survey also supplement our arguments concerning the maintenance of nomadic patterns even within housing and the socio-cultural importance to housed Gypsy/Travellers of retaining extensive localised networks, factors discussed in depth in Chapter Eight.

Purposive studies of housed Gypsies and Travellers

In Table 3 we summarise the data from our targeted (purposively sampled) projects designed to focus on the experiences of housed Gypsies and Travellers through a more in-depth qualitative approach. Within these studies (all utilising the same questionnaire albeit with some slight differences in focus group topic guides dependent on area) we explicitly refined the data capture tools to enable us to develop certain themes and capitalise on information pertaining to housing tenure and ethnicity of respondents.

Table 3: In-depth qualitative studies – respondents by housing tenure and ethnicity

	Housing tenure					Ethnicity			
	Number of households	Social housing	Owner-occupier	Private rental	Other/B&B/ temporary	English Gypsy Romany	Irish Traveller	'New' Traveller	Other/ mixed
South West	28	85%	5%	8%	2%	17	I	8	2
South East	20	80%	15%	0%	5%	18	0	0	2
Inner London	10	70%	0%	30%	0%	0	10	0	0
Outer London	10	50%	40%	10%	0%	9	0	0	I
Total	68	71.25%	15.0%	12.0%	1.75%	44 (64.7%)	11 (16.3%)	8 (11.7%)	5 (7.3%)

Although via our GTAA data sets (and focus groups connected with those studies) we were able to access owner occupiers, amongst our 'targeted' sample (Table 3), we were only able to include a significantly smaller number of such respondents (albeit this is an artefact of our deliberate targeting of residents of a local authority housing estate for our initial foray into research with housed families) than would be expected in the wider Gypsy and Traveller population based on GTAA evidence. Of those individuals whom we surveyed for the South West study of Gypsies and Travellers in housing, by far the largest numbers of participants were co-residents on two closely linked estates. Subsequently, snowballing to obtain interviewees almost inevitably led us to those in similar property types. Although social housing tenants are over-represented in Table 3 the percentages are not totally disproportionate if one breaks down GTAA data to examine the smaller local area within which the small-scale qualitative studies are located, as the high value of housing stock in those areas excludes all but a relatively small number of housed Gypsies and Travellers from entering into the private market. Another factor which helps to explain this demographic is that our respondents were generally younger people (or in a few cases, divorced or separated people who were living with relatives and lacked adequate capital to purchase property or enter the private rented market, preferring instead to reside with family members who could offer them a spare room or a sofa). In such circumstances unless an individual expressly states (as did one interviewee: "I am looking after the flat for a friend, I have a van I sleep in and then I stay with family sometimes – I am not interested in getting a council place like they offered me I would be trapped") that they do not consider themselves to be a resident of the property identified, we have classified them according to the tenure of the property in which they are dwelling. It was noteworthy that in our South West area study we identified that perhaps as many as 15 per cent of household members who were present in the home of the key respondent were siblings or 'other'. The high percentage of extended family co-residence would be interesting to compare with household demographic surveys amongst other populations.

The South West region has the highest proportions of Gypsies and Travellers living in social housing with 85 per cent of participants renting their homes from either the local authority or registered social landlords followed by the South East, at 80 per cent. The relatively high numbers in social housing is further supported by GTAA survey findings and the commissioned survey discussed above (Tables 1 and 2). Despite remaining cautious about generalising from relatively small sample sizes the London sample appear to demonstrate lower levels of social renting. In Inner London this is likely to be a reflection of high demand for social housing stock combined with a greater reliance on the private rental sector while in Outer London participants were more likely to be owner-occupiers, a trend explained by the fact that they were generally older, with 60 per cent of those interviewed aged over 55. This group had, with the exception of the South West region, been housed for longer than other respondents, with over half having lived in their current house for over 10 years compared to just 20 per cent in Inner London and the South East (Table 4). Nearly two thirds of the Outer London participants cited work-related reasons as important reasons for settling into housing in contrast to respondents in the other localities. Subsequently many ran their own businesses (or had done so prior to retirement) and had access to greater financial resources allowing them to purchase their own homes, with a few buying their council homes through 'Right to Buy' schemes.

As referred to previously, and considered in more detail in Chapter Six, we were interested in exploring the relationship between duration of residence in housing and the extent to which respondents felt that they 'settled' into such accommodation. Accordingly, wherever possible we sought to identify the length of time for which respondents had lived in 'bricks and mortar' and correlate this by degree of satisfaction and 'best' aspects of housing. In a number of cases of young people participating in the focus group we have had to 'guesstimate' >10 years of residence based on their age and statements such as "we moved into housing when I was a little chavvy and the site closed down", while others were clear that they "were born to housing". Overall we found that amongst the South-Western respondents (partially as a result of our selection of young people to take part in a focus group) we had a large percentage of respondents who have remained in housing for a considerable period of time (see Table 4). This apparent slanting of the data is however remedied when we take into account data from GTAAs which provides a wider range of respondents and rather clearer view of the patterns of housed residence and duration of such accommodation.

Table 4: Interview respondents by length of residence in current accommodation

	0–1 year	1–5 years	6–10 years	10 years +
South West	1%	11%	28%	60%
South East	20%	35%	25%	20%
Inner London	10%	40%	30%	20%
Outer London	0%	10%	40%	50%
Total	7.75%	24.0%	30.75%	37.50%

In terms of household structure, the largest proportion consisted of a couple with dependent children although this varied between regions with the South West sample consisting of 55 per cent of households in this category compared to Outer London where only 30 per cent had resident dependent children, reflecting the older demographic profile of the latter group (Table 5). Conversely, 60 per cent of the Outer London sample had children who had grown up and established their own homes compared to only 10 per cent in Inner London. A significantly higher proportion of single person households were interviewed in Inner London at 30 per cent compared to an average of just over 13 per cent of households, which is still considerably lower than the national average of 29 per cent single person households (ONS, 2011).

Table 5: Composition of household and household size

	Composition of household				Household size					
	Couple with children/ dependents	Lone parent household	Couple no children/ left home	Single person	1	2	3	4	5	6+
South West	55%	20%	17%	8%	8%	12%	15%	25%	20%	20%
South East	50%	30%	15%	5%	5%	25%	20%	15%	10%	25%
Inner London	40%	20%	10%	30%	30%	20%	0%	10%	20%	20%
Outer London	30%	0%	60%	10%	10%	60%	0%	10%	20%	0%
Total	**43.75%**	**17.50%**	**25.50%**	**13.25%**	**13.25%**	**29.25%**	**8.75%**	**15%**	**17.50%**	**16.25%**

Household composition was also significantly larger, with nearly half of those interviewed living in households consisting of four or more people compared to 20 per cent of the general population (ONS, 2011). However, recording family size accurately was problematic due to the dynamic and fluid nature of household structure, fluctuating according to the circumstances of different family members. Thus it was not uncommon to record household groupings such as 'couple, two children and woman's cousin'; 'couple; three young adult daughters; oldest daughter and three children' or, as one older gentleman recorded, 'me, my wife, a couple of grandchildren always here and other grandchildren that come and go'. Another respondent noted that their household consisted of herself and her dependent children living at home and that in the garden they had a trailer which at the time of interview was home to her 'niece, nephew and one of her grandchildren'. The extent of overcrowding is therefore sometimes extreme, although it was rare that respondents identified this fact unless explicitly prompted. Only one focus group participant in the South West area (single person household) reported that he had "left home –

it was too crowded with all my brothers and sisters and my mum and her boyfriend and my sister's boys". It has been noted elsewhere that Gypsies and Travellers tend to tolerate greater levels of overcrowding than many other communities would consider acceptable and it has been suggested that this may relate to expectations of both family duty to assist those in need, and familiarity with the less spacious conditions found in caravans and mobile homes (Home and Greenfields, 2006).

Finally, in Table 6 we show the number of housed individuals in each area who participated in focus group discussions and who lived in 'bricks and mortar'. Thus for example in one area our focus group explored social relations and community cohesion and all but two respondents lived in housing; whilst in another locality we looked at the impact on women's health of residence in particular forms of accommodation (sites and housing), and a focus group with young people only included those youth who were resident in social housing on a particular estate. To date we have not undertaken focus groups in London due to difficulties in convening such gatherings when we are carrying out opportunistic interviews with a dispersed population. However, it is anticipated that as we continue to work with housed families we may be able to organise such groups within the study areas to explore household demographics and inter-ethnic community relations.

Table 6: Constituents of focus groups

	Number of participants	Male	Female
South West (adult women)	11	–	11
South West (young people aged 5–25)	11	3	8
South East (young people aged 10–17)	6	4	2
South East (adults)	12	7	5
Total	40	14	26

Having discussed the varied data sources that are utilised in this text and outlined the housing-related and demographic characteristics of the sample, the remainder of this book explores the empirical and qualitative data concerning the lived experiences of formerly nomadic or sited residents now residing in conventional housing. The following chapter explores the routes through which many arrived in housing, highlighting key regularities in those routes, situated as they were within the wider structural and policy-driven forces discussed in the previous chapters.

Note

[1] See Greenfields et al (2007) for a discussion on the use of various data sources such as Schools Census Data Traveller Education Service records and population projections based on typical household size.

FIVE

Routes into housing

In all of the research locales outlined in the previous chapter, significant Gypsy and Traveller populations are resident in conventional housing as a consequence of the broader legislative, social and historical forces previously discussed as well as resulting from individual preferences and circumstances. In recent decades, the housing 'careers' and residential characteristics of minority groups have received extensive attention (Sarre et al, 1989; Somerville and Steele, 2002; Robinson and Reeve, 2006), with research consistently showing that despite significant differences between BME groups they tend as a category to be disadvantaged in relation to housing; 26 per cent of BME households reside in social housing compared to 18 per cent of all households in England and Wales. Evidence also indicates that these households experience higher levels of over-crowding and are more likely to be concentrated in deprived areas (Shelter, 2010b). Since 1997 levels of homelessness among BME households have risen at over twice the rate of the general population (Shelter, 2004). This trend may well accelerate in coming years as a result of their concentration in urban centres, particularly London due to its high concentration of BME groups. More recently concern has been expressed that a combination of housing benefit caps, a severe shortage of affordable housing and high rents in the private rental sector will result in a rise in homelessness and a significant relocation of low income groups beyond the boundaries of the capital to areas where rents are lower (Radical Islington, 2012) in essence creating ghettos for the poor similar to the 'banlieues' of Paris (Silverstein and Tetreault, 2006). Families with more than three children will be particularly affected as the number of London neighbourhoods that are not 'largely unaffordable' for housing benefit claimants will be halved (from 75 to 36 per cent) by 2016 as a result of reforms to the Local Housing Allowance (LHA) (Shelter, 2010a). This process of spatial restructuring (as we saw in Chapter Two) is global in nature: as nation states have become more spatially polarised between a 'network of globalized metropolitan centres' and 'non metropolitan localities and peripheries' so the poor, economically inactive and those minorities who are unable, or unwilling, to participate as global actors and consumers are subject to new forms of spatial zoning and control (Bancroft, 2005, p 5).

As discussed, one aspect of spatial management has concerned the control, surveillance and sedentarisation of Gypsy and Traveller communities which has been enacted through making nomadism progressively more difficult to maintain and by settling them on permanent sites and/or into conventional housing (Belton, 2005; Richardson, 2006). This chapter will examine the micro-level expression of these broader processes on the accommodation careers of the research respondents prior to considering (in Chapter Six) the impacts of such enforced movement on family and individual well-being. Central to the analysis are the reasons for entering housing and the routes by which those interviewed arrived there. Typically, attempts to understand the settlement patterns of minority groups have centred on the 'choice/constraint' debate. Accounts emphasising 'constraints' argue that BME housing outcomes result from external forces such as discrimination by housing agencies and in the allocation policies of housing authorities, thus restricting housing options and stratifying minority groups into 'housing classes' characterised by tenure (Rex and Moore, 1967).

Other accounts place more emphasis on 'choice' and preference in the creation of ethnic enclaves, such as a desire to live in a familiar ethnic and cultural milieu where newcomers can easily access informal social support systems and the chances of encountering racial hostility are minimised (Dahya, 1974, and see further Chapter Eight). Questions surrounding choice and constraint are a reflection of the core sociological question over the relationship between structure and agency. The two cannot be separated in reality since choices are constrained by both structural location and individual circumstances (Sarre, 1986). Choices are further shaped and expressed through collective strategies that themselves emerge in response to external circumstances such as experiences of prejudice, exclusion and group solidarity (Greenfields and Smith, 2010, 2011). The testimonies in this chapter reveal a multiplicity of constraints regarding preferred type of accommodation; the suitability of available housing and other considerations such as proximity to kin and social networks, which are all important factors in determining housing preferences. These external forces are not insurmountable, however, and the power to constrain and restrict choice is always tempered by the 'counter-agency' of individual citizens. Prior (2009) argues that policy discourses construct distinct identities that embody particular modes of behaviour for recipients of welfare services and are situated within particular forms of governance. Access to a raft of services has thus become increasingly conditional on adopting behavioural standards, for example policy interventions designed to deter 'anti-social' behaviour, instill self-discipline and promote the development of human and social capital imposed on social housing tenants (Burney, 2009). However,

> Citizens are not 'empty vessels' waiting to be filled with the attributes and potentialities prescribed for them by dominant discourses ...They respond to policies and engage with practitioners with their own understandings of the situation, their own sense of what would constitute a just or unjust outcome and their own capacities for action, including alternative sources of knowledge. (Prior, 2009, p 22)

Constraints on action are therefore partly offset by individual agency and preferences such as an apparent desire for self-segregation (Phillips, 1998; 2007). Choices are further facilitated and enabled through collective strategies that provide a degree of autonomy and maintenance of accustomed lifestyles such as high levels of mobility as well as the recreation of spatially segregated communities within the housing system (Chapter Eight). Accommodation options are also dependent on the social and economic resources that individual households can access. Harrison, for example, highlights the importance of economic divisions within particular minority groups in shaping housing options and notes that 'each minority group has not only its own specific settlement geography but also its own potential for internal socioeconomic polarisation' (2003, p 108). Cemlyn, Greenfields et al identify a changing pattern of caravan site provision in recent years with a decline in public site provision and the greatest rise in pitch numbers occurring through private site applications (2009, p 8). The scope to resist moving into housing therefore and the accommodation options of what were, until quite recently, mobile communities, have developed and diverged, depending upon differing socioeconomic circumstances. Much academic and policy-related literature tends to homogenise Gypsies and Travellers, failing to acknowledge either the disparate origins from which different travelling groups have evolved, or the wide variations in the income and financial assets of family groups (Okely, 1983, p 63). Given limits on the lifestyle and accommodation options facing all Gypsies and Travellers, it is, nevertheless, those with the most economic resources who are able to maximise their accommodation and lifestyle choices.[1] Thus, in common with many other minority groups, it is the poorer and least-skilled sections of those communities who lack the resources to purchase their own land or homes (bungalows tend to be the favoured type of 'conventional' housing; see further Chapter Six), and who now face the most severely circumscribed choices due to the shortage of vacancies on public sites and the difficulty of maintaining a nomadic lifestyle.

In reviewing our findings, it is important to note that the method of 'purposive sampling' that was employed in many of the studies on which we draw (whereby community members were employed to access respondents from their own kin and community networks) tends to yield a sample that is relatively homogenous in its attributes rather than providing linkages to groups who may possess different attributes and characteristics. Thus the sample may be skewed towards those with the fewest housing options and under-represent the more successful community members who are more likely to be owner-occupiers or have the resources to purchase their own land. Nevertheless, we have sought to include data from owner-occupiers, typically accessed through GTAAs on which we have worked, and as demonstrated in the previous chapter, even allowing for regional variations it is the widespread move into social housing that has been most significant for the community as a whole. Furthermore, residential concentrations of housed Gypsies and Travellers are more prominent in social housing, largely due to the circumstances through which many entered 'bricks and mortar' and partly due to the flexibility that such accommodation affords, as such forms of tenure allows households to remain relatively mobile within housing. Consequently the potential to consciously recreate traditional communities on housing estates is maximised, providing individuals and families a limited degree of autonomy and choice in relation to selection of neighbourhood and the maintenance of community and kin structures (see Chapter Eight).

The structure of this chapter and the selection of examples were guided by the research aims which set out to explore the relationship between choice and constraint in shaping housing transitions. Accordingly we interrogate the data to analyse the routes through which different households arrived in conventional housing, of which by far the most common reasons were insufficient capacity on public caravan sites; the increasing difficulty of sustaining nomadism as a viable lifestyle and the necessity of accessing public services for dependents, although the decisions of housing officials and front-line housing department staff in the allocation process were often perceived by respondents as a factor in limiting housing options. Core secondary elements which impacted on housing choice and need related to individual circumstances such as caring responsibilities; obligations to family and kin; and life-cycle factors such as the structure and size of the household. For analytical purposes those factors are separated in the following sections in order to highlight the main processes that shape housing transitions and subsequently determine the respondents' quality of life and experiences in 'bricks and mortar' residences. In the testimonies, however, the categories were closely intertwined and frequently overlapped, revealing the dynamic and interconnected nature of the constraints and opportunities encountered in relation to housing. The following discussion sets the context for a consideration of how respondents' desire to exercise autonomy and control over their housing options shapes their sense of well-being (or otherwise) in housing, a subject addressed in Chapter Six, and the ways in which these perceptions are themselves mediated by the presence (or lack of) social networks. These themes are elaborated further in the remainder of the book.

Site provision and 'enforced' housing

The most common reason given for moving into housing was a lack of site vacancies. Among the in-depth qualitative studies this was cited by just under half of the total sample. Respondents repeatedly indicated that a lack of control in response to external forces was perceived as having a damaging impact, playing a significant role in generating a sense of 'cultural trauma'. In some cases it could be argued that it is the sense of being forced into housing as much as the experience of living in housing that stimulates and intensifies the traumatic experience of life in conventional accommodation:

> "I'm not very happy here. We miss the site, we don't like houses. It's too lonely, I feel closed in and it's much more expensive with all the bills. We'd really like to live down on the site. We've been on the waiting list for 12 years now."

Similarly, in the GTAA surveys that overlap our study areas, a lack of accommodation on sites (often after new household formation) was a major reason for entering housing, while the qualitative studies expand upon this to include information on difficulties gaining permission to develop private sites and repeated evictions, citing this triumvirate as the other main reasons for entering housing. Table 7 shows that the highest numbers referring to site shortages were respondents in the South East (where high pressure on rural and peri-urban land exists) and, surprisingly, the lowest numbers were found in Outer London, although the latter had settled significantly earlier largely in the 1960s and displayed a greater degree of economic rationality and choice in their decisions (Smith and Greenfields, 2012).

Table 7: Primary reason cited for residence in housing

	Health/ education	Family reasons	Evictions/ site shortage/ failed planning application	Other
South West	17%	25%	52%	6%
South East	15%	25%	55%	5%
Inner London	10%	20%	50%	20%
Outer London	10%	30%	30%	30%
Total	13%	25%	47%	15%

The figures from our data are consistent with the national picture. Cemlyn, Greenfields et al (2009, p 6) note that between 2003 and 2005 only 15–25 per cent of identified site demand was met, whilst between January 2009 and January 2011 there was only a 2.1 per cent net growth of caravans on public sites nationally. In the South East this constituted a 7.6 per cent increase in numbers from 1,288 to 1,386 caravans, while the South West experienced a 9.5 per cent increase from 682 to 747 caravans. Over the same time period, only London experienced a fall – of over 12 per cent – in the number of caravans which could be accommodated on on local authority sites, down from 719 to 630, adding to the pressure on families struggling to obtain a place on over-subscribed sites in the metropolis. Despite the growth in local authority site capacity over the period it has failed to keep pace with demand, which has grown steadily due to population increase and intensifying legal pressures to prohibit unauthorised encampments and developments. Over the same two-year period, unauthorised encampments fell by 28 per cent nationally, and unauthorised developments (where the land is owned by Gypsies/Travellers but planning permission has not been granted) fell by 7 per cent (DCLG, 2011). In the light of changing and more punitive planning policies in relation to site development (Ryder et al, 2011), it is likely that increased evictions will place further pressure on the demand for public sites. A series of studies have highlighted the cumulative effects of a shortage of public pitches, criminalisation of unauthorised camping and the subsequent drift into conventional housing on inequalities experienced by Gypsies and Travellers. In the Cemlyn and Greenfields et al review, they argue that:

Accommodation, the lack of appropriate or adequate site provision, and the issue of enforced movement into housing of Gypsies and Travellers, raises concerns over fundamental human rights to privacy, home and family life. (2009, p 29)

A major aspect of an individual's sense of security and well-being is the capacity to exercise a degree of control and autonomy over major life decisions (Doyal and Gough, 1991). A lack of control, particularly when combined with low social status, can have negative impacts on psychological and physical health (Van Cleemput, 2008). Many respondents complained bitterly about 'enforced' settlement in housing due to a lack of more culturally appropriate alternatives and the closure of local authority sites. One middle-aged woman in the South West for example recounted how

"... we was forced out [of the local authority site] when it shut down but it wasn't how we was brung up not to be in a house – but it was that or go on the road again and we couldn't do that with our son being disabled and me being pregnant again. It did get better and I wouldn't want to go back on a site now ... but it was very hard for a long time."

In the survey of 158 Gypsy and Traveller households conducted in the South East a lack of public sites and shortage of stopping places was viewed as the most pressing issue facing the Gypsy and Traveller community (Smith, 2008) with these findings confirming data gathered in GTAAs from across the UK. The pressure to settle felt by many families is widely regarded as a politically motivated assault on their traditional lifestyle with many respondents in all study areas complaining that "they don't want Gypsies on the road no more" or "they won't let us live how we want". Belton (2005, and see further Chapters One and Two) may be correct that post-war legislation restricting travelling lifestyles had a wider purpose than a racially motivated attack on a relatively small and insignificant minority of Gypsies and Travellers. However, what is of relevance here is what the functions of legislation were perceived to be by those directly affected. As Goffman (1981) notes, for stigmatised groups, disdain for a society that rejects them is reinforced and confirmed through personalised interpretations of the motives of the 'self-appointed wise' and the policies they implement. Limits on mobility are a major cause of the social dislocation felt by many members of this community since it violates one of their most fundamental symbols of cultural and ethnic identity while simultaneously eroding cultural values that prioritise independence and autonomy. During a focus group interview in the South East one woman commented:

> "... there is no choice to live on a site – you don't have that choice. People would actually like a choice about their lives."

Others added that "most don't want to be in houses. Our culture and ways are being taken from us and we can't live how we were raised". One respondent in the South West when asked if she had wanted to move into a house replied, "not really but I feel we were pushed into it", a view expressed by many in all study areas. Many compared the situation and social status of Gypsies and Travellers unfavourably to other minority groups and there is a widespread feeling that the emphasis on diversity and social inclusion has bypassed their community. As one Gypsy in the South West observed, "I'm not being funny but if we was black they wouldn't treat us like this". Indeed, despite clear attempts to provide equality of treatment to housing applicants, public service employees are not immune from the internalisation of negative stereotypes, while the prevalence of racist attitudes towards nomadic peoples is a significant though latent factor in shaping public policy, particularly in terms of implementation and practice at the local level. One woman in the South East, echoing the sentiments of many, noted that

> "We don't get treated the same as other groups. Our kids are still getting bullied, the police are always at my house. Our way of life is being wiped out. We need more sites."

One man in the South West, having failed to gain planning permission on his own land, was then classed as technically homeless following eviction and placed into social housing on an estate. In the context of severe shortages of affordable housing, the irrationality of preventing self-provision and forcing Gypsies and Travellers into housing where they did not want to be was not lost on him, as he noted:

> "There's people as want to live in houses and we don't and it's making us ill and unhappy and my wife is not good with her nerves. Why can't they just let us live how we want and let someone that wants to be a kerret [house dweller] be one instead of making us live like gorjers?"

In the rural areas of the South East there was also a palpable sense of injustice that the achievements of other minority groups are celebrated while the contribution that Gypsies made as a mobile rural workforce is unacknowledged and largely forgotten. At the same time as the region's rural heritage is being destroyed to make room for housing developments, Gypsies and Travellers often experience extreme difficulty gaining planning permission to develop private sites, while an insufficient supply of pitches on public sites means that many are being forcibly settled alongside the wider population with whom they find little in common. During a focus group in the South East one elderly Gypsy male commented:

> "See what you've got to understand, is that our people kept the countryside, we kept them fields, grew new crops, kept the farms and fed this country through two world wars. By rights, as we never always got paid for the work, that countryside is ours and we get very upset when we drive through and see obstructions like housing estates rather than the willow tree. The hassle [hazel] tree and the old cobnut tree have all been uprooted for monstrosities these settled folk choose to live in."

The shortage of sites in London noted above was confirmed in the interviews with the London-based Irish Travellers, where a lack of pitches on public sites was cited as the main reason for moving into housing by over half of the sample, although, as mentioned above, this factor was frequently provided in combination with other elements such as the difficulty of accessing health and education services on the road. As Power notes (2004, p 26), Irish Travellers often faced a double bind due to their ethnic identity as Travellers and their Irish nationality. The 1968 Caravan Act led to site provision (albeit inadequate) for 'indigenous' Gypsies but often resulted in the exclusion of Irish Travellers from council sites as they were not considered 'indigenous'. One woman had come over from Ireland as a child in the 1970s and spent much of the next two decades travelling between England and Ireland with her extended family. After getting married she lived 'by the roadside' with her husband on the outskirts of London, Essex and Kent for a year until she became pregnant and needed a more settled life. As no council pitches were available they were considered homeless and placed in temporary accommodation before moving to their current home, a council house in North London where the family have lived for ten years. She recalled;

> "We went in housing after I got married. We lived in bed
> and breakfast and temporary accommodation in Tottenham
> because there was nowhere in England that had a pitch on a
> site where we could stay. So the council gave us this house.
> I would have preferred to bring my kids up on a council
> site but was never able to get a pitch."

Many entered housing after being registered as homeless, since
under the 1996 Housing Act a person eligible for accommodation is
considered homeless if they are living in a caravan but have no place to
legally reside in it (Johnson and Willars, 2007). Another Irish woman
living in a council house in North East London with her five children
recalled that she was registered as homeless before being accommodated:

> "We weren't allowed to stop for long in places and campsites
> were becoming harder to find. I had five small children and
> was getting moved from pillar to post. You can only stand
> so much and in the end we just got fed up of it."

As the quotation implies, site shortages often combined with a series of
other factors in shaping housing transitions. A man in the South East
lamented his move into housing but argued that the options facing his
family were extremely restricted and thus "we needed to, because it's
getting more and more difficult to travel. It's too much hassle being
moved on every day". These sentiments were repeated in all study areas
with the following man in the South West reporting similar motivations
(in addition to hazardous stopping places and fear of violence from
locals) for entering housing, "I was sick of living on unsafe sites with
abuse from the locals. It's better for the kids having the security".

The detrimental health effects of constant evictions in terms of
accessing and ensuring continuity of health care and of the psychological
impacts of stress caused by insecurity has been well documented (Parry
et al, 2004; Van Cleemput, 2008). The following 60-year-old respondent
from South London estimated the extent of settlement into housing
among his own network of formerly nomadic kin to be around 75
per cent. He argued that environmental conditions combined with the
manifold pressures of life on the road can be a significant factor in the
deterioration of health that frequently precedes the move into housing:

> "Constant hassle and being moved along is the biggest
> health risk 'cos it creates a lot of worry and stress in the
> parents and that's why there's heart problems, bad nerves

makes people not look after themselves and drink and smoke too much and that rubs off on the kids and is carried down the generations."

A further important determinant of settlement in housing was deterioration of physical health, the recognition of chronic illness in household members and the need to access health services. After entering housing, however, many subsequently feel that they have merely substituted one set of problems for another set. Studies indicate that social isolation, 'nerves' and depression are extremely common among housed Gypsies and Travellers with a deterioration in mental health frequently following the move into housing (Parry et al, 2004; Greenfields and Smith, 2010). One man, for example, noted that since moving into housing his wife's health "is better on one hand because we have easier access to a doctor here, but worse because my wife hates it here and is depressed". Van Cleemput (2008) argues that lack of control over one's life circumstances leading to pressure to settle produces direct psychological effects that influence well-being and may contribute to morbidity and mortality levels. Thus whilst the majority of our respondents were relatively powerless to resist the structural and legislative forces which drove them into housing, the residential settlement patterns of Gypsies and Travellers are shaped not only by their personal obligations but also by the decisions of housing department bureaucrats, who hold (or are perceived of as holding) the power to exacerbate or ease the transition into 'bricks and mortar' accommodation.

Housing officers and housing allocation

The majority of our respondents were housed on run-down estates characterised by higher than average levels of poverty, economic inactivity, unemployment and attendant social problems. Whilst ever increased demand for, and deterioration of, the diminishing stock of remaining public and social housing (King, 2008a, 2008b) is undoubtedly a major factor in the quality of housing into which many Gypsies and Travellers are housed, settlement patterns are also influenced by what Henman and Marston (2008) refer to as a 'social division of welfare surveillance', a phrase which refers to variations in state control of access to social, fiscal and occupational forms of welfare benefits. Populations accessing these different forms of welfare payments are variously classified in both popular and policy formulations into 'deserving' and 'undeserving' categories, each accompanied by differing degrees of scrutiny and assessment for the same services. Under conditions of housing scarcity, and tasked with accommodating growing proportions of the most vulnerable and deprived sections of society, front-line decision makers play a key role in recreating and legitimating social and spatial divisions. Housing managers are thus increasingly required to act as agents of social control through the screening of prospective tenants according to 'need', which itself is 'socially constructed by bureaucracies and is not only different from organisation to organisation but also from situation to situation' (Saugeres, 2000, p 589). Deploying social distinctions as a determinant of housing allocation based on stereotyping of households and expectations of location serves to spatially marginalise and concentrate elements who offend dominant norms, manoeuvering such groups into accommodation in the most disadvantaged areas (see further Chapters Six and Eight).

For stigmatised groups such as Gypsies and Travellers a consequence of these processes is that many are channelled into poor quality, 'hard to let' housing. As one woman complained, "they put you in the worse council estates that you could imagine because you're the villain because they know you're, as they say, the pikeys". Many felt that they were deliberately offered properties on the worst estates with the highest levels of anti-social behaviour and disorder, viewing this as symptomatic of their low social status and part of a broader experience of discrimination. One man in the South East, highlighting the relationship between the high levels of depression among the housed population and the influence of environmental factors, noted:

> "Mental illness is big in the housed Gypsies, I've seen it. It's massive and I see it all throughout the country. They put them in substandard housing because that's what they think they are, substandard people."

In contrast, interviews with housing officers indicate that rather than negative stereotyping leading to such accommodation offers, often Gypsies and Travellers are allocated housing after presenting as homeless following evictions from unauthorised camps and, depending on the availability of housing and the urgency of their situation, may thus find themselves living in the same neighbourhoods as others from their community (see further Chapter Eight). Some housing officials, however, suggested an unofficial policy of accommodating Gypsies in the same neighbourhoods in recognition of the communities' own preferences, combined with an aversion among many non-Gypsies to living close to them and the conflict that sometimes results from enforced co-residence (see Chapters Six and Seven). In both the South East and South West study areas the move into housing was largely stimulated by the local authorities' aim to eradicate unauthorised encampments in their localities and to spatially manage their Gypsy and Traveller populations. In the South East many were housed in the mid 1980s following the clearance of two large, and previously tolerated, stopping places. Many respondents still feel betrayed that the public sites that were offered as a condition of vacating the unauthorised sites never materialised. One woman, who had entered housing during this period but was unable to settle and later moved onto a private site, recalled:

> "They told us if we got off the marshes and went into housing they'd build sites for us and we could move back out onto the sites. It never happened. The only ones who got a place on the sites were the roadsiders who wouldn't go into houses."

Official explanations for the residential settlement patterns of their local Gypsy and Traveller populations thus emphasised the role of choice and the desire for ethnic segregation, which occurs as an artefact of housing policies, since applicants with family connections to an area are prioritised, as well as conscious use of the housing transfer system as a strategy to live close to family and community members (see Chapter Eight). Indeed one housing officer in the South East reported:

> "If they've come into housing off a site or the roadside they've generally lived a very social and communal existence and to be put into a house where everybody lives their own lives between closed doors is a difficult adjustment for most to make [so] they tend to bunch together in particular estates and live in the same manner that they're used to."

Whilst the strategies by which communities are reformed and networks of social relations maintained in housing are elaborated in Chapter Eight we noted repeatedly that the locally based networks of extended kin in which many respondents were immersed were a major source of emotional and social support providing solidarity and collective protection in what were often hostile and unwelcoming neighbourhoods (discussed in Chapter Seven). However, despite their benefits, close-knit networks characterised by high levels of 'bonding' social capital and a deficit of 'bridging' capital to other social groups can also impose excessive obligations and responsibilities that themselves can increase stress and hardship (Ferlander, 2007). The nature of social ties and strength of reciprocal obligations between kin members also shapes the social composition of particular neighbourhoods, as family responsibilities such as childcare, the provision of care for elderly and sick family members and providing support following bereavement or a family crisis (see further Finch, 1989; and Finch and Mason, 1993) play an important role in preferred residential location.

Family, responsibility and housing

Approximately one quarter of those interviewed cited 'family reasons' as a major reason for entering housing, typically referring to the desire to live near family members and/or to provide care for elderly and sick relatives. Our findings thus support the 'lifecycle approach' to housing careers which focuses on how different housing needs are generated by the relationship between choice and the nature of the household at various stages of the lifecycle (Gilbert and Varley, 1991, p 96). For our sample, spatial requirements are directly related to childrearing, with options shaped by the supply of available accommodation: thus overcrowding on many public sites and a shortage of pitches may necessitate a move into housing with the arrival of new family members. One man, for example, who moved into housing due to overcrowding in his caravan and a lack of pitches on their former site for an additional one said: "we needed the room. The family are growing and there was no more room on the site". The close-knit and dynamic nature of family life meant that many households were extremely fluid with different family members temporarily residing at the same address as a result of personal circumstances such as the death of a spouse, relationship breakdown or eviction from a roadside site (see further Chapters Six and Eight). This indicates a cultural norm of reciprocity (Finch, 1989), with mutual expectations that family members will provide accommodation (whether on a site or in housing) for a relative who is stopping in the area or with nowhere else to live, regardless of their own circumstances or any overcrowding which might occur.

Housing officers also noted that where an established community of housed Gypsies and Travellers exist, second and subsequent generations often request housing on the same estate frequently citing family support and caring responsibilities as a reason for requiring housing in a particular locality. One woman in the South East for example reported that "mother is poorly and lost our dad to heart attack so she came here", and another that "we had another baby and my mum has moved in to help out". A Romany Gypsy woman in the South West recalled that she had

> "[gone into] housing temporary to look after my grandad when my gran was poorly and then she died. There wasn't any sites near to them with pitches but we managed to move to where we are and there are other Travellers near us. I'd like to live on a site again one day but we're alright here while my granddad needs me and my parents are on the site so we're up and down the road."

Despite reliance on housing officials to assist with allocation of properties, suspicion and mistrust of 'authority' is confirmed in the often conflictual and negative nature of relations between Gypsies and Travellers and front-line employees of public services and welfare agencies, making respondents more dependent on informal kin and community-based forms of care than official sources of 'help'. A former 'roadsider' from the South East commented that they would have preferred to have remained in caravans but entered housing "because dad's sisters live round this way and they helped out after dad died". The choice between maintaining one's preferred lifestyle and the performing of familial duties, however, is deeply restricted by policy induced factors such as a shortage of transit (short-term) sites and restrictions on parking caravans outside local authority and social housing thus making visits by nomadic family members logistically difficult. One woman in the South East who entered housing with her children after separating from her husband noted how these restrictions can lead to previously close-knit families becoming fragmented and ultimately impacting on their sense of isolation in housing.

> "I needed my family after the separation and going into a house for the first time was really hard. They would all come and stay but there were complaints about the trailers and vans outside and we were told they're not allowed. There's no transit site either and the gavvers [police] wouldn't give them a stop – so it got hard for them to stop anywhere round here and I can't see as much of them as I'd like."

Two of the Irish women in Inner London had entered housing after fleeing from domestic violence. Power (2004, p 27) notes that Traveller women who leave a violent partner can be shunned by their extended family due to the stigma attached to ending a marriage. Accordingly, if a woman is determined to remain separated, such a lifestyle change will frequently necessitate a complete break from the community. One woman living in North London, for example, recalled:

> "Travelling life with my husband was not easy. I was married to an alcoholic who was drinking every minute of the day and was very violent towards me and I spent many years running to women refuges from my husband. I had seven girls and four boys and spent most of the time bringing them up in women's refuges. I received help from the support workers and that's how I settled in houses."

When figures were averaged across all study areas, we found that around 13 per cent of respondents stated that gaining access to health and/or education was an important factor influencing their decision to enter housing. However, a significantly higher proportion stated this element combined with other issues (such as repeated eviction) to encourage them to make the transition. One woman noted that one of the few advantages of life in housing was that "my child can go to school and nobody knows he's a Traveller". Another woman highlighted the trade-off facing many families when considering accommodation options. She was highly critical of the labelling of caravan dwelling as deviant and pointed out that a 'normal' house-dwelling existence, while providing the opportunity for her children to attend school, also exposed her family to extreme levels of socially unacceptable and previously unexperienced behaviour such as racial prejudice and violence:

> "I only went into the house for the school. I only went in so the kids could go to school. There's nothing normal with my little boy being kicked to hell every day at school. There's nothing normal about dog poo being put through my door."

Our respondents stressed that accommodation choices are therefore frequently made as a last resort in the context of years of experiencing significant barriers to accessing public services such as (contrary to both the law and official policies) the refusal of some schools to accept nomadic children, or GPs failing to register families for treatment without a permanent address. One man in London discussed how a combination of factors – site shortages and the need to utilise health and education – foreclosed the options facing his household (and many similar) families:

> "[We] couldn't get nowhere else to live, they said it was a ten-year wait for a pitch and my wife were ill and two of the chavvies [children] they needed a doctor regular and you can't get that on the roadside – so we went into a house."

The need to be settled in conventional housing in order to access services also led to a degree of instrumentalism over housing options. The following woman (interviewed for a GTAA on which we worked) reported that following a diagnosis of cancer the difficulty of finding a stopping place close to the hospital meant a move into housing was necessary, although shortly after her recovery the family moved out onto a private site:

> "I ended up going in because I had the cancer cell things and we'd been evicted so many times there was no other stop … we'd already asked if we could bring the trailer into the hospital grounds but they said no so I had to move into a house to know that once I was in there I knew where the children would be. Then when I came out I had to have a salty bath every day and that's the reason I went in there."

Similarly, a 'new' Traveller interviewed in the South West recalled that it was expedient to enter housing temporarily in order to become a foster parent for a friend's child following the death of the caring parent. This narrative is not especially uncommon, as across Europe there is a long history of Gypsy children being removed from their children by social workers following official 'concern' and disputes over accommodation and employment-related practices. Studies have revealed discriminatory and negative attitudes towards Gypsies among many social workers and the anti-nomadic stance of social services is well known among travelling communities who regard social workers with suspicion and as being largely concerned with the removal of children from families (Cemlyn, 2000a, 2000b; Titley, 2008). Fear of institutional prejudice and the potential implications of such attitudes for those on the receiving end can thus foster a highly instrumental approach amongst Gypsies and Travellers who come to the attention of the authorities.

> "My reason for going in a house six or seven years ago is that I fostered a young lady whose mother had died and social services were keen for me to foster her but not if I was in a caravan so we had to go through this whole rigmarole of getting a three-bedroom house that nobody wanted and at the end of the year when we all moved back out again they forgot about us which was very good. Yes, nobody wants to be seen as a Traveller when you're under that amount of scrutiny and social workers don't want to be seen as soft on Travellers, that's the other thing."

A female respondent who had been living on unauthorised encampments and who had her children removed by social services due to mental health problems following separation from her husband was told that she would only have her children returned to her care if she lived in a house where supervision and official support could be provided. As she recounts, it was only after returning to living on site that her condition improved and she was deemed capable of raising her children.

> "The reason I went into a house they said to me if I were to go into a house they would let me have my children back. Well, I was in that house for three years, the worst years of my life. I would have rather gone and pitched a tent anywhere than be in a house ... but it wasn't until I moved back to my land back with my husband ... the people kept coming to visit and they could see the difference in me ... And this happens all over. There's a lot of Travelling women out there that have had nervous breakdowns in their homes and the pills make it worse, they take the children."

Whilst the following chapter explores the psychological aspects of housing transitions amongst our sample in more detail, it is self-evident (holding true, we suggest, for all communities) that the capacity to exercise a degree of autonomy over major life decisions such as household stability, residential location and the cultural appropriateness of accommodation are major factors in individual health and well-being (Propper et al, 2007; Bond et al, 2012). In this chapter we have highlighted the main routes through which the respondents arrived in conventional housing, using this data as a 'jumping off point' to explore how structural determinants combine to limit the accommodation choices facing many families, and how pre-existing stressors are often exacerbated by the constraints of familial obligations, fear of racist attacks by neighbours, and continued (or perceived) resistance to the delivery of appropriate or preferred accommodation from some housing market institutions (Ratcliffe, 2000, p 211). Despite these multitudinal factors, we found that many participants in all study areas were able to exercise a degree of agency over their choice of accommodation and to carve out, as far as possible, lifestyles in conventional housing that were congruent with cultural mores and practices. The ability to maintain a sense of continuity in response to the massive upheaval that entering housing often involves is therefore key to shaping communal and individual responses to settling, or resisting the transition into being a 'housed Traveller'.

Note

[1] Notwithstanding the fact that 90 per cent of planning applications for private Gypsy sites are initially refused often following organised local campaigns (CRE, 2006).

SIX

Housing transitions

The previous chapter highlighted the main routes through which the Gypsies and Travellers interviewed in the different locations included in this study arrived in housing. While a degree of autonomy could often be exercised in relation to neighbourhood (see Chapter Eight), for many the move into housing was experienced as a severe limit on individual agency and an attendant diminution of accustomed lifestyle. As noted in Chapter One, fundamental and rapid changes in one's social landscape can impact traumatically at a group level, and 'supply the prevailing mood and temper, dominate its imagery and its sense of self, [and] govern the way that members relate to each other' of a collectivity (Erikson, 1995, p 190). At the individual level, such transformations may constitute a 'blow to the psyche that breaks through one's defenses so suddenly and with such brutal force that one cannot react to it effectively' (Erikson, 1995, p 187). This chapter addresses the participants' experiences of moving into housing and the multi-layered sets of concerns that must be addressed when moving into what is frequently an alien type of accommodation while simultaneously having to deal with an unfamiliar and foreign set of circumstances.

Bennett (1998, p 215) notes that 'culture shock' refers to the 'anxiety that results from losing all of our familiar signs and symbols of social intercourse'. This anxiety arises due to the loss of perceptual reinforcements from one's own culture and exposure to new stimuli which can be disorientating in terms of disruption to familiar cultural patterns. The concept is pertinent in understanding the transition from sites or the roadside into housing, which also involves a deeper-rooted transition from a cultural framework that emphasises a 'we' consciousness, collective identity, emotional dependence and group solidarity towards one premised on an 'I' consciousness defined by emotional independence, individual initiative, the right to privacy and personal autonomy (Kim, 1995, p 4).

> Our adaptive processes fail to meet the needs of the moment, and we find ourselves overwhelmed by the stimuli we are forced to assimilate. Therefore, if transition shock is a state of loss and disorientation precipitated by a change in

> one's familiar environment that requires adjustment, then
> culture shock may be characterized as transition shock in
> the context of an alien culture. (Bennett, 1998, p 216)

For many Gypsies and Travellers the difficulties encountered following initial settlement into housing are extremely traumatic and encompass practical, environmental, spatial and social dimensions that frequently serve to 'undermine or overwhelm one, or several, essential ingredients of a culture or the culture as a whole' (Smelser, 2004, pp 38–40). For those accustomed to a communal kin-based existence characterised by frequent social interaction and a relative lack of privacy, not only are they separated from community ties (often for the first time in their lives) but they have to attend to a very different set of unfamiliar practical and daily concerns. The following section examines the transition process in more detail focusing, in particular, on the initial move into housing.

Adapting to 'bricks and mortar'

The financial aspects of life in housing threw the differences between nomadic and settled understandings, attitudes and practices regarding consumption into stark contrast. The interaction between time and money is central to budgetary planning and is shaped by habit, custom and external circumstances rather than purely rational decision making (Chattoe and Gilbert, 1999). While observers such as Lewis (1968) and Ashkam (1975) identified a present time orientation and inability to plan for the future as consistent with a 'culture of poverty', Valentine's (1968) critique of this perspective views culture as a collective response to situational constraints, with 'material responses ... prior to, and separate from, the culture of any collectivity' (p 6). For many recently housed Gypsies and Travellers, budgeting for household expenditure and coming to terms with the use of credit for gas and electric as opposed to the immediate expenditure involved in purchasing a gas bottle, for example, is a difficult adjustment, rendering customary spending patterns and budgetary practices obsolete. The shock of budgeting for central heating bills and/or numerous hot baths could be profound, plunging households into debt which could be difficult to surmount. One woman in the South West for example recalled:

> "I couldn't believe the bills – I was having hot baths twice a
> day and the kids were running the taps and it was all kushti
> but the price they charged for it when I got the bill in – I

didn't know what to do – we'd only had gas bottles afore that and changed them when they run low. I just ignored the bills until it all got too bad and I knew we had to do something."

Two thirds of participants across all study areas estimated that their economic situation had worsened since moving into housing, a combination of reduced opportunities for casual work and the higher costs associated with housing (Smith and Greenfields, 2012). Additional expenses and financial management issues can greatly exacerbate the stress experienced by many respondents often leading families into a spiral of debt (Gidley and Rooke, 2008). Commonly reported problems included: having to select a gas or electricity supplier and negotiate credit over bills which need to be met on a regular quarterly or monthly basis instead of paying for a gas bottle and filling up with fuel when required; coping with tenancy agreement regulations; and applying for council tax and housing benefits. For individuals who did not possess a bank account or who had moved around frequently and could not provide evidence of former addresses to enable them to participate in banking systems this was particularly problematic (Cemlyn et al, 2009). For families with limited literacy in particular, the sheer extent of bureaucracy involved in obtaining, moving into and retaining a property was often daunting, with anecdotal reports of tenancies lost or given up because of the maze of paperwork and regulations which some felt were too complex to negotiate (Shelter, 2008).

Whilst, theoretically at least, assistance with budgeting and making a transition into housing was available in at least one of our study areas through the 'Supporting People' scheme current at that time, the interrelationship between newly housed residents and local authorities predicated against the use of this service. As Prior and Barnes (2011) note, policy outcomes represent 'a field of complex interactions between reflexive subjects, the outcomes of which are necessarily contingent' (p 267). Parry et al (2004) identified a 'defensively hostile' demeanor among Gypsies and Travellers when dealing with officialdom, based in past experiences and the anticipation of prejudice. Given the internalisation of widely held negative stereotypes held by some front-line staff, having to deal with bureaucratic demands while placing oneself in a potentially conflictual situation with public agency staff can be both stressful and humiliating and is avoided where possible. One respondent in the South East argued that in his experience institutional racism was extensive in public agencies, fuelling distrust, reluctance to engage with agencies and shaping interactions between Gypsies and local officials:

> "They don't like Gypsies and they treat you like dirt. We're rejected by some services because they don't want anything to do with us – we need equal rights to be recognised as an ethnic minority and for other people to have more understanding like they do for the others."

Studies have indicated that while Gypsies and Travellers experience high levels of racism they are more resigned to it than other minority groups, rarely lodging official complaints against officials or reporting racist hostility (Netto, 2006), which is unsurprising given the poor state of relations with the police. Narratives of resignation were common in response to questions surrounding why they felt they received so much hostility. For example, one Romany female in the South East replied, "Please you know the answer to that. Because we are Gypsies of course", with another responding, "Because we are Gypsies. Do you need another reason?". Accordingly, reluctance to engage with public agencies means that most are reliant on informal sources of support and advice from their own community. In turn, this increases the importance of localised networks and access to community members conversant with life in housing, as sources of emotional and practical assistance in supporting housing transitions.

Difficulties adjusting to economic and bureaucratic demands are compounded by the unfamiliar physical layout of conventional housing compared to trailers or chalets. A frequent theme in studies of housed Gypsies and Travellers – and a central element of 'cultural aversion' arguments – has been the profound difficulties that many experience in adapting to the confined nature of housing and the damaging effects on well-being of this (Thomas and Campbell, 1992; Power, 2004; Shelter, 2008; Fordham Research, 2009). It was striking how frequently respondents referred to the physical and spatial differences between living in a caravan and housing and its effects on the dynamics of social life and family relations (Seymour, 2011). A sense of perplexity and bewilderment over not being able to see and hear other family members as they dispersed into separate rooms rather than remaining within the trailer or sharing social space in the immediate vicinity outside was frequently voiced by those new to housing. These differences greatly exacerbated the stress experienced on moving into bricks and mortar and were in many cases accompanied by feelings of enclosure, claustrophobia and panic attacks, which themselves are aggravated by adverse life events (Naficy, 2003).[1] Those who were accommodated in flats experienced these symptoms more severely: being surrounded by strangers whom they could see but not hear; the abnormal sense of having people living above and below oneself – "people over your head it's not natural" – and without easy access to 'outside' had in many cases, adverse impacts on mental health. One man in the South West described himself as feeling "like a rat in a cage pacing, pacing, staring out of the window". The feeling of being imprisoned and unwillingly fixed to one place was frequently voiced. One man for example, reported that "I feel trapped, I like open space. I get itchy feet and would like to shift in a trailer", capturing the sentiments of many.

The layout of housing, the relative lack of natural light and smaller ratio of windows to wall space, could intensify feelings of confinement. Moreover, the clear separation of inside and outside, which is less distinct in a caravan, added significantly to feelings of disorientation, as one woman explained:

> "It's just staring at the four walls that does my head in. It's terrible really terrible. I know in a trailer it's smaller but you've got windows all around you and can see out in all directions who's coming and what's going on so it just feels bigger."

Apart from the implications for mental health and psychological well-being (discussed below), many considered housing to be injurious to physical health and related anecdotes of children and family members developing asthma and other conditions after entering housing. The contrast between the 'natural' nomadic life and the 'synthetic' nature of house dwelling with its negative impacts on health, was commented on by a resident of south London:

> "Travellers get ill when they first go in houses because the air and light are different, it's artificial not fresh air and daylight [so] a lot of breathing and lung problems start then. Central heating dries the air and is dangerous to the lungs and heart. Travellers are in housing now living in artificial atmospheres with chemicals and breathing it when they sleep. Living under electric light is bad for the eyes and causes headaches."

Other aspects of the layout of housing that house-dwellers take for granted were highlighted as adding to transition difficulties.

For example, getting used to stairs caused significant problems and demonstrates the pitfalls of applying universal notions of trauma and its causative agents as these vary widely between individuals and cultures with some seemingly innocuous changes in an individual's circumstances causing considerable stress (Laungani, 2002). For those unaccustomed to stairs they posed additional difficulties, as one woman in the South West explained:

> "Can't cope with the stairs I hate those stairs and the children were always falling up them and down them 'cos they'd not been used to them before and then if they got bruised the school look at you funny."

Most were used to living on one level and were not familiar with an upstairs which was frequently not utilised or used for alternative purposes, as one man reported, "I hardly go up there [upstairs]. We sleep downstairs, the dogs stay upstairs and we keep the kid's toys and stuff up there". In replicating their past lifestyles as far as possible and in denying the reality of their new surroundings, some families reported sleeping downstairs in one room. One woman in the South East revealed that she and her children were "moving down a mattress so you're all sleeping downstairs together at night then dragging it up in the day so they (health visitors) don't think you've gone funny in the head". Others gave anecdotes of friends and relatives who slept in trailers parked outside or in the garden leaving the house unoccupied at night, a strategy which would undoubtedly be adopted by many others if it were possible (see below). Thus unsurprisingly many of those who expanded on their desire to leave housing and return to a caravan or a site argued that their unhappiness and strongly negative experiences of housing was grounded in a complex web of social and cultural factors. When asked whether he could identify any positive aspects of living in a house, the following Gypsy male from the South East replied:

> "Everything is bad [in housing]. Too many bills, I don't like the stairs. We can't have a fire in the garden or cook outside or sit outside talking round the fire 'cos the neighbours would call the police. We can't even have family funerals like we would in a trailer."

A profound sense of spatial disorientation was articulated which related to the different conceptualisations and usage of internal and external space and contrasted sharply to the practices of their non-Gypsy neighbours. One woman in the South East said that her family were "only using one room and a kitchen like – there's too much space in a big house like they put us in and no real space outside either so it's topsy turvy". Indeed the use of outside space could create tensions which further problematised the transition process as respondents indicated that modes of socialising which were customary for site residents such as gathering outside trailers and having an outdoor fire were perceived as threatening and intimidating by their 'gorjer' neighbours. One or two related families living in the same neighbourhood or a household with a large family could result in large numbers of youths gathering outside, which was frequently interpreted by the police or housing officers as anti-social and a potential cause of disorder. One woman in the South West retorted, "but that is just our way. It don't mean nothing and how can you say to [son] that he can't see his cousins and his friends when they come off the site to call?"

The feeling of being 'trapped' in housing was linked in many cases to the inability of social housing tenants to keep a caravan outside their premises. Seventy per cent of social housing tenants reported that tenancy restrictions meant they were unable to keep a trailer on the roadside or on hard standing outside their premises, restricting the ability of family members to visit. Such regulations were widely regarded as an attack on their cultural identity and lifestyle, with one participant in the South West arguing that "It's because they don't want us to travel no more now they've put us in houses they don't want no more Travellers around here". Similarly, feelings of incarceration were intensified by restrictions forbidding cultural practices such as the keeping of animals. One man noted that his family "can't keep no dogs here or horses and we've always had dogs. They're part of our culture". A woman in the South East who moved into housing after losing a planning appeal for a private site explained how rules concerning the keeping of animals resulted in a loss of livelihood: "I used to keep chickens and sell eggs. When we moved here they says 'you're not allowed to keep chickens here' so we've got none 'cos we can't keep them". As Smelser (2004, p 40) notes, the language of affect provides a link and continuity between the cultural and psychological levels. During a focus group in the South East one participant expressed a clear recognition of the corrosive impact of local policies to rehouse their Gypsy/Traveller population and the impact on his individual and collective identity:

"I've been stuck in this council house so many years now and living here has ruined my way of life. I would've liked to live on a site but only with my family and no other ... there's a lot of housed Travellers who would give up their houses and go back to living their way of life and who should be given that opportunity to decide."

Thus the practical physical and spatial contrasts between living on a site or on the road and life in conventional housing constituted a huge contrast which could fundamentally disrupt the individual's frame of reference and sense of identity. The accumulation of these interrelated factors was experienced most intensely by those who also experienced social isolation and loneliness due to being accommodated far from their relatives and community members and therefore lacked the mitigating effects that such networks could provide. In contrast those who reported that they were satisfied in housing repeatedly indicated that the presence of kin and community members made the transition easier, even where they reported significant initial difficulties settling into conventional housing (see further Chapter Eight).

Perceptions of neighbourhood

In common with other minority groups, many of those interviewed regarded public spaces in their immediate vicinity as spaces of fear and were avoided where possible (Peters, 2011). This avoidance intensified feelings of isolation and stemmed from perceptions of their environment and the possibility of encountering racism. Respondents made frequent reference to the bleakness of their surroundings when accommodated on housing estates, "no garden, no greenery, a dirty filthy area" (female, South West). This was compounded by an accompanying moral and social discord within their neighbourhoods. One man in the South East, for example, commented that "the estate is rubbish. You can imagine scag heads, rubbish, gorjer kids being naughty. This is just a shit council estate". A woman resident on the same estate identified a breakdown of intergenerational methods of social control contrasting their non-Gypsy neighbours unfavourably with her own community, "kids drinking, robbing the old, walking round all night with weapons and the adults are too scared to tell their own kids off" (see Chapter Seven). Another woman in the South East viewed her neighbourhood and its residents with suspicion due to the perceived permissiveness of 'gorjer' society and a concern that

"There's too many perverts and dirty old men about …
and the drugs, a lot of it is through drugs and drink. When
I was a young girl it was all under the carpet, you'd never
hear about drugs or nothing like this."

Our findings surrounding the relation between perceptions of
neighbourhood and use of public space bore out the conclusions of a
study of Gypsies and Travellers in East Anglia where it was noted that
among housed community members

> … many revealed they had developed a constant expectation
> and anticipation of encountering racism which often
> made them wish to minimize or avoid contact with non
> Travellers. Public areas such as parks and local shops were
> actively avoided by some children, indicating how racism
> contributes to a restriction of children's movements and
> their growing isolation. (Warrington, 2006, p 1)

Many of the women interviewed who lived in local authority or social
housing expressed fears about their children's safety and apprehension
concerning the relative anonymity of their surroundings compared to
a site "where everyone knows each other". The difference between the
hustle and bustle of site life where there was always someone present to
keep an eye on property and where any stranger who entered would
be noticed and challenged was frequently expressed in relation to the
potential for property crime. These concerns made many reluctant
to leave their houses vacant and precluded extended periods away
travelling, with one man in the South West commenting that "we are
worried that when we leave to travel the property is left to the mercy
of the world as various things happen". Anxiety over the safety of the
home-space was so profound for one family living on a council estate
in the South East that the father reported: "I don't travel no more, as
my house would not be secure if left. If we go away we make sure that
my grown sons are home". Notions of the outside world as corrupt and
threatening served to constrain networks of social relations, inhibiting
the development of bridging ties to the wider community and were
also an important motivating force behind the desire for mono-ethnic
communities where a semblance of security and reciprocal networks
of support could be accessed (see Chapter Eight). Moreover, housing
transitions and perceptions of life in housing also displayed marked
intergenerational differences (Chapter Nine) and were also profoundly
shaped by gender. These are explored in the following section.

Gendered transitions

Okely (1983, pp 172–3) notes the tendency for Gypsies to form alliances between families with a long association, which due to their flexible and shifting nature she terms 'clusters' rather than extended families. As discussed in the next chapter, the sharp division of gender roles in Gypsy and Traveller culture and the preponderance of gender stratified networks makes women more immersed in, and reliant on, these localised clusters of extended kin and community members than men. The residential proximity and frequent interaction that was a feature of site or roadside life promotes densely knit connections, mutual awareness of problems and reciprocal support (Wellman and Wortley, 1990). As a result of these gender-based and spatially bounded patterns of sociability, women in all localities were much more likely to refer explicitly to social isolation and concerns over loss of family contact upon entering housing. One woman in the South East for example stated that "we're all in housing now and it's not our way. It's scattered our people", while in the South West another woman noted that the hardest thing about housing was "loneliness. Not got your sisters, not got your mum, not got your aunties – you've got nobody with you". Whilst the transfer into housing from sites or the roadside clearly impacts on both men and women, the qualitative experiences of house dwelling vary substantially between the sexes, with women bearing an especially heavy burden in terms of being primarily responsible for engaging with external agencies and balancing complex new budgetary requirements whilst supporting their families through the transitionary period. In the absence of social support these demands can prove overwhelming, as one young woman who participated in a focus group in the South West recalled:

> "… you'd go literally three months and you might just say good morning to someone outside because they lived their own lives never spoke to each other. I didn't want people in my house but you didn't visit people and it got to the stage when I had the children and post natal depression kicked in."

It has been argued that social engagement is a major factor in explaining health outcomes and a number of studies have emphasised the health benefits of localised social networks and circuits of social capital (Marmot, 2004). A woman interviewed for a GTAA in the South East region evocatively expressed the impact of enforced social isolation on her mental health:

"I stayed there [in housing] 12 months and it was the worst 12 months of my life. I ended up in a nutty hospital where I'd tried to kill myself. I don't know what it does to us. I think it is because we are away from our people. You can get up in the morning [on site] and shout over the fence to somebody and they're there."

For a significant number of newly housed Gypsy and Traveller women (particularly female lone parents), residence in housing and the cumulative outcomes of fundamental dislocations from accustomed ways of living can result in symptoms of mental ill health consistent with indicators of cultural trauma (Alexander, 2004). In such circumstances it is perhaps unsurprising that a significant number reported that they suffered from 'nerves' or were prescribed anti-depressants by their doctors (ranging from between 40–60 per cent of the housed samples in some GTAAs). While women were generally reticent to discuss their own use of alcohol and illegal drugs, one woman in the South East commented that she needed "a bottle of vodka and diazepam" to cope with her new surroundings. Even among long-term housed women (10 years or more) who had been living in housing for several years, women were particularly likely to highlight the impact of community breakdown on their mental health. An Irish Traveller woman interviewed in Inner London noted the bitter frustration and loss of personal sovereignty experienced by individuals who had also become estranged from their social ties as a result of circumstantially enforced settlement, "there is nothing good about living in a house. You lose contact with your community. I don't have any choice".

The qualitative interview data and discussions over many years of working with Gypsies and Travellers also revealed that women are often perceived as the guardians of their culture and primarily responsible for ensuring that young people are socialised in a manner which ensures their familiarity with cultural mores and a sense of continuity with their collective past.[2] For families who are adapting to a new and alien environment while experiencing separation from communal support systems, the burden of trying to keep their children on the 'straight and narrow' can be overpowering and accompanied by a sense of shame and guilt if their children "get in with the wrong – and that is usually a gorjer – crowd" (male, South West). This became particularly salient since disruption to social networks and dilution of the inter-mutual basis of Gypsy culture also undermines mechanisms of social reproduction. Such mechanisms traditionally operated through proximate social ties and group responsibility for the socialisation and surveillance of children, and for policing the gender stratified routes to adulthood (Formoso and Burrell, 2000). One woman in the South East related how the collapse of these mechanisms impacted on her own children and on her ability to adequately control them. Erosion of the symbolic boundaries through which Gypsy/Travellers define themselves in relation to the wider society and weakening of the social control mechanisms that upheld such boundaries is a constant concern, as the following mother recounted:

> "I think it was the breaking point when the children started getting into things they shouldn't be ... I think that did it for me because they just stopped listening. They got to the point that all the other children they live with don't listen to their mums and that's how the children started to get where they stopped doing what they would normally do and there ain't no support, is there? You can't just knock on the trailer next door and have a cup of tea and a chat there was none of that."

As discussed in the previous chapter, familial and community based support are, as with many minority groups, often the major and preferred method of social support for needy community members. In certain circumstances housing allocation systems and residential clustering have facilitated the maintenance of such mechanisms in conventional housing (Chapter Eight). In other cases over-zealous local authority efforts to settle families in housing can erode systems of informal support and devalue the role of women as the providers of practical and emotional support to kin members. A woman in the South East recalled bitterly that planning restrictions barring family members from staying on site meant that "when my dad died they [local authority] wouldn't even let me pull on my mum's [self owned] site to look after her, to comfort her as it would affect her permission". In another case a couple in the South West gave up their long-standing legal battle with the local planning authority who were trying to evict them from their privately owned site when "[wife] had a stroke and [husband] thought for her safety and sanity moving to a house would sort her out". The combination of stressful legal challenges and planning restrictions forbidding amendments to the property and prohibiting family members from co-residing on site and providing daily assistance as they had previously, precluded them from remaining in trailers as their health needs changed. Subsequently the family unit was dispersed as the couple reluctantly entered housing curtailing the intergenerational transmission of support and assistance and increasing the couple's reliance on formal systems of welfare support.

Consequently older relatives who would otherwise have been able to continue their preferred lifestyle and remain living on sites with family members providing necessary care, were sometimes forced into housing (along with their carers) or had to move as a family group and attempt to find elusive adjoining pitches on sites together. This weakening of gender-based social roles, support mechanisms and traditional notions of responsibility was a frequently articulated dimension of cultural dislocation among women in all study areas. As one woman remarked, housing "isn't like a site with all your family around you, is it? The home life's good for the gorjers but not for us, we're used to trailers and I'd like us to be in one again".

In contrast to the women who, during interviews, were generally disposed to discuss the injurious impacts of settlement on themselves and on their status and role in family and community structures, men were more likely to refer to the adverse aspects of sedentarisation vicariously, attributing the worst impacts of transition to the effect on their wives, children and future generations of Gypsy and Traveller youth. Comments such as "it's worse for the wife she's on tranquillisers" or "my wife finds it really tough" were common among the men interviewed. Similarly, references were frequently made to the hardships experienced by their children. One Irish Traveller in London noted that the hardest thing about housing was "having to hide your identity and your kids having to pretend they're not Travellers so people won't call them pikeys or dirty Gypsies". A Romany Gypsy man in the South East voiced his fears for the future of his community, adding that

> "... the travelling lifestyle is being killed off. There won't be Travellers in the future. There's more evictions for unauthorised camps, no sites and more hardship for our people. There's nothing for our lads to look forward to, just houses like this one."

Reticence to elaborate on the impact of settlement in housing on their own social and emotional functioning may reflect cultural attitudes that emphasise stoicism, self reliance and fatalism (Van Cleemput et al, 2007). In addition women are generally more willing to admit, discuss and seek treatment for depression and anxiety than men (Bird and Rieker, 1999). One female, for example, noted that

> "... men don't act like us. They get unhappy too, but they
> just bottle it up or go off somewhere and don't let on – and
> we're unhappy and they're unhappy – but we can talk to
> our sisters or mum about it."

However, many women were of the view that men suffered less, due to their wider network of social and work-based contacts outside of the immediate vicinity, and a greater degree of freedom than women. Gossip acts as a powerful method of ensuring conformity and social control, with its potency related to the strength of one's social ties (Hannerz, 1980). Women's narratives of constraint – of being constrained not only by their new physical environment but by collective norms and gender expectations – were exacerbated by concern that their own and their families' reputation and social standing would be damaged if they were seen to mix too freely with non-Gypsies/Travellers, which restricted their social relations to mono-ethnic networks and limited spatial boundaries. Men were differentiated on the basis of not being so affected by these constraints and were therefore not considered as experiencing the same degree of trauma. In addition women noted that men did not bear primary responsibility for dealing with the external world, which women often found difficult to accomplish. As one woman interviewed for a GTAA in the South East remarked:

> "It's one of the loneliness things that can happen to a
> travelling woman. It's alright for the men 'cos they can go
> off to the fairs and everything else. It's the women – men
> aren't in the house for 24 hours, the men probably won't
> come in until 8pm and they've been out all day and they
> just go to bed but we've been there all day. It's been really
> really hard." (Richardson et al, 2007, p 111)

Whilst the assumption of the woman quoted above is accurate to some extent, as males are undoubtedly less socially constrained than women, there is abundant emergent evidence that the transition from sites into housing has a detrimental impact on men's employment patterns and social status. In nomadic cultures there is a less sharp distinction between 'home' and 'workspace' than in settled society: a loss of amenities such as storage space and restrictions which prohibit conducting work-related activities at home has made it difficult to maintain traditional forms of work (Smith and Greenfields, 2012). Ober (2000) refers to 'repeated traumatisation' which has its roots in institutional racism and oppression from the dominant culture. Over time the reiteration of trauma erodes individual coping mechanisms, which increases the potential for pathological and self-destructive responses. Anecdotal evidence indicates that males are experiencing depression, grief and loss, with these negative emotions revealing themselves in rising alcohol and substance misuse, domestic violence and marital breakdown. Through these manifestations of individual trauma the phenomenon can acquire a collective and inter-generational momentum. McAusland (2008), writing in relation to Australian Aboriginal and Torres Strait Islanders who have also experienced extreme and culturally corrosive forces and displayed similar patterns of destructive responses, argues that:

> not only were these types of problems to be expected within a context of prolonged and repeated traumatisation, but that it was possibly to transcend such experiences ... That is, historical trauma becomes re-enacted in families, separation leads to poor internalised models of parenting and coping with stress, and carries forward as intergenerational trauma. (McAusland, 2008, p 60)

In a health project for Gypsy and Traveller women which one of the authors coordinated (unpublished to date) 70 per cent of participants were aware of families experiencing drug and/or alcohol abuse, domestic abuse and family breakdown which they attributed to the strains of living in housing. Participants commented that men commonly refused to acknowledge depression or poor emotional health but masked the symptoms with harmful behaviours and self medication. As one woman observed, "men are more likely to go out hard drinking or something if there is family trouble rather than show their feelings". Increasing substance misuse is also made easier through the breakdown of patriarchal systems of social control, the decline in communal living and greater privacy and scope for secrecy that house dwelling affords compared to life on a site where collective surveillance and monitoring of behaviour is the norm. One Romany female in the South East noted bleakly:

> "You have a drive down [the] High Street and have a look at the boys I grew up with and chat with them. They're either out of their head on drugs or on Tennants Super [strong beer] or whatever because they're getting rid of the day. There's no point in them having a day. They'd sooner be where they are out of their face. They're all stuck in houses now all stuck in the council estates they don't want

to be there but where they going to go?" (Richardson, et al, 2007, p 114)

Cemlyn et al (2009) note that a number of advice workers and community members who responded to the Equalities and Human Rights Commission survey report the dissolution of hitherto stable marriages following the move into housing, linking this phenomenon to the strains and distress following the transition. Where this occurs, the authors identify increased female caring responsibilities and gendered poverty coupled with the grief of relationship loss (Cemlyn et al, 2009, p 230). Under such circumstances a number of women found the weight of supporting their family to be unbearable. The oft-reported concern amongst isolated families to conceal their identity from their neighbours led to increased strains on families, which negatively impacted on household functioning and family dynamics. In some cases family functioning became so impaired that it necessitated intervention by social services who undoubtedly interpreted such impairments as symptoms of individual dysfunction, rather than as manifestations of a collective phenomenon that has arisen in response to a concerted assault on the cultural foundations of nomadic people.

Authenticity and identity

In addition to the often destructive emotional and psychological impacts of settlement in housing, the ramifications of such a dramatic change of lifestyle were widely regarded as violating the most fundamental aspects of Gypsy/Traveller identity. Ethnic identity is represented by symbolic signifiers including physical attributes, appearance, behavioural patterns, family relations and group rituals. These are interpreted and manipulated by social actors in the course of interaction as they categorise themselves and others in a process of negotiation (De Andrade, 2000, p 272). Of crucial importance in this regard is the notion of ethnic 'authenticity' or the 'negotiated outcome of interactional processes of authentication' which is informed by socio-historical processes and founded in similar past constructions and discourses (Shenk, 2007, p 194). Greenfields and Smith (2010, p 401) discuss how in a sample of more than 200 GTAA respondents over 92 per cent of English Gypsy and 64 per cent of Irish Traveller interviewees defined their 'way of life' as being key to their social identity, with over half expanding on their answers to include a shared history of nomadic lifestyles and close-knit family bonds. As discussed at various points in this book, the vast majority of respondents who had previously lived in trailers articulated a strong sense of loss and regret over the demise of their previous lifestyle, even when recognising, as did the man interviewed in the South West, that "this way of life's come to the end of the road – you just can't be a Traveller no more".

In the qualitative interviews conducted in all study locales, 'histories of mobility' were employed as signifiers of authenticity and to 'establish identity in ruptured life courses and communities' (Eastmond, 2007, p 1). The possession of a caravan and maintaining the ability to 'just get up and go' was a significant symbol of cultural capital and in maintaining the belief that the respondents still possessed independence and, in principle, the ability to travel. Regulations prohibiting the stationing of caravans outside social housing or concerning the duration that houses can be left vacant, however, place significant constraints on semi-nomadism and can be experienced as a further assault on cultural identity, heightening feelings of distress. One participant commented that "I can't keep a trailer here. I'm a lone parent. I have four children and would love to travel but I just can't do that as we are". Given the centrality of nomadism as a facet of individual and collective identity the importance of 'travelling' was reiterated in the interviews and focus groups where over 65 per cent reported travelling at some point of the year even if only to attend one or two horse fairs or other culturally important events, though in the South East survey undertaken by Smith (2008) only 42 per cent of those in housing had travelled in the previous five years (p 21). Others, as discussed in Chapter Eight, have adopted new forms of nomadism by moving through a series of houses or alternating living in housing with staying with relatives on sites.

The family remains the primary means through which ethnic identity is transmitted and ethnic self-consciousness acquired (Alba, 1990, p 164). To sustain cultural identities and values a number of parents reported sending their children off to spend time with relatives who were living on sites or who still travelled, to ensure, as one woman said "they don't forget their roots just because they are growing up in housing". In other cases, a 'rediscovery' of core cultural values, a reclamation of identity and return to traditional lifestyles may feature as a strategy of cultural resistance to enforced assimilation (Croasman, 2006). One Irish Traveller woman living in a flat in London for example reported:

> "My children did not know anything about their culture as they were very young when I moved into a house. They had to hide the fact that they were Travellers while here. They have both got married and have moved back to Ireland to my brothers and have gone back to their travelling life."

For households who are relatively isolated, the move into housing and dislocation from their community and forms of intermutual obligations which previously integrated populations can leave individuals in a state of disequilibrium (Durkheim, 1933). Thus, some respondents felt themselves abruptly torn away from a community engaging in a 'shared project' of the type envisaged by Giddens who, reflecting on contemporary notions of identity, noted the desire to 'keep a particular narrative going ... [to] continually integrate events which occur in the external world, and sort them into the ongoing "story" about the self' (Giddens, 1991, p 54). The feeling of anomie and estrangement from customary ways of life can have a deeply disturbing psychological effect, as discussed above (Lau and Ridge, 2011). Across all localities, the number of respondents who reported that "nothing" compensated them for living in housing or that they "hated everything" was consistently reported by 10–16 per cent of interviewees, whose transition to housing included symptoms of claustrophobia, loneliness, insecurity and loss of autonomy, as encapsulated by an Irish Traveller in London who noted that "my life is not my own. I feel trapped and get depressed looking at four walls everyday". Others referred to concepts of cultural authenticity and of feeling 'out of place' in housing, with one respondent in the South East arguing that "it's just not our way of life, we don't belong in houses, we're born to roam the roads". One respondent in South London, despite having spent over 25 years in housing, still felt a strong aversion to housing, viewing sedentarisation as incompatible with cultural mores and values and resulting for many, in a process of cultural demoralisation and decline:

> "We spend a lot of time outdoors not like those in housing and a lot of us feel shut in and enclosed [in housing] the home life is alright for the comforts but it's not what I was raised to. Governments took away the right to lead a travelling life and it's the cause of all the Travellers' problems, if you can't travel you can't earn money, the work's gone and too many lads have never even worked. There's too many in jail and too many dying young. [We] can't keep our culture or pass it on to the next generation so a lot are drinking heavily and taking drugs to block it out. The end of the travelling way's what's causing the ill health, in the old days it was poverty that killed a lot of Travellers."

A common concern was that if respondents lived in housing and could not maintain adequate contact with relatives and other Gypsies and

Travellers their identity would become 'diluted'. One woman in the South West commented on the fear of being regarded by her relatives who lived on sites as "settled now – not like them – different things going on so you can't join in the talk in the same way about who is doing what or where you just been". Studies indicate that among immigrant minorities in the USA (while distinct ethnic identities were maintained over time), successive generations became progressively detached from their cultural origins. However, assimilation was hindered by resistance from the dominant society, residential segregation and the extent to which social ties, cultural expression and economic opportunities could be met within the boundaries of the ethnic group (Sanders, 2002, pp 332–3). For housed families whose relatives were either living on sites some distance away or who were nomadic 'roadsiders' there was a similar fear that long-term separation from the community would weaken their resistance to assimilation. Moreover, increasing divergence of lifestyles and the difficulties of sustaining the frequent social interaction to which most were accustomed could, over time, have connotations for one's social identity and intensify a sense of 'difference'. One woman in the South East for example recounted her experiences of "[waiting] until the evening when some of your family may turn up for you and they will do but after a while they think you're settled and they're going to be moved on". Many housed Gypsies experience the denial of their ethnic identity acutely, the same woman continuing that "the worst thing is when you move into the house they count you as settled, you're not part of the population, you're not a Gypsy any more". Another participant in a focus group in the South East recalled how on going onto a site some distance from her home to visit relatives, she encountered open hostility from a female site resident who recognised her as a 'kennet' (someone who lived in housing and was perceived as having discarded their cultural heritage). The woman would have turned her off the land had not an older man intervened who knew both of the respondents' parents and recognised her due to her physical resemblance to her family members. In this way, not only do the mainstream population denigrate the ethnic identity of 'settled' Gypsies and Travellers, but friends and relatives who still live on sites or travel may gradually become more distant from housed families who may be perceived as 'different' and perhaps less 'authentic', thus exacerbating their isolation (Greenfields, 2010).

Successful transitions

GTAA data relating to Gypsies and Travellers' levels of wellbeing and satisfaction with housing cannot be matched on a 'like for like' basis across locales as questions varied depending on the purpose for which data was gathered. In the commissioned survey in the South East, 45 per cent would leave housing if a pitch on a site was available, rising to 64 per cent among those housed for between one and 15 years, indicating both the duration and extent of unhappiness with conventional housing. Almost half of those wishing to move out of housing cited family/ cultural and lifestyle reasons for wishing to return to site life (Smith, 2008, pp 30–1). In a GTAA in the South West, 39 per cent of housed respondents reported that they were planning to move from housing or were uncertain whether they would remain or not in such properties if another option existed (Home and Greenfields, 2007). Returning to the road always remains a possibility in theory if not in practice, with comments such as "The Gypsies will be moving out of housing because some of them hate it and they'll be going on the road again" and "I'm always thinking of hitching up a trailer and leaving this place [house] for good" universally voiced. The qualitative studies allowed issues of 'best' and 'worst' aspects of such accommodation to be explored in greater depth and indicated that the relatively 'successful' transitions into housing were associated with a series of interrelated factors that could alleviate the more traumatic aspects of settlement. Firstly, a degree of autonomy over place and type of residence, which was inevitably more marked among owner occupiers. Secondly, proximity to family and networks of other Gypsies and Travellers, which again was more available to homeowners who were able to purchase property close to relatives; those able to apply for social housing close to their family or a local site; or who were accommodated en masse following site closure or clearance of unauthorised camps (Chapters Five and Eight). Finally, experience and knowledge of housing acquired either through previous housing careers, through access to informal networks of social capital or (to a lesser extent) from specialist services such as Supporting People or local community projects.

Despite the extent of negativity and ill feeling expressed with regard to residence in housing, a small minority had moved into conventional accommodation through choice, either to 'try something different' or because of marriage to a non-Gypsy (Chapter Eight). One woman commented that she had long aspired to house dwelling: "I had always liked the look of those little houses when we was on a site and I really fancied having all that space, lovely big bathroom and a nice garden to sit in so we put our name down". Such conscious choice to experience house dwelling alleviates the frustrated anxiety articulated by the majority of respondents, highlighting the fundamental importance of individual autonomy as a basis for judging personal well-being (Dorman, 1996). Similarly, those who opted to enter housing due to old age or health-related reasons were more sanguine about their accommodation, and more likely to stress the benefits of house dwelling, frequently citing access to running water and heating, "it's warm and cosy" (Irish Traveller woman, London). Physical comforts were regarded as the main 'positive' aspect of housing, cited by 43 per cent of participants. Freedom from harassment and evictions meaning that roadside families are constantly moved on and find it difficult to access or maintain continuity with health and education agencies were the next most commonly cited positive aspect. The benefits of "not being moved every day" and not "[getting] hassle from the gavvers [police] all the time" were mentioned by over one third of housed participants. Around 18 per cent stated that the ability to access health and education was the best aspect of housing and these considerations were often implicated in their initial decision to enter housing (Chapter Five).

Moreover, housing tenure, type of accommodation and neighbourhood demographics also impacted on the success or otherwise of the transfer from caravans to 'bricks and mortar'. In all areas (apart from Inner London where property prices made the possibility of buying a property impossible for those we interviewed) owner occupiers consisted of relatively long-term housed Gypsies and Travellers. This particular sub-set of respondents, whilst often entering housing after failing to get planning permission on privately owned sites and articulating a preference for "our own site with my family all around me" tended to report the highest levels of satisfaction with their accommodation. One owner occupier in the South East who had lived in housing for 12 years observed that the freedom to keep a caravan and to continue nomadic cultural practices was a key facet shaping their attitude to housing:

> "We had the money and the council estates here were bad back then. Not only that but the garden was big enough to put a caravan in. It's our daughter's bedroom. I paid for it [house] so I'll do as I please."

A marked preference was found amongst respondents for residence in bungalows, a type of accommodation that mirrors the physical layout of mobile homes and static caravans and which are analogous to the chalets which, under planning and caravan site regulations, are permitted on Gypsy and Traveller sites. In all GTAAs that covered the study areas and where questions of preferred 'type' of housed accommodation were included, bungalows/chalets were identified by over 70 per cent of those surveyed. In addition approximately 45 per cent of 'sited' respondents identified this form of housing as the preferred type where someone could not reside on a site due to poor health and infirmity. A preference was also expressed for incorporating bungalows into the design of caravan sites, essentially a design similar to the 'group' housing schemes such as are in use in Ireland. These incorporate a mixture of bungalow/chalet properties and caravan pitches which are typically occupied by a series of inter-related households (DELG, 2012). Given the scarcity of publicly owned bungalows in all of the study locales only a tiny percentage of participants living in local authority or social housing (<2 per cent) lived in a bungalow. As discussed in various sections of this book, a further, and probably the most significant, determinant of how well individuals settled into housing was the existence of social contacts in a locality; particularly when an element of choice existed over neighbourhood. As the following Romany woman in the South West recalled:

> "... well, my love, we had a bit of money after we sold up so we could choose where to live and we had family near here and we like it here as it's near to my cousin's site."

The adverse and detrimental aspects of the relocation into housing formed the dominant theme in the participants' narratives and the totality of experiences exhibited the four traits that Sztompka (2004) identifies in relation to traumatic change summarised in Chapter One. First, the mass sedentarisation of nomadic communities has been sudden and rapid, 'occurring within a span of time relatively short for a given kind of process' (p 158). Second, in relation to the scope of change in the lives of those interviewed, 'it touches many aspects of life – be it social life or personal life – or that it affects many actors and actions'. Third is the particular content of change, affecting 'the core aspects of social life or personal fate'. The fourth trait is the specific mental frame through which settlement was received by those affected. It is 'at least to some extent unexpected, surprising, precisely "shocking" in the literal sense of the term' (p 159). While the narratives presented above are located within wider socioeconomic forces and policy-induced constraints that have stimulated large-scale settlement into housing and provide the framework within which lives are experienced, they tell us little about the collective practices and strategies through which settlement and assimilation is contested and resisted.

Indeed, overemphasis on the culturally traumatic elements of far-reaching social change minimises the capacity for individual and collective defiance to those changes or the innovative and resistive responses to policies that are perceived as oppressive (Glasgow, 1980). As demonstrated above, the more severe and deleterious aspects of housing were frequently offset through the exercise of 'bounded autonomy' in relation to tenure, type and location of residence and proximity to community members (Chapter Eight). In practice, however, the ambivalent nature of, and mutual hostility between, Gypsy/Travellers and their non-Gypsy neighbours was the single most important factor in structuring patterns of social relationships at a micro-level, a theme which is explored in the next chapter.

Notes

[1] In Smith's survey of 103 housed Gypsy/Travellers in the South East, 17 per cent wished to leave housing due to claustrophobia, anxiety and/or feeling shut in (2008, p 33).

[2] The concept of women as 'guardians of culture' and transmitters of traditional practices has been identified by anthropologists in numerous texts (Okely, 1983; Rosaldo and Lampshere, 1974).

SEVEN

Gypsies, Travellers and gorjers: conflict and cooperation

We have identified how settlement into conventional housing can entail significant psycho-social and practical challenges for former caravan dwellers. In our subsequent exploration of the various difficulties in adjusting to housing experienced by respondents we will focus on how living in proximity to close kin and being able to access networks of social relationships act as a protective factor in preserving wellbeing (Dawkins, 2006; Fletcher, 2009). The community-based nature of Gypsy/Traveller culture centred around principles of 'bounded solidarity' – in-group oriented and with a strong sense of collective solidarity engendered by external threats to the group – has been observed amongst these communities in various historical and geographical contexts (Okely, 1983; Gmelch, 1986; Sanders, 2002). This and the following chapter investigate the structure and nature of these social relations in the study areas and delineate the patterns of interactions that simultaneously generate social closure and boundary maintenance along cultural and ethnic lines *and* characterise inter-group relations with co-resident neighbours from outside of the travelling community. As explored in previous chapters, inter-group relations and a merging of boundaries between Gypsy/Travellers and largely low-income groups is not a new phenomenon though we posit that in recent decades the pattern of such engagements may be changing in the light of increased diversity within low income areas of dense public housing (Rutter and Latorre, 2009). This chapter thus examines how neighbourhood-level factors influence the cohesiveness of social relations that exist between housed Gypsies (see further Chapter Eight), the nature of inter-group contacts and the extent to which social ties transcend their own boundaries to include their 'gorjer' neighbours.

While structural and societal level factors have most commonly been invoked to explain the persistently marginal status of Gypsies and Travellers this status manifests itself, and is contested, in everyday social interactions. For Bottero and Irwin (2003) issues of identity and difference are located within grounded accounts of social practice that consider the relational aspects as 'elements and outcomes of social changes'. Social relations, they point out, are variable across different historical and cultural contexts, and 'a focus on their particular articulation helps to shed light on the shaping and reshaping of social experiences and inequalities' (p 464). In the context of relations between Gypsies/Travellers and the wider society, Powell notes the tendency to offer structural explanations and correctly argues that 'there is a need to link these structural factors and their characteristics to this process of disidentification and the everyday relations within and between groups' (2008, p 106). Processes of marginalisation and 'othering' described by social scientists generally incorporate whatever are deemed the essential properties of difference and then proceed to explain how boundaries are constructed on the basis of those (real or perceived) differences. The abstract nature of theoretical constructs and their inability to adequately account for individual agency means that such accounts fail to capture the complexity of neighbourhood dynamics or of the shifting and overlapping nature of kin and friendship patterns at the micro-level. Subsequently, the emphasis on inter-group divisions has tended to neglect the development of commonalities between often conflictual groups and the manner in which these relationships are constructed and reconstructed through social and spatial practices. Anthias (2001) criticises the reification of social categories that polarise the material (class) and the symbolic (gender and ethnicity) aspects of stratification while downplaying connections between those categories and arguing that:

> social categories of differentiation and stratification…involve both processual social relations (which are analytically distinct) and embodied social outcomes which are difficult to desegregate … contradictory and in-between positions construct identities and actions that constitute important points of departure for understanding the dynamics of social stratification on the one hand, and social integration on the other. (2001, p 387)

Settlement and discrimination

It has long been recognised that increasing numbers of ethnic minority groups in low-income areas can fuel resentment among existing residents (regardless of ethnicity), due to increased competition for scarce resources, particularly housing and labour market opportunities (Rex and Moore, 1967; Beider, 2011), the more so in rural locales which do not traditionally have a large number of minority ethnic residents and which conversely have limited public housing stock (CRC, 2006; 2007).

The extent of prejudice directed towards minorities, or conversely the degree of acceptance towards different groups, is not uniform, however, and varies with those less obviously 'foreign' often finding it easier to integrate into their new area (Robinson and Reeve, 2006; Hickman et al, 2008). As discussed in Chapter Two, prejudice towards Gypsies and Travellers draws not on physical or linguistic differences so much as on the dominance of 'sedentary' ideology and historical stereotypes. Those stereotypes have persisted regardless of whether they are nomadic or 'settled', indicating that it is not nomadism in itself that generates such antipathy towards Gypsies (ni Shuinear, 1997; Clark, 2006). Despite sharing many attributes with the majority 'white' population minorities such as Gypsies may be viewed as 'not quite white' since their lifestyles and values are denied legitimacy and they are excluded from the forms of cultural capital and privileges that accrue to people of majority status (Garner, 2007). Contemporary liberal societies are distinguished by such contradictions: continuing to tolerate extreme and illiberal civil, religious and political groups and allowing for the denigration of certain minorities while espousing equality of rights and diversity (Zafirovki, 2007, p 107). However tolerant and inclusive a society purports to be, it is a sociological fact that all societies require the presence of pariah and other 'outsider' groups as these populations constitute a necessary element for the construction of material and symbolic hierarchies and provide a reference point from which the 'in' group draw their own moral and social boundaries (Van den Berghe, 1981; Elias and Scotson, 1994).

The role of Gypsies and Travellers in fulfilling this function can be demonstrated clearly by the findings from Stonewall's (2003) survey on 'outsider communities'. Their findings indicated that whilst two thirds of people in England cited at least one minority group towards whom they feel negative, the most frequently listed were Gypsies/Travellers (35 per cent) followed by refugees and asylum seekers (34 per cent). A more recent study in Scotland (2010) found that 37 per cent reported that they would be unhappy if a relative formed a close personal relationship with a Gypsy or Traveller (Ormston et al, 2011). These negative feelings manifest themselves in an almost universal desire among the sedentary population for spatial separation: thus, contradictorily, while the 'settled' community demands that nomads cease travelling and 'settle down', there are countless examples of local communities mobilising to oppose Gypsy sites or the provision of housing to members of these communities in their neighbourhoods (Cemlyn et al, 2009, p 214). Indeed there are few issues that vex and galvanise a community as effectively as the possibility of Travellers settling in their vicinity. Unsurprisingly, housed Gypsies and Travellers are particularly prone to racism and prejudice from their neighbours (Greenfields and Smith, 2010, 2011). Indeed in all geographic areas and neighbourhoods in the series of studies reported here, social relations with their non-Gypsy neighbours were distinguished by hostility, mistrust and mutual avoidance. Pat Niner's (2003) study found that 54 per cent of local authorities who responded to a survey reported that 'problems with neighbours' were one of the main reasons that housed Gypsies and Travellers ended their tenancies, second in frequency only to 'inability to settle in a house', cited by 79 per cent of respondents (2003, p 56). Experiences of prejudice ranging from obvious avoidance and a refusal to speak to Gypsy/Traveller neighbours through to overtly racist attacks (both verbal and physical) from their neighbours were reported by many of the sample. Thus, typical reports include narratives such as these, recounted during a focus group interview in the South East.

> "They gave me and my sister a flat and they [neighbours] put all the windows out, 'cos they had found out it was Travellers [moving in] ..."

> "That happened to us as well, when we first moved in ... when we was allocated the house, you should see what they did to the house, they ruined it, broke into it."

In Elias and Scotson's (1994) classic study of community divisions on a housing estate, *The established and the outsiders,* newcomers were frequently perceived of as a threat, due to the fear that associating with them would tarnish the status of the established group and of the local area. For Gypsies and Travellers, the prevalence of deviant stereotypes with which they are commonly associated, means that their move into housing is often accompanied by a fear among their neighbours of further social decline, disorder and crime on already deprived estates; anxiety which sets in motion processes of social closure and division. In relation to the above discussion, two issues are relevant in understanding the negative social relations between Gypsies/Travellers and their non-Gypsy neighbours, as well as the nature of their mutual interdependence and affinities. Firstly, the marginalised sections of the working class who have been progressively excluded by social, economic and cultural changes have been repeatedly labelled as a feckless welfare-dependent underclass in recent decades (Smith, 2005; MacDonald and Marsh, 2005). This has been accompanied by the residualisation and stigmatisation of housing estates and their residents (Hastings, 2004; Webster, 2007). The demonisation of both groups thus provides the social climate for a collective awareness of shared social locations and low status, yet also sets the context for inter-group struggles over relative power and status making membership of such communities particularly contested and salient in this context. Again, Elias and Scotson observe that 'As soon as the power disparities ... diminishes ..., the former outsider group ... tends to retaliate' (1994, p xxi). Secondly, as Nadel's (1984) study of a stigmatised community of former fisherman in Scotland illustrates: such groups do not necessarily accept the views attributed to them by outsiders and may develop a 'virtuous counter image of themselves, a negation and a denial of stigma' (1984, p 113). Differences in intra-group cohesion between housed Gypsies/Travellers and their neighbours accordingly reflect residential settlement patterns, the particular social composition of different localities, and the strength of collective identities and allegiances which allow for counter-stigmatisation whilst acting as a powerful riposte to negative stereotypes.

The following sections will examine how these issues are played out in the daily interactions between the research participants and those who live in close spatial (if not always social) proximity to them.

Stereotypes and social closure

Drawing on Max Weber's account of how social and status differentiations are maintained and reproduced through exclusionary practices, Frank Parkin (1979) notes that 'exclusionary closure' involves attempts by one group to enjoy a privileged position in relation to another group through a process of subordination. However, this is only one side of the coin: he also identifies 'usurpation' or 'that type of social closure mounted by a group in response to its outsider status and the collective experience of exclusion' (1979, p 74). When this involves groups such as women and minority groups who lack the industrial strength of organised labour (given the strength of unionisation at the time when Parkin wrote), 'outsider groups' rely heavily on social and expressive forms of collective mobilisation. These tend to be based on a defensive pride and solidarity that raises the self-esteem of group members by highlighting contradictions between the conduct and supposed values of the majority group (Barker, 2012). Parkin notes that

> One common, if slightly paradoxical, form this takes is the
> attempt to manipulate the belief system of the dominant

group by pointing up the inconsistencies between its advertised doctrines and its actual conduct. (1979, p 85)

One such method is through the inversion of stereotypical images and derogatory discourses. Thus Barker, in his study of youth homelessness in Australia, notes that:

> the cultural capital that is prized by homeless young people is recognized by other people within their social field as a legitimate claim to power. The capital that is prized in the social field of homeless youth is recognised by the broader community, but negatively, hence the term 'negative cultural capital'. The capital of the homeless young people is recognised by others and seen as anti-social which nonetheless positions homeless youth in a place of power, respect, fear or recognition. (2012, p 4)

If we apply this model to the social relations pertaining within our own field of study, we find that the very fluidity and malleability of stereotypes allows the long-held associations of Gypsies with dirt, crime and disorder to be reversed and levelled against their 'gorjer' neighbours in a manner which retrieves and utilises power to strengthen the cultural capital possessed by members of the former communities. Elias and Scotson (1994, p xxvii) identify the labelling of outsider groups as dirty and unhygienic as a universal feature of insider-outsider relations and the attribution and denial of such claims are an important element in the symbolic struggle over group status at the neighbourhood level. Amongst our own sample, their neighbours' hygiene practices and standards of cleanliness were frequently described pejoratively and held in stark contrast to their own, as the following male in the South-East commented:

> "You go to any Romany Gypsy places, their places are spotless, they take pride in cleaning their places ... But in houses they put us in with the people that never washes their places from one end of the week to the next where the grease is that thick on the gas cookers, I mean the gas cookers honestly."

Generalisations that classify the 'gorjer' as impure and polluting, contribute to what Powell (2008, p 97) terms a 'process of collective identification [which] contributes to a "we image"' among Gypsies surrounding standards of cleanliness and morality. As discussed in Chapter One, many Gypsies believe in their own superiority in relation to the settled population and this sentiment was frequently articulated by distinguishing their own hygienic practices with those of their neighbours:

> "You get some gorjer just coming in from the street laying on the bed, shoes on, hair dirty never showered for about two years. Us: clean socks, clean trainers, shower gel, there's a towel over there."

By applying stereotypical classifications of their neighbours, social closure strengthens the boundaries between different sections of communities since, in the words of one participant "I don't get on with them at all. They're the dirtiest people I've ever met". Patterns of social interaction in turn become restricted to those of similar ethnic and cultural backgrounds; as one commented: "I don't bother with them much. I like to keep my distance from them". Another participant in the South West reported that he didn't have "many gorjer friends. Far more Traveller ones, feel more comfortable with other Travellers". Parkin (1979, p 98) notes that exclusionary social closure normally relies on *legalistic* strategies, (such as the legislative offensive against nomadism and policies that have spatially segregated Gypsies and Travellers on caravan sites). In contrast, usurpationary closure resorts to *solidaristic* tactics which, particularly when strengthened by hostility from the outside society, heightens a sense of intra-group solidarity and awareness of inter-group differences:

> "Because our own race are the only people who welcome us with a nice cup of tea, a sandwich, it don't matter, wherever I pull in in this country, if I pull into a site even if I don't know them ... Do you know what I mean? That's the difference about us."

Another woman in the South East observed how mutual denigration and negative labelling contributed to social divisions and inhibited the development of wider social networks noting that relations on her estate were "not good, not bad, but would be better if we mixed more. They think we're dirty gyppos and we think they're dirty gorjers so we don't mix". The perceptions that each group holds towards the other foster intolerance and an overly sensitised awareness of trivial inconveniences that would be ignored under different circumstances. As one woman in the South West reported:

> "It's like anything if you know someone hates you, you puts up the barrier and think why be nice to these people. It makes you a different person ... we put our hand up to the people [wave] they turn away, and one woman kept complaining about the music but it wasn't loud. But the gorjer neighbour had the music twice as loud nothing was said."

Such minor problems are a frequent source of disagreement with many feeling that they are unfairly singled out by their neighbours even where relations are relatively good, as the following participant remarked: "When I was in my first house, I used to get on with the neighbours but if anything happened the fault was always ours".

Intolerance, prejudice and a willingness to complain to the authorities add to the perception of Gypsy and Traveller deviance and criminality. As one participant in the South East commented: "I hate it here. I haven't got my family here and the police are always at my door". Indeed, a major area in which participants contested negative stereotypes and positioned themselves favourably in relation to the settled population was with respect to criminal behaviour. Most are acutely aware that, fuelled by inflammatory and selective media reportage, they are closely associated with crime by the majority society, making them subject to increased policing and surveillance (Richardson, 2007b). During a focus group of young Gypsies and Travellers in the South West the participants discussed how these stereotypes shapes their social status and daily interactions:

> "You know what it's like [there is an assumption that] these people are all lazy bastards and all on the dole, don't want to work and all that – you know what I mean?"

A young girl who participated in the focus groups (Chapter Nine) noted:

> "We don't really get 'grief grief' but if we go into a shop that's the main thing because they think you're a Traveller and you ain't got no money and you're going to chor [steal]."

A lack of interaction between groups entrenches these firmly held views, which derive from the settled population's sense of moral superiority. However, in circumstances, where equally discredited co-proximate groups share similarly marginalised social and economic positions, a sense of collective superiority is more fragile and difficult to sustain. Complaints over the dishonesty and predilection to criminality of 'gorjers' was a recurrent theme within our interviews with older Gypsies and Travellers, placing limits on inter-group relations and contributing to the respective groups' ignorance of each other (Sanders, 2002).

> "The estate is full of unruly kids with no respect, the neighbours are still as bad as they used to be. We get hassled all the time by bad names. [We've] been broken into many times. Gorjers are the wors,t really badly raised."

Thus constructions of negatively 'othered' communities, as noted by Bloul (1999), overwhelmingly lead to:

> exclusionary identity politics [which] structure various 'ethnic communities' in parallel isolation relative to a dominant centre … [the] stress on partial and multiple character [therefore] fail to explore adequately the conditions for solidarity between different 'Others'. (1999, p 8)

While attributions of criminality against their 'gorjer' neighbours were commonplace the distinctions were often more nuanced than the blanket stereotypes often applied to them by the majority society and recognised internal differences within both groups (Powell, 2008, p 100). One lady in the South East for example pointed to the contradictions in dominant discourses and perceptions of Gypsies and Travellers, commenting:

> "Some of 'em won't accept us because we're Gypsies. They think that because one or two of them, are pinchers, and don't get me wrong but both sides do it … you can't make like one side is all angels and the other side are dirt. So it's both sides. But because we're Gypsies … 'Oh, you might pinch something.' 'Have you ever seen me before?' 'Well no.' 'So how come you think I'm going to pinch something?'"

Conflicts over children's behaviour and the appropriate response to misbehaviour and anti-social behaviour were another frequent source of discord between our respondents and their neighbours, and an arena where their own child-rearing practices were seen as superior. As one woman remarked about the non-Gypsy parents on her estate "they should all be under social services for the way they treat their children". Given that the socialisation of children in nomadic cultures has traditionally been based on collective responsibility for the supervision and guidance of children (Formoso and Burrell, 2000), several respondents were critical of their neighbours' parenting skills and their refusal to accept criticism of their children:

> "We don't [get on]. We had an argument a few years ago about a neighbour's kids being naughty. I don't see anything wrong with telling other children off as I would if they were Travellers [misbehaving]."

Inter-group variations in the degree of social cohesion and the extent of locally based social networks were therefore regarded as a key factor in facilitating collective supervision of children, and many respondents were of the view that the close social and kinship ties in their own community acts as a form of social control. However, informal systems of social control require consensus concerning the appropriate method of sanction, and social relations in their own community were contrasted with the apparently more isolated lives of their settled neighbours. As a result, the lack of communal responsibility for supervising and disciplining children is often seen as fuelling declining behavioural standards.

> "They [non-Gypsies] cannot take criticism of their own families and if you complain it'll end up in a fight whereas Travellers they will take advice and sort their kids out when they play up 'cos we all know each other so 'I'll tell your father' normally does it."

Conversely, limited interaction between housed Travellers and their settled neighbours; contrasting attitudes and practices towards children combined with mutual suspicion and ambivalence can intensify problems by drawing in family members and inflaming community tensions. The following woman remarked during a focus group in the South East that the parents' reluctance to deal with an incident involving her granddaughter meant that she had no choice but to get involved herself:

> "... half the time they're [gorjers] worse than what our children are. There's a few round our way. They let them do what they like. My grand-girl got threatened by a gorjer yesterday with a knife and I'm not having that 'cos I'll go after them first. They won't do it again."

Incidents of physical attacks and verbal abuse were common in all study areas, and were a significant source of concern for many of the participants, particularly the mothers in the sample, many of whom discussed their worries surrounding their children's safety in their neighbourhoods: "it is that you're frightened that the neighbours are going to know your babies are Gypsy children and that's what started my panic attacks off quite badly". Borgois (1996) argues that through 'cultures of opposition' that emerge in response to external threats and discrimination, individuals may actually *reinforce* negative stereotypes through developing aggressively defensive reactions, a theme which is further elaborated in the current context below.

Responses to racism: masculinity and solidarity

For Gypsies and Travellers the hostility described above is experienced and internalised from a young age, and the coping strategies utilised to defend against such experiences are similarly learned and refined in childhood. Over three quarters of the Gypsy and Traveller students in Derrington's (2007) study had experienced racism at school, and in the GTAAs on which we have worked, we frequently found over 90 per cent of respondents identifying immediate household members as having such experiences. Accordingly, there is a preference among many parents for their children to attend schools where there are other Gypsy and Traveller pupils, creating a cohesive critical mass of children to defend each other against external attack or hostility (Bhopal, 2000). This concentration of Gypsy and Traveller pupils in certain schools has thus been facilitated through their settlement in certain localities and neighbourhoods, such as those within our study areas. Link and Phelan (2001, p 371) note that having a devalued status in the wider society can result in 'very concrete forms of inequality in the context of social interactions within small groups'. This can reveal itself in various ways, for example through a reactive cohesiveness making individual members aware of their collective status as outsiders. We found abundant evidence of this theory in our study, with one man in the South East commenting:

> "... when they go to school they also take their culture to school and the wider community don't understand what their culture is about ... they congregate with each other because they feel the rest of the school is threatening to them."

Similarly, a male Gypsy in the South East youth focus group acknowledged that the cohesiveness of Gypsies and Travellers in school could often inflame tensions with other pupils noting that "That's our trouble, we stay together instead of going around with gorjers and gorjers turn on you". Gypsies are therefore very aware of the stereotypes that the wider society holds towards them and are not wholly passive victims in this process, sometimes manipulating these stereotypes for their own advantage (ni Shuinear, 1997). Derrington (2007) identified one of the coping strategies adopted by the pupils he interviewed was to cultivate a reputation for being 'hard' and to respond with violence to physical and verbal threats, a common response also found in Levinson and Sparkes' study (2003). This is a strategy encouraged through socialisation and through cultural values that place a premium on fighting ability. As ni Shuinear notes this is a rational strategy when seen from the insiders' perspective:

> a tiny minority group, always scattered into tinier units of a couple of families at most, living in among a huge majority who make no secret of their hatred, must use every possible means to prevent physical attack. The best way of achieving this is by making the majority afraid to do so. (1997, p 32)

During focus group interviews with young people it was apparent that aggressive and frequently excessive responses to external threats were part of a culturally grounded repertoire for dealing with such incidents. These reactions in turn, fuel stereotypical associations of Gypsies with violence, since, as Goffman notes, when an individual plays a role he/she is implicitly requesting that the audience believe that the character actually possesses the attributes of that role (1982, p 28). One teenage boy in the South East remarked:

"I keep fighting all the time. I like a fight. The gorjers come up to me all the time and give it a big 'un and think they'll get away with it. They don't. We beat the shit out of them."

Such narratives and examples of fighting in response to racist abuse or attacks were common among the young men interviewed in the focus groups. While these undoubtedly reflected an element of adolescent braggadocio, they also highlight the complex nature of social boundaries and hybridisation on housing estates where Gypsies and Travellers have had a long presence (see Chapter Nine), as the following example recounted during a focus group with young people in the South West illustrates.

"He was calling me a dirty gyppo and all that and he was calling me a scumbag and he said, oh I'll get my cousins to beat you up. Well, I said, I thought you said you wasn't a Traveller. No, he said, he was a gorjer and proud of it. I said his cousins were Travellers and he still kept calling me a dirty gyppo so I beat him up."

Indeed, accounts of discrimination and racism were paralleled by a wry acknowledgement by some that the behaviour of some of their family members is not conducive to good community relations: "if you met my cousin ... she just starts on anyone for no apparent reason. It is people like that that give us a bad name". In the context of continuing institutional racism and the reluctance of schools and other public authorities to address racism against Gypsies and Travellers, the reputation and potential for violence is an important protective strategy through combining concepts of masculinity and honour. This provides a certain kudos and grudging status among sections of the male working class who display similar attitudes and value similar concepts (Polk, 1999, p 26). This is particularly the case when demarcating forms of dominant masculinity amongst young men displaced from the labour market (Nayak, 2006, pp 826–7). Hobbes for example observes that: 'While strategies are symbiotically modified, violence and the expression of tough masculinity remain resilient, ever-present features of the youth and parent [working-class] culture' (1989, p 125). The use of violence as a protective strategy and historical associations of Gypsies with criminality (for example, the very use of the derogatory term 'chav' and its associations with the Romany language to connote 'rough' working-class culture) also has wider implications in terms of intercommunity relations, as they are avoided by many of their more 'respectable' neighbours, with those predisposed to 'chavishness' or violent criminality often the only non-Gypsies willing to socialise with their Gypsy and Traveller neighbours. One Romany man in the South East discussing drug use among the housed community reported that:

> "… the only people that'll talk to them on these estates are people that are on those type of things [drugs] … it's only a criminal element will talk to them that have anything to do with them. The only house dwellers that mix with Travellers are the villains."

Given the preference for residential and social segregation discussed further in the following chapter, evidence suggests that minorities' settlement patterns have a rational basis in the economic and social benefits harnessed through membership of locally based networks (Hudson et al, 2007) which also, by lessening contact with the wider society, minimises experiences of racism and discrimination (Ratcliffe, 2002). Accordingly, the possibility of racial harassment and the perception that certain areas are unsafe for minority groups in contrast to the solidarity that spatial concentrations of such groups can offer, may act as a major constraint on choices over locality (Bowes and Sim, 2002; Musterd, 2008); findings which feed into the debate on the impact of ethnic enclaves on community cohesion in areas of low socioeconomic status (Letki, 2008). Indeed our findings demonstrate that the often conflictual nature of social relations between Gypsies, Travellers and wider society was a key aspect of the 'chain migration' processes and residential concentrations of Gypsies and Travellers identified in all study areas (see Chapter Eight). Many of our respondents mentioned the sense of security that comes from being part of a localised and close-knit community, which both expresses and reinforces solidarity:

> "I got family all over this estate there's so many of us the gorgers wouldn't dare give us any trouble and that's the best thing about being here me aunts and cousins are always in our place."

As considered in greater depth in Chapter Eight, even where relations between different co-resident Gypsy and Traveller households are not marked by strong social ties, the existence of another (formerly) travelling family in the vicinity can provide reassurance and where necessary, vital allies against local hostility with solidarity based on shared experiences of prejudice and conflict. When discussing the Irish

Traveller family who lived in the same road as his own family of English (Romany) Gypsies in South London, for example, one man remarked:

> "Yes, some [live] up the road from me. Irish Travellers, they're alright. We don't talk much but we do look out for each other. They backed me up when all the neighbours lied to the gavvers [police] and said it was me who started a fight with one of the neighbours. [They] were the only ones in the road who did."

These experiences of intra and inter-ethnic solidarity are therefore important motivations towards the residential concentration of minorities, and relevant also to wider concerns over the development of 'parallel communities' and deficit of 'community cohesion' (Letki, 2008), which has received increasing governmental attention, becoming a key policy objective of the New Labour government (Home Office, 2001; Cantle, 2005). Those who advocate greater cohesion through imposing their own ideals of the 'good community' on citizens with less economic and political power generally demonstrate a scant knowledge of neighbourhood-level social dynamics in the poor and deprived locales that are the focus of their concern. This is particularly so given that research indicates that the extent of socioeconomic deprivation is frequently a key to understanding diminishing levels of 'neighbourliness' (Hudson et al, 2007; Letki, 2008). Thus, 'top down' recommendations about what poor communities 'need' may neglect residents' desire to live in ethnically or socially homogeneous communities *within* diverse neighbourhoods, a key finding from our research. Secondly, and despite efforts to stimulate greater 'social mix' in new urban housing developments, concerns over 'parallel communities' are rarely levelled at urban professionals, presumably because such groups are able to implement strategies of closure through creating exclusive communities (regardless of ethnicity, see Hinsliff, 2008) while disengaging from other social classes through a process of 'middle-class disaffiliation' (Watt, 2009).

Thus the processes of social closure and construction of ethnic boundaries described here represent the collective responses of Gypsies and Travellers to the perceived dangers and threats within both their neighbourhoods *and* wider society. Without a widespread determined and long-term commitment from government, public bodies and the media to proactively challenge and oppose racism against Gypsies and Travellers with equal vigour as when other minority groups experience discrimination, specific policy objectives to engender community inclusiveness will have, at best, a negligible impact on inter-ethnic relations. Furthermore, public concern over segregated communities is often presented most vocally by professionals whose status as 'moral entrepeneurs' depends on identifying and proposing policy solutions for social problems (Becker, 1963). As a result the focus is overwhelmingly on the *lack* of inter-group relations which necessitates an appropriate policy response and professional intervention, rarely on the existence of such relations. In contrast to this apparent static picture of conflict and antagonism at the micro-level, social boundaries are seldom insurmountable and are in a constant state of flux: constructed and reconstructed through shifting loyalties and friendships, as well as material and practical necessities (Hickman et al, 2008; Bailey et al, 2012). These stimulate interactions between people of different social and ethnic categories based on what Suttles (1968) termed a 'personalistic social order'. This social order evaluates individuals not solely on the basis of collective identity but against their own biographical precedents and reputation and through localised cultures which shape 'the distinctive connections of places to the "outside" which therefore becomes part of what constructs the place' (Shimoni, 2006, p 220).

Social mixing and intergroup classifications: locals and outsiders

Silverman (1988) is critical of the tendency to study Gypsies and Travellers as an isolated bounded group and like others, notes their tendency to settle in low-income areas where their way of life is more likely to be tolerated (Burney, 1999). Thus, an innovative feature of this book is the exploration of the interactions between Gypsies and Travellers and other white working-class communities who share experiences of marginalisation and stigmatised identities (Beider, 2011; Garner, 2007). Accordingly, notwithstanding the conflict and animosity between the communities described above, one of the few positive aspects of their estates' environment was the relatively permissive and tolerant atmosphere. A man in the South West for example pointed out that "we're near the site and it's a 'rough and ready' estate so no one complains about anything and we all get on OK". Acton (1974) argues that the historic impact of urbanisation and settlement has been to increase cultural contact between Gypsies and the wider population bringing a greater range of the population within the Gypsy cultural spread (see further Chapter Three). Neighbourhood diversity he adds, represent 'the nodal points of cultural change' and that 'in considering cultural change and culture contact it is ... precisely the marginal cases which are interesting: situations of culture-contact are where race relations occur' (1974, p 17). In certain aspects the desire to differentiate themselves and construct boundaries between themselves and their non-Gypsy neighbours described above, is paradoxically a reaction against processes of acculturation occurring between Travellers and those who live on the same estates and in the same neighbourhoods (see Chapter Nine). The emphasis placed on all that symbolically sets them apart may thus reflect what Shimoni (2006) refers to as a sense of *uncertain* boundaries, creating a need to affirm Gypsies' and Travellers' own cultural borders by portraying their norms and practices as superior to those of their neighbours.

Despite the prevalence of social segregation and the often antagonistic nature of relationships between housed Gypsies and their neighbours, the boundaries between these groups sharing analogous socioeconomic locations and a similarly discredited social status are hence permeable and fluid. Particularly among younger Gypsies and Travellers many of whom have spent most, or all, of their lives in housing, a degree of convergence and hybridisation of identities is occurring between themselves and other youth in their neighbourhoods (see further Chapter Nine). However, social inclusion has not generally accompanied these processes of acculturation due to structural determinants that have excluded both groups and it is within this context that inter-group relations and a merging of categories has occurred. Anthias (2001) identifies three dimensions of stratification as a method of integrating class, ethnicity and gender. The first is in terms of outcomes and life conditions; the second is the predispositions and opportunities that are structured by the individual's location; while the third is in the dimension of collective allegiances and identities related to struggles over resources. She argues that:

> ... these manifest disjunctions may produce a range of local struggles, contestations and proclamations, on the basis of organising around the category of class, or that of ethnicity or that of gender. On the other hand, a coincidence in the individuals that share both life conditions and life outcomes (ie shared outcomes and shared exclusions/opportunities) might have the effect of naturalising the similarity and lead to the formation of more permanent solidarity groups. (2001, p 384)

As discussed in Chapter Three, and despite the emphasis in both academic and popular literature on the physical isolation and social distance of Gypsies and other nomadic communities, evidence suggests considerable social, economic and cultural exchange have always existed with the wider society. In fact the economic survival of nomadic groups depends on such interaction (Gmelch, 1986). Silverman (1988) observes that, largely due to this necessity, Gypsy identity has always been situationally dependent, interacting with the wider society so that they 'freely adopt and adapt many aspects of it, redefine them and incorporate them into their own culture' (1988, p 267). While low levels of cross-group interaction encourages stereotyping, where social relations do exist, those stereotypes are challenged. One man in the South East for example observed: "I've known quite a few people round here anyway. All my life and there's good and bad in all. I've had a few rows with gorjers and that. Some are good, some are bad".

Similarly, an Irish Traveller lady from North London clearly differentiated between those 'gorjers' who accepted her as a Traveller and those to whom her identity was unknown:

> "I do my own thing around here you cannot get too involved with people you don't really know. I know a lot of gorjers near the site. We know them and they know we are Travellers. We get on well with them."

Sibley (1995, p 18) notes that stereotypes are a central element in understanding spatial and social exclusion and can only go unchallenged when there is minimal interaction with 'others'. The following example demonstrates how stereotypes can be overcome through challenging them. A woman in the South West recalled how she dealt with her non-Gypsy neighbours' initial prejudices after she had moved into housing:

> "... you heard the neighbours talking about 'Gypsies this and that' when they read something in the paper so I had to speak up and say 'excuse me, I'm a Gypsy' but it's alright now. They know me, they know us, and they apologised for thinking like that. So we're alright where we are and we have a nice house and the children are settled and we have nice friends."

One of the primary means through which the division between Gypsies and non-Gypsies has been breached is through intermarriage and partnership formation (considered in Chapter Nine). Dawson's

(2005) genealogical research indicates that since the 1700s one third of all Gypsies in every generation have 'married out', undermining myths often perpetuated by Gypsies themselves over 'pure bloodedness'. When discussing the state of local relations many of the participants' differentiated their neighbours on an individual basis and sharply distinguished the majority from their own 'gorjer' relatives. The following man in the South East for example, stated that "both of my boys have got gorjer wives and they're nice, they're nice people". Another added, "yes, most gorjers don't like us, [but] some are more down to earth like us. My brother's married a gorjer girl and her family are lovely people".

However, the tendency for Travellers to settle in localities close to former stopping places and their historical association with certain areas (Chapter Three) means that clear demarcations were drawn between 'local' gorjers, with whom many have had a long and close relationship marked by both conflict *and* cooperation, and outsiders (see too Chapter Eight). This was especially evident in the South East, which has a high Gypsy/Traveller population due to the prevalence, until recently, of seasonal agricultural work and the region's proximity to economic opportunities in London and its environs. The decline of agricultural work and the social mixing that occurred between Gypsies, Travellers and locals during such work was frequently cited as an important factor in eroding a sense of solidarity that previously existed between the two groups. During a focus group interview one woman said:

> "Everyone used to be on farms whether they be Travellers
> or whether they be gorjers we were all on farms and we all
> worked together. But nowadays that's not there. That's gone.
> And because that's gone I think that is the reason attitudes
> towards us has got worse."

Moreover, while the pace of settlement has intensified over the past 20 years, the process of sedentarisation has been occurring throughout the post-war period resulting in long-established communities of Gypsies/ Travellers on certain housing estates and significant levels of social interaction with the non-Gypsy locals. One man reported that "Even though me mum and dad was in wagons years ago, then they moved them to a house, so most of the time you've known them [gorgers] all your life". Another noted:

> "I live with mostly Travellers up the same road as me but
> I live with gorjers as well. I get on quite well with them

actually. 'Cos I've been brought up with them I've known them all my life. Most of them live up my road anyway."

At a micro-level inter-group relations were reported as taking widely divergent forms ranging from close and lasting friendships and intermarriage/partnering through to open hostility and avoidance. Nevertheless the major source of racism against Gypsies and Travellers and of organised local prejudice against them was regarded as having a clear class dimension. Collective opposition and mobilisation to new sites or unauthorised camps were rarely identified among 'locals' where conflict is more likely to be of an individualised and personal nature, but among the influx of commuters moving out from the cities following the proliferation of private housing developments that pepper semi-rural locales in the Home Counties (Boyle and Halfacree, 1998).

> "The problem is, I think our biggest problem is people from outside the area moving in. Local people know us, they know the families, they growed up with us. Right, and we all get on well, but what happens is when you get people come into the area like here and they don't know there is a big population here that is Traveller."

Watt's (2008) study of Londoners moving out to the suburbs explored how residents of a private housing development construct boundaries based on notions of dirt and purity that took two main spatial forms: one with respect to undesirable localities – the local council estate, amenities and the local Traveller site. The other referred to the presence of 'dirty' people in their localities whom they socially and spatially distanced themselves from – 'undesirable' elements moving out of London, the residents of local housing estates and Travellers. These processes result in socio-spatial segregation between newcomers and the longer-established residents on one hand and the development of social and spatial solidarities among similarly excluded sections of the population on the other.

> "You've got Londoners moving in and all our locals, all the original old locals that we grew up with, me dad grew up with, me aunties and everyone else their children have never had that chance to grow up [together]. All they've grown up with is these Londoners coming in and everyone else from up-country and the cities saying how bad we are. How do they know? They've never lived with us."

This chapter has indicated the complex and often contradictory nature of social relations between housed Gypsies/Travellers and the majority population that they live amongst, drawing attention both to the prevalence of antipathy and conflict between Gypsies and non-Gypsies and to the existence of social relations that cross such boundaries. Nevertheless many of those interviewed in all study areas expressed a strong desire to live close to other family members and among 'their own kind'. The following chapter is concerned with the situational adaptability of Gypsy and Traveller culture in the face of external pressures and, more specifically, how recourse to collective strategies have allowed many to resist assimilation and reformulate an approximation to traditional communities within conventional housing.

EIGHT

Recreating community

As explored in the previous chapter, social relations between housed Gypsies and Travellers and their sedentary neighbours are not infrequently characterised by tensions, and the use of (mutual) negative stereotyping which can sporadically flare into open conflict. As a response both to the potentially hostile environment in which some housed Gypsies and Travellers find themselves and as a mechanism for preserving and asserting their own cultural identity, specific strategies are utilised. Holloway (2005) examines how white rural residents in the vicinity of Appleby horse fair construct and racialise Gypsies and Travellers, which subsequently shapes how they relate towards them. She argues that general attitudes towards these groups, as well as discursive constructions of differences *within* the travelling population (between 'true' Gypsies and 'hangers on'), are based on certain physical and cultural markers. In contrast to 'passing', whereby individuals from stigmatised groups attempt to pass as members of 'mainstream' society, one strategy involved the accentuation of these physical and cultural markers and adoption of an overtly 'Traveller' identity demonstrating the range and adaptability of collective strategies which may be employed depending on the specific situational context. Strategies may involve avoidance of contact with individuals from other communities or use of Romanes or Gammon/Cant as an exclusionary tactic. Matras (2010, p 169) notes that the use of Romani vocabulary among British Travellers is a result of 'insiders insisting on the maintenance of a group-particular form of speech, coupled with the functionality of an in-group lexicon in the social context of a tight knit peripatetic group'.

Other tactics include the manipulation of stereotypes for personal advantage such as cultivation of an aggressive and violent demeanour or the feigning of illiteracy, all of which may feature within an armoury of techniques utilised by informants. The maintenance of cultural boundaries and retention of distinctive minority identities through distinctive strategies are common to a number of diasporic communities (Song, 2003; Hewstone et al, 2007). Conversely, as considered in the following chapter the cultural markers which signify membership of the Gypsy or Traveller community can, in certain socio-spatial contexts, be seen as a desirable form of cultural capital by young people from a range of ethnic groups. Fernandez Kelly (1994) highlights the close relation between social and cultural capital: both are defined by physical factors like the characteristics of space and also by collective categories such as class, gender and ethnicity. The main difference lies in their location:

> Cultural capital consists of a symbolic repertory whose meaning individuals learn and use as members of particular social networks. By contrast social capital often depends on relations of reciprocity among individuals and groups. Cultural capital issues forth as expressive behaviour. Social capital hinges on relations of trust and cooperation which facilitate access to scarce resources. (Fernandez Kelly, 1994, p 89)

Over time, shared social space facilitates cross-fertilisation as some neighbours and co-residents of 'Traveller areas' either consciously mimic and/or unconsciously absorb aspects of the argot, interactional styles and other culturally specific characteristics, actively seeking to become assimilated into Gypsy/Traveller society. The complex hybridised identities which can be created within families, social groupings and geographic locations allow residents of those areas to circulate in social networks that include Gypsies and Travellers and other co-resident social groups, developing distinctive forms of cultural and social capital attuned to the specificities of particular economically and socially excluded neighbourhoods (Brah, 1996). Such networks, however, when evolving on a neighbourhood basis and comprised largely of similarly marginalised yet heterogeneous members, may also hinder the development of bridging forms of capital and access to opportunities beyond the immediate locality, which is addressed in more depth in the following chapter (Granovetter, 1973; Putnam, 2000). In this chapter we address intra-group relationships and the ways that communities are consciously recreated by Gypsy/Traveller residents of housing estates by resorting to various strategies that are accessed though social networks and the flows of social capital circulating through them.

Despite the cordial inter-ethnic relationships which can exist in close-knit marginalised communities, Gypsy and Traveller respondents from all of the study areas, overwhelmingly stated a preference for living amongst 'our own kind'. The notion that animosity and mutual suspicion is the starting point from which relations with the 'settled' community proceed is frequently confirmed when interacting outside of their own community and shapes the structure of social relations in their neighbourhoods. One female participant in a focus group noted that "I think that we're so comfortable in our own community because we feel that no one really likes us anyway. And it's a funny feeling". Thus for a large number of respondents a feeling of alienation from the surrounding community and a lack of continuity in their social environments consistent with ontological insecurity was reported (Giddens, 1991). These experiences often existed despite their apparent degree of attachment to the local neighbourhood and reflected an oft-articulated sense that in engagements with their 'settled' neighbours "we always have to try to prove ourselves. And when you try to prove yourself its bloody hard work trying to prove that you're capable of being a part of the community". For individuals (particularly women, see Chapter Six) who were geographically isolated from other Gypsies and Travellers a combination of social isolation and fear (or actual experiences) of enacted racism perpetrated by neighbours could create a toxic mix which not infrequently led to psychological symptoms such as 'nerves', reliance on prescription and illegal drugs and mental breakdown (Parry et al, 2004). The potentially damaging consequences of social isolation, which are recounted in anecdotes that circulate through social networks, provide a powerful incentive to recreate communities and live in close spatial proximity to other community members.

Smelser (2004, p 36) notes that for an event to qualify as a cultural trauma it must render problematic something considered essential to the integrity of the affected society. Given the primary importance attached to family and community in Gypsy and Traveller culture and the ubiquity of narratives surrounding loss of community among those who had moved into housing, it was unsurprising that a series of tactics existed to minimise isolation and maintain contact with the wider Gypsy/Traveller community. These tactics fostered an approximation to traditional community structures *within* housing (Greenfields and Smith, 2010, 2011). The following sections will outline some of the main methods through which community structures are reformulated and maintained in the face of spatial management through large-scale settlement. The first is an outcome of the interrelation between central overnment policy and its execution at the local level, while the other represents an assertion of autonomy and cultural opposition which 'collectively resists and avoids changes that other groups, especially other agents such as development workers, view as expedient, good, correct or necessary' (Fortier, 2009, p 164).

Spatial management and residential segregation

As indicated in previous chapters, the main 'push' factor in the transition from nomadism to sedentarisation has been policy relating to accommodating Gypsies and Travellers on one hand and legislation concerning the management of unauthorised encampments on the other. The aim of government policies continues to be the eventual sedentarisation and assimilation of nomadic communities. Kabachnik (2009, p 472) argues that this objective, in combination with the legal construction of Gypsy status as opposed to an ethnic or cultural definition, 'deemphasizes the cultural practices of Gypsies and Travellers'. However, while official and legal discourses minimise the cultural and ethnic aspects of Gypsy and Traveller identity, this does not necessarily weaken the continuing salience of cultural identities and practices for people at the receiving end of those policies or how in certain circumstances, their implementation provide opportunities for the retention of those practices, albeit adapted and refashioned to a new environment.

As discussed in Chapter Five, in some localities the residential concentration of Gypsies and Travellers was a direct outcome of local authority approaches towards managing their nomadic populations. In both the South East and South West areas (comprising of relatively large post-war estates) the majority of housed Gypsies and Travellers were dwelling in socially and spatially cohesive communities where they and their families had often resided for several generations. These locally based extended family networks generally preceded settlement in housing, with many older community members, in particular, having previously travelled or resided on sites in the area with other Gypsies who were subsequently housed in the immediate vicinity. The location of these relatively dense groupings of housed Gypsies and Travellers in both areas were directly connected to long associations with travelling people in those localities, resulting from seasonal employment opportunities and/or traditional stopping places. Initially, a tradition of working on a local 'circuit', and in some cases intermarriage with (other) local Gypsy/Traveller or sedentary families had led the parents and grandparents of many informants to settle or travel relatively close to the respondents' current place of residence (Chapter Three). Thereafter the concentration of housed Gypsy and Traveller families in our studies could be traced in several cases to a conscious local authority policy of 'settlement' in the 1950s and 1960s whereby residents of long-used stopping places or small family sites were firstly accommodated in pre-fabricated huts following the compulsory purchase of land and later required to move en masse into newly built council house accommodation (Stanley, 2002; Evans, 2004). A second wave of settlement into housing could be traced to the closure of a number of local authority provided sites in the wake of the 1994 Criminal Justice Act (Chapter Two). In the South West study area for example, of the 38 housed respondents who participated in the research, over 70 per cent reported that either they or their parents had been resettled into housing as a result of closure of a local authority site in the vicinity.

The development of sizeable communities of housed Gypsies and Travellers in the South West and South East areas is generally a more recent phenomenon than in London where, as discussed in Chapter Three, significant housed communities have been recorded since the mid 19th century. The settlement patterns and community structures are similar, however, and distinguished by several large and related extended families settling in an area where they remain over successive generations. Historical associations and collective memories associated with certain localities generate strong attachments to and identification with, certain places. In a study of racism and minority experiences in rural Kent it was found that of all the minority groups interviewed, the sample of Romany Gypsies articulated the strongest affiliation to place identifying closely with both their local area and with the wider national and international Romany community (Ray and Reed, 2005). One elderly resident housed in south London clearly expressed a sense of 'belonging' based on an awareness of his community's historical connections to the area and the changing demographic make up of this locality:

> "Travellers were here a long time before they moved the blacks in after the war. Then the yuppies started coming and now the black folk are being pushed out. We were here first, there's a long connection, my grandfolk and their people came from down-country in the 1920s and camped in [local] yards ... this was a good area once but its changed for the worst since the property developers and professionals started moving in."

Of those respondents who had grown up in 'bricks and mortar', even when individuals had moved house there was a reported preference for remaining within a narrowly defined area. One respondent in the South West, for example, cited a common pattern among the sample "born a few roads away, went to school local, married away – the next estate – then we come back when we got a chance. We're local people". The attachment to what are often deprived housed estates has also been observed among marginalised working-class populations and is related to 'the embeddedness of these individuals in close, locally concentrated family and socially networks' (MacDonald and Marsh, 2005, p 156). Moreover the maintenance of nomadic patterns *within* housing (discussed later in this chapter) tends to be of a highly localised nature with moves out of the area relatively rare and many moves occurring within the same estates. Settlement patterns and the reconstitution of social networks on housing estates therefore entails the conflation of place and cultural identity with a number of respondents 'belonging' not only to a particular ethnic group, but also by attachment to their neighbourhood in a manner which cuts across generations and complicate narratives of ethnic and social boundaries in a manner similar to that identified in sites of urban super-diversity (Hudson et al, 2007).

Ruptures in established and taken-for-granted ways of life, therefore, do not necessarily dislocate social networks and may provide openings to create new solidarities while reaffirming old ones (Grand'Maison and Lefebvre, 1996). In one focus group, participants had been rehoused from two separate sites within a few weeks of each other on a particular estate estimated by local authority officers as having approximately 50 per cent of housing stock occupied by Gypsies and Travellers. Participants referred to the fact that despite the significant difficulties involved in learning to live in housing, the fact that other Gypsies and Travellers lived in the neighbourhood offered a sense of security and helped them to recreate a familiar community milieu within an alien environment, as remarked on by one woman in the South East: "The estate's full of them [Travellers] and that's good 'cos we'd go mental if there was only gorjers, I don't have much to do with them [non-Gypsies]". Where several clusters of families or site residents were allocated properties within a single neighbourhood, old (and on occasion, moribund) contacts could be reactivated as part of the process of recreating community. Respondents occasionally reported that they discovered distant relatives in unexpected contexts, as a man in the South West recalled:

> "… we went down the pub one night with me sons – and I saw Jim – I hadn't seen him for 20 year since we were pulled on the same site and there he was living quarter of a mile away they put him in a house too – him and his missus."

Contrary to the implicit policy objectives of assimilation, an important mechanism facilitating the spatial concentration of Gypsies and Travellers and maintenance of cultural identities and practices has been policies pertaining to settlement on caravan sites and in conventional housing. As mentioned, a combination of explicit housing policies and 'waves' of settlement created by site closures in the 1960s and again in the 1990s, meant that groups of Gypsy and Traveller families (predominantly in the South West and South East study areas) were relocated in their entirety within a short time frame. This enabled them to recreate relationships within a new physical environment with only a temporary (albeit frequently significant) disruption caused by their decanting from sites into housing. For respondents living in London, the situation is more complex given the widespread shortage of public housing stock. In these cases, respondents tended to utilise a combination of tactics, including the use of Choice Based Lettings and mutual exchange of public sector housing, or to obtain private rented accommodation in a locality close to family and community networks, leading once more to clusters of Travellers residing in relatively small areas throughout the city and displaying similar residential patterns to those observed in studies of 'urban' Gypsies in various cities and countries (Gropper, 1975; Kornblum, 1975; Sutherland, 1975; Gmelch, 1977).

Rebuilding community: housing exchanges and Choice Based Letting

Another important mechanism through which community structures and social relationships were conserved was through a conscious and strategic approach to the housing allocation system and exploiting opportunities that the social housing system provides. As priority is given to those with existing family connections in an area, respondents living in public housing stock had often applied to be accommodated at a specific location where a network of relatives were in close proximity, either residing on the same estate or in the immediate vicinity, as one respondent in the South East noted:

> " … didn't want to be in a house but there were no places [on the official site] I said if it had to be a house the only place I'd go was on [local estate] it's full of Travellers and I had loads of family on my mum's side there. I knew a lot of the gorjers from school so it weren't like I'd be around strangers."

However, there were marked geographical differences in participants' ability to access social housing in their preferred areas, with some individuals reporting less opportunity. Those who were accommodated as a result of an emergency – for example after being housed from the roadside and officially homeless; following domestic violence – or those resident in inner-city urban locales where housing stock is at a premium reported less choice over the type and location of housing. The Irish Travellers living in different parts of Inner London had few options regarding location due to the high demand for housing and in many cases, large family sizes which further limited their alternatives in the public sector. One woman who lived with her husband and four children recalled for example that: "we needed somewhere to live. The council offered us this place because it's big enough for us and the kids so we took it". Evidence also suggests a high usage of private rental stock amongst inner-city Irish Travellers, with the relative ease of attaining short-term tenancies in this sector supporting a rapid movement between premises as tenants change accommodation frequently. For some inner-city respondents, an element of inter-ethnic competition could be traced in their narratives of applying for public sector housing as other minority ethnic residents of an estate were at times perceived as being in competition for internal housing transfers and associated resources, strengthening their own community networks at the expense of Gypsy and Traveller and other longer-established residents (Dench et al, 2006; Hickman, et al, 2008). One woman living in a self-owned former council property in outer London remarked on how intensifying competition was making it more difficult to maintain spatially grounded networks of kin:

> "I'm not being racist but we're born here and my daughter can't get nowhere to live round here so they've moved out to X with my grand-boy. There's not many people I know from years back now [round here], but they come in and get housed just like that in a house that's got room for a lot of chavvies. I know a lot of travelling people, local people, what would like that house with space and a garden and all."

Bancroft (2005) notes that while state policy has tried to restrict the choices open to Gypsies and Travellers by attempting to fix them spatially, they also provide 'spaces of resistance to marginalization and exclusion, spaces of survival' (p 51). Collective adaptations and access to informal sources of knowledge have allowed the recreation of communities and a significant degree of nomadism even *within* the confines of conventional housing. Gropper's (1975, pp 174–5) study of Gypsies in New York identified a continuation of nomadic patterns marked by 'sporadic and superficial' contact with other groups and a distaste for what they saw of those groups within the metropolis. High levels of mobility represent one element in a 'reservoir' of culture allowing them to resist assimilation and continue accustomed ways of living. A study of Irish Travellers in London reported greater mobility among those in housing than among those living in trailers, as many were unable to settle and moved through a succession of housing between squatting on sites or on unauthorised encampments (Emerson and Brodie, 2001). One female in the South East, for example, estimated that on average she moved twice a year, commenting that housing actually afforded more scope for nomadism than caravan dwelling:

> "if you get a stop [somewhere to park a caravan] you'll stay long as you can. In houses though I can't stay for long, six months is enough ... we've been here three months now and we'll give it another month or two then swap with my cousin for a bit and come back here in the new year."

The trend of frequent movement between houses has been identified in various contexts: for example, in a study of Finnish Roma it has been suggested that such rapid shifts of accommodation equate to a new form of 'travelling' for individuals who have become sedentarised over two or three generations and who are unaccustomed to feeling chained to one locality (Berlin, 2012).

Evidence from the South East study locale found that just under half of the housed sample of 103 Gypsy/Traveller households had moved at least once in the previous five years, including over 20 per cent who had moved three times or more as respondents sought to exchange premises through complex networks of opportunistic and carefully planned transfers until they were able to settle closer to their family and wider support system (Smith, 2008). As noted by one Gypsy participant in a South East focus group:

> "As much as people try to separate Gypsies and Travellers in housing in this area they are wheeling and dealing to be in houses near their own families, so then you end up around this area with estates full of Travellers, and unfortunately people around them don't understand why they want to be together. But it is that family network."

One local authority housing office in the South East region drew a connection between mutual transfer systems within social housing stock and the development of communities amongst housed Gypsies and Travellers. During the interview, and based on her experience of working with this community, she highlighted a degree of mobility which was, in her experience, unusual for tenants of conventional secure accommodation and related this transience to the maintenance of traditional lifestyles observing that:

> "Through the mutual exchange system they are very mobile in housing, they're moving around and using houses like wagons. The lifestyle doesn't stop just because they're in housing."

In both the South East and South West localitie,s housing officers reported that on certain estates half of the population comprised Gypsy and Traveller households, with initial housing allocation failing to account for the size of the population. The same housing officer also observed that often by the time housing staff became involved in a housing transfer, community networks had already ensured that an individual with reason to live in a certain locality was 'organised' as the mutual exchange system was underpinned by, and reinforced, networks of reciprocity: "It's all done through ties and someone knows someone who wants to move onto this or that street and we'll get them turning up having arranged a 3- or 4-way exchange".

The advent of Choice Based Letting (CBL) has also impacted on the increased density of Gypsy and Traveller populations in our study areas. Manley and van Ham (2011) report that the intention behind CBL was that accommodation demand would be stimulated in 'hard to let' areas as households selected properties and locations suitable for their needs. This has created a perfect market model for the Gypsies and Travellers we have interviewed and assisted them in locating closer to their families and existing networks. In practice, whilst such 'choice' may meet the immediate needs of families to reside in areas where they can live in close proximity to family and allow the conscious creation of ethnic enclaves, the outcome is often that minority ethnic households using CBL mechanisms are likely to end up in deprived ethnically concentrated neighbourhoods (Manley and van Ham, 2011).

In response to the disruption of family patterns and accommodation preferences caused by shortage of sites, and as a form of conscious protection from local residents' hostility (or anticipatory fear of such hostility), patterns of 'migration-settlement' are emerging which parallel 'chain-migration' processes identified among other minority ethnic groups (Pillai et al, 2007; Haug, 2008). Thus, local authority policies are frequently the catalyst for the *initial* accommodation of Gypsies and Travellers near to a former or existing local authority site, while familiarity with an area also appears to influence owner-occupiers and some private rental tenants. This model of conscious community building replicates that identified by Greenfields (2006) in relation to owner-occupiers in Southampton who reported that as a neighbourhood gained a reputation of being a 'Gypsy area' it became easier for would-be purchasers to put in an offer for a property as local network members would advise them someone was moving away. Once a particular spatial density of Gypsy and Traveller residents is reached the process becomes cumulative as non-Gypsy households tend to move away and only those aspiring residents who are 'Traveller-friendly' or who have familial or other pre-existing links relocate to such an area, increasing the sense of community cohesion amongst neighbours. Through these processes relationships become increasingly strengthened through family, social and employment connections whilst weaker ties between individuals who are neither members of the Gypsy/Traveller communities or who do not circulate in those networks dissolve as newcomers are immersed in localised networks of social relations.

The capacity to develop adaptive trajectories and maintain minority lifestyles and practices in spite of adverse changes designed to limit and oppress those lifestyles is a hallmark of cultural resilience (Theron et al, 2011). The coping mechanisms and strategies that reformulate Gypsy and Traveller community structures are based in historically grounded and highly developed mechanisms that foster adaptation without assimilation (Sutherland, 1975, p 290). The distinctive communities of housed Gypsies/Travellers which result largely replicates site life. Community members requiring housing in specific areas can frequently be accommodated in a manner which mirrors the ways in which plots on caravan sites may be traded or temporarily lent whilst someone goes travelling, or relatives will 'double up' to support someone at a time of crisis (Greenfields and Home, 2008; Cemlyn et al, 2009). At the same time the ability to remain mobile within the housing system facilitates the continuation of culturally approved methods of defusing feuds and conflicts with other Gypsy and Traveller families (Gmelch, 1977). As one participant in south London recalled, "I moved here because another travelling family moved onto my old estate. Our families never got on going back a long time so I got a swap down here 'cos I'm getting too old for the grief". Thus while housing can be experienced as extremely isolating and restricting (Chapter Six), the mechanisms through which housing is allocated, exchanged and secured means it can also be utilised in an extremely versatile manner and traditional community structures and patterns of sociability continued in a new context. The ability to deflect external pressures and maintain a dense web of social relations is essential to a sense of collective identity and individual well-being, as a female resident on a private site in the South East noted:

> "the condenseness of the travelling community keeps it alive. Without that we'd disintegrate which is what the government want but that'll never happen even if they put us all in houses and places we don't want to be they'll always be who they are."

Gender, networks and community

Studies of the relationship between family structures and external social relations in working class communities have long posited that the extent to which gender roles were differentiated within the household was related to the spouses 'connectedness' to local family-based networks. High segregation in the conjugal relationship was accompanied by the existence of close-knit networks and vice versa (Bott, 1957; Young and Willmott, 1957). In Gypsy and Traveller culture gender roles within the family are often highly segregated with women overwhelmingly occupied with housework and child-rearing. Consequently they tended to have a greater density of localised networks which acted as an important source of emotional support and informal welfare in addition to exerting a considerable normative pressure to conformity (Hannerz, 1980). Attitudes towards women working, for example, made it difficult for some to find work outside traditional family-based working practices, as one woman noted, "If you wanted to work, you couldn't marry a Traveller". It was noteworthy that female respondents were more likely than males to refer to greater social contact with people from other social groups although these were predominantly focused around children and family settings, "at the school – we get on ok; I chat to the other mums outside the school, we're all mothers whatever colour we are". However, their social contacts were overwhelmingly single-gendered and very few had relations with males outside their immediate family network due to the conservative nature of Gypsy/Traveller culture and the normative pressures to conformity mentioned above, "my husband wouldn't want me speaking to gorjer men". Interestingly, those women who had social contact with non-Gypsies/Travellers tended to provide a *reason* for such cross-boundary contact rather than citing pure friendship, "friends with a couple of gorjer families because the boys play with ours. They invite ours to birthday parties".

While more interviews were collected from women than from men, overall (Chapter Four) evidence indicates that females were more likely to actively initiate or engage in network-development activities than were men, a trait which appears common to women from both mainstream populations and minority ethnic groups (Gilchrist and Kyprianou, 2011). On the occasions where males did refer to new social contacts or friendships which were emergent after moving to a new locality, these appeared to 'grow' as a result of casual neighbourhood contacts, "over time they [non-Gypsy neighbours] got to see we were ok – now we're friends"; common interests such as football, or as a result of contacts initiated through female relatives or children. In general, males circulated in more homogeneous Gypsy/Traveller networks than did the women and rarely did they actively initiate new relationships in the local area. An important counter example, however, was in the sphere of economic and work relationships. These frequently transcended their own social ties and proceeded on the basis of mutual financial advantage, linking together previously isolated individuals ,as one man noted: "I don't care who they are as long as we can both make some nice money".

Network homophily refers to the desire of individuals to interact with people who are similar to themselves (McPherson et al, 2001). The evidence concerning patterns of male interaction support the homophily principle which states that personal networks are most commonly homogeneous and defined (in ascending order) by ethnicity, gender, occupation, educational status and age, providing a useful model for explaining the rapidity with which respondents identify and network with others from the same ethnic group. Accordingly, in the fertile context of Gypsy and Traveller settlement into a new locale both genders developed relatively close social ties as points of commonality were discovered, or created through the recognition of being a member of a minority community within an 'alien' or potentially threatening environment (Gill and Bialski, 2011). The search for intra-community networks was common to residents at all locations studied. In some cases respondents reported that they had initiated contact with strangers whom they tentatively identified as a member of the Gypsy/Traveller community. An Irish Traveller woman in the South East recalled:

> "I saw this woman in the street on my estate and I knewed her for a Travelling woman so I says to her 'you're a Traveller, aren't you?' and she said 'no' but then she said – quiet like – 'don't you tell nobody and I'll not tell about you neither'."

In other cases it was reported that another individual had made the original contact. The ability to establish and identify differences often function as Bourdieu notes, below the level of consciousness and includes 'the primordial, tacit contract whereby they define "us" as opposed to "them"' (1984, p 473).

> "I went to the hospital the other week with my mother-in-law and this woman, she was a Traveller but I didn't know she was a Traveller, she was laying in the bed and she had no gold on but she said to me 'are you a Traveller?'. I went 'yeah, why?' but she was a Traveller herself but I didn't know she was a Traveller."

Such signifiers are embodied in one's bodily hexis – by which Bourdieu means 'deportment, the manner and style in which actors "carry themselves": stance, gait, gesture' and which fuse the individual's subjective world with the cultural world into which they are born (Jenkins, 2002, p 75). The often subtle signs indicating that somebody is a Gypsy/Traveller are not readily discernible to many 'outsiders' since many signifiers are shared with the white working class who they live amongst and where a significant degree of acculturation and cross-fertilisation has occurred both historically (Chapter Three) and contemporaneously (Chapter Nine). Nevertheless such distinctions are recognisable to community members and to working-class individuals who, through dint of sharing the same social space, generally have a more refined and nuanced understanding of Gypsy and Traveller identity than many professionals and other self-appointed 'experts'. Recognition results from the 'practical sense' that operate on the basis of shared normative assumptions and understandings about common interests that can be advanced through social exchange. The benefits that accrue from those exchanges are the foundations of the group's solidarity through encouraging mutual recognition (Bourdieu, 1985; 1986). One woman in the South West for example observed:

> "We can tell each other ... we might not know someone but you like recognise someone's a Traveller. Down the shop like she looks at you and you look at her and then

you find out – like when Minnie asked if you were Dan's girl or related to Katy and then you know how you fit [in] and you're not really so alone."

Similarly, during a focus group with Gypsy and Traveller high school students conducted in the South East one young man remarked:

"Good thing about Travellers, walk down town. Even if you see Travellers you've never seen in your life, they know you but you don't know them you still knows they're Travellers straight away. Don't know how but you can pass one and you just know right away."

Overall, a theme which emerged across all study areas was the impact of repeated experiences of rejection or discriminatory treatment on respondents' willingness to seek contact with non-Gypsies and Travellers and a heightened sense of boundaries between themselves and those who were unrelated by ties of kinship and culture. These findings broadly mirror those identified by Jayaweera and Choudhury (2008) who explored barriers to social inclusion for new migrants. They found that participants repeatedly referred to the impact of racism in reducing trust in their ability to be accepted by society and that their closest social relations were with members of their own family and ethnic group. As noted previously (Chapter Six), participants in our studies (especially women) have stressed the sense of isolation on moving into housing and in contrast, the importance to their wellbeing of 'being in and out of each other's houses all the time'. Iddenden et al's (2008) public health survey in Hull (an area with a long-established and settled Gypsy/ Traveller community) found that 89 per cent of Gypsy and Traveller respondents reported daily or almost daily contact with relatives who were not members of the same household and 81 per cent reported similarly high levels of contact with friends, compared to approximately 50 per cent for other residents including those from minority ethnic communities. The report also found that over half of all Gypsies and Travellers interviewed had at least five relatives or close friends living in their immediate vicinity compared to 20 per cent among other respondents. Where Gypsies and Travellers become resident in housing the importance of creating or sustaining a community network to stabilise their family and to access social capital and a range of resources becomes of paramount importance in mitigating the cultural trauma of an abrupt change of lifestyle. For individuals who were offered public accommodation in isolated situations, a tendency to seek to move house as rapidly as possible and to relocate to an area of greater density of Gypsy/Traveller population was common.

Self isolation

Nevertheless, dense and spatially bounded networks characterised by high levels of social interaction are not without their own stressors: feuds, grievances and intra-community conflict were reported during the interviews, with some expressing a preference for living at some distance from 'Gypsy' areas. Moreover, while a dense web of social ties can offer a structured system of practical and emotional support and a vehicle for sustaining community solidarity and identity they can also impose excessive obligations on network members and enforce overly restrictive behavioural norms, which can thwart social mobility and aspirations outside of those norms. The localised networks in the study areas are intermeshed with larger networks of extended family and associates that transcend the immediate vicinity and which comprise a highly effective informal system of surveillance and monitoring. In cases where individuals had deliberately separated themselves from their community as a result of a family dispute or leaving a violent spouse, they reported feeling insecure and concerned that their location would be revealed via these networks. Subsequently they avoided developing any form of social relationship with other Gypsies or Travellers in case their whereabouts became known. For example, whilst undertaking a GTAA in an area of southern England, a community interviewer reported that on encountering a Traveller woman on a housing estate and seeking to obtain an appointment with her to undertake the accommodation survey, the potential interviewee initially denied she was a member of the Traveller community, then became angry and upset that her identity had been revealed. The woman finally indicated that she was hiding from a violent ex-spouse and wanted nothing to do with anyone from her own community as she was afraid that if it was known to other Irish Travellers that she lived locally, her husband would track her down. Even being reassured that the GTAA interviews were confidential did not alleviate the lady's fears and she remained distressed that she had been identified as a Traveller stating that she had not thought that there were members of her community living nearby when she was rehoused.

Anecdotal evidence received from charities and community organisations confirm that reluctance to be accommodated near other Gypsies and Travellers is not uncommon, particularly amongst gay or lesbian couples, if an individual has been released from prison following intra-community violence or has been involved in activities regarded as reprehensible such as involvement with social work agencies as a result of neglect or physical abuse of children or elders. Indeed, the best-selling popularist autobiography 'Gypsy Boy on the Run' provides fruitful grounds for discussion on the potentially negative consequences of membership of a close-knit community whose members are able to recognise and identify someone's family connections with considerable ease (Walsh, 2011). Staff at Solas Anois, the Irish Traveller women's refuge, have referred to service users at their refuge returning to violent situations, after having been identified by other members of their community following rehousing and subsequently experiencing community pressure to return to their marriage (Clark, 2009).

For owner-occupiers who had voluntarily moved into housing and who had higher levels of financial capital, respondents generally articulated a greater degree of agency in selecting the area to which they moved (Chapter Six). In some cases this meant waiting until they were able to buy a house in a road with long-term historical connections with Gypsy settlement (Greenfields, 2006) but in other cases indicated a conscious desire to spatially distance themselves from the community thereby electing to remove themselves from the intense and, for some, arduous atmosphere of a communally centred life on site. One Gypsy woman whose work involves extensive work with the Gypsy and Traveller community noted:

> "I moved off the site because I didn't want the hassle ... You get burnt out and you want some family time – not people coming to your trailer, knocking on your door or phoning you all the time – I get it all the time at work and we wanted some family time and somewhere I could come in and shut the door and that was that."

For others, marriage outside of the community resulted in a desire to maintain a degree of social and spatial separation although as the following English Gypsy woman in the South West recalled, this was initially a difficult transition;

> "I'm married to a gorger, don't get me wrong my family get on with him alright but we didn't want to live in the middle of it all, we wanted something a bit different – a house – where I could see my family and the kids could spend time on the site but we wanted somewhere not right next door. But it was really lonely when we went in

the house and I got really depressed to start with – up my mum's every day."

Those who expressed a desire for spatial distancing and a degree of social distance from the Gypsy and Traveller community were very much in the minority. Smith's (2008) survey of 103 housed Travellers in the South East broadly mirrors Iddenden et al's (2008) findings from Hull. 85 per cent of respondents to the South East survey were aware of other Gypsies and Travellers in their area and the majority expressed positive attitudes towards this. Only 13 per cent had no local ties, mostly as a result of moving into the area from elsewhere and over 60 per cent of these voiced negative feelings about this, confirming the social isolation experienced by many which, in turn, shapes their transitional experiences of housing (Chapter Six). One single parent, who had moved to the area following conflict with her ex-partner for example, commented that she felt "among strangers. I don't feel safe and I've got no family support. I hate it here" (2008, p 15).

Whilst it is clear that local authority (and indeed private sector) housing allocation procedures can be related to patterns of ethnic segregation, neighbourhood clustering by ethnic group has been associated with assisting new migrants (or in the current case newly housed Gypsies and Travellers) to obtain access to support networks and mechanisms (Peach, 1998; Temple et al, 2005). The benefits of residence in areas with a high degree of co-ethnic density have, however, only relatively recently been subject to more sustained and nuanced analysis amid concerns over the impact on both broader society and individual ethnic communities of over-reliance on 'bonding' social capital. Thus an unintended consequence of using housing exchange mechanisms and Choice Based Letting to provide people with greater choice over where they live may be increased rates of neighbourhood segregation. Manley and Van Hamm (2011) argue that, contrary to expectations, ethnic minority households who make use of Choice Based Letting are far more likely than white groups to rent a home in a deprived neighbourhood or a locale with a high density of ethnic minority tenants. Inevitably this has potential impacts for the degree of economic and social inclusion and future prospects of subsequent generations of Gypsies and Travellers growing up in such locations.

The overall implications for community cohesion amongst residents of such segregated estates would therefore appear potentially rife with conflict, with clashes between distinct communities occurring periodically as a result of racism, arguments over children's behaviour or cultural practices such as large family gatherings. In practice, however, we were able to identify a tendency in some areas for 'parallel communities' to become 'syncretic communities' where large numbers of Gypsies and Travellers were residing in close proximity and inter-cultural partnerships and friendships were formed (Chapters Seven and Nine). Thus it is arguable that over time, the key issue facing Gypsies and Travellers in housing will be the geographical, class and spatially exclusionary elements experienced by the majority of *all* estate residents rather than any specifically ethnically based issues.

NINE

Young people in housing: aspirations, social relations and identity

This chapter draws predominantly on two focus groups conducted in the South East and South West research sites in addition to data gleaned from secondary analysis of GTAA focus groups and household interviews conducted in the primary research locales.[1] It explores the experiences of young housed Gypsies and Travellers (aged 25 or less) and the evolving nature of spatially bounded social relationships among these youthful cohorts, for many of whom life in conventional housing has been their predominant experience. The chapter focuses on the dynamics of intercommunity and interpersonal relations and discusses how an increasing social and cultural convergence with non-Traveller youth generates generationally specific understandings of Gypsy/Traveller identity as well as intergenerational divergences in those conceptualisations. These differences predominantly coalesced around notions of collective identity; the differing emphasis placed on the symbolic role of nomadism; in attitudes surrounding intergroup relationships and the importance placed on boundary maintenance and corresponding perceptions of 'authenticity' (see further Chapter Six). The timing and intersection of radical social transformations (such as the move from nomadism towards settlement) and generation-specific attitudes are central to understanding the tension that emerges between older cultural precepts and an emergent youth culture more attuned to new social circumstances (Sztompka, 2000).

Under such conditions new solidarities and identities develop, which express two contradictory forces: inter-generational conflict, in addition to a simultaneous desire for identification and continuity with the parent culture (Smith, 2005). Edmunds and Turner (2002, p 6) argue that a 'sociology of generations' and of generational consciousness must begin with the historical context and shared experiences through which that consciousness was formed. Such a perspective was utilised by the Birmingham Centre for Contemporary Cultural Studies (CCCS) in their analyses of post-war working-class youth culture, and is relevant to a fuller understanding of how the undermining of nomadic traditions and the transplanting of Gypsies and Travellers into housing is mediated by both gender and age-cohort. Collective responses and adaptations to external change are differentiated on the basis of both, whilst still retaining an overall adherence to more generalised shared values and worldviews. As Clarke et al (1993) note:

> Here we begin to see how forces, working right across a class, but differentially experienced as between the generations, may have formed the basis for generating an outlook – a kind of consciousness – specific to age position: a generational consciousness. (Clarke et al, 1993, p 51)

Accordingly, we locate the generationally specific narratives recounted in this chapter in the context of the specific opportunity structures and historical locations within which such narratives were formed. This perspective, argues Wangler (2012), is particularly fruitful in exploring the aftermath of traumatic cultural changes and emergent ways of coping with, and interpreting, such disruptions.

> This approach is particularly effective and beneficial for the study of the dynamics of national minority groups with regard to their integration into society and the adaptation of new lifestyles as well as the formation of a new historical consciousness. (Wangler, 2012, p 66)

We found it noteworthy that concerns over boundary maintenance and cultural contamination (Barth, 1969; Okely, 1983) were more apparent among adult Gypsies and Travellers than this younger cohort, with a balanced tension existing between people from surrounding communities, and primary relationships overwhelmingly mono-ethnic for those of older age groups (see further Chapters Seven and Eight). In relation to Acton's (1974) typology of collective responses to external change outlined in Chapter One these patterns of engagement represent a culturally conservative response that involves maintaining traditional cultural values and practices by minimising contact with the outside world. Social segregation is further reinforced through external social prejudice and racism. Gilchrist and Kyprianou (2011, p 8) warn that extensive reliance on ethnically segregated social groups among second generation immigrants can be 'limiting in the longer term, restricting their choices and aspirations for education and careers' although we found that the responses of many younger people were more congruous with a culturally adaptive strategy where influences from the outside world that were beneficial were adopted leading to a reformulation rather than a rejection of Gypsy and Traveller identities. Amongst young people in both focus groups less explicitly negative attitudes towards non-Gypsies and Travellers were articulated than by their parents and grandparents, demonstrating a counter-tendency to the development of inward-looking housed communities discussed from Chapters Six through to Eight. One grandmother in the South East, for example, indicated the ease with which her granddaughter was able to cross ethnic boundaries according to the fluid nature of friendship among young children without the reciprocal suspicion and incomprehension that characterised their parents' experiences when interacting with 'gorjer' society:

> "… my grand-girl she plays with Travellers. When she falls out with them, she'll go and play with the gorjers. When she falls out with them she goes back to square one and plays with the Travellers."

In the following section we address educational and employment aspirations, as a precursor to discussing the frequently conflicting influences of familial expectations ethnic identity and local youth cultures on young Gypsies and Travellers. The dynamic and fluid nature of youthful networks frequently transcends the social and cultural boundaries that are enforced most vigorously on both sides (Gypsy/Traveller and gorjer) by parents and elders, with the result that aspirations often reflect these opposing tendencies whilst also differing along gender and intra-community ethnic (Romany Gypsy and Irish Traveller) lines.

Gender social reproduction and transformation

The relatively short time frame within which a substantial proportion of Britain's previously nomadic families have been settled has resulted in a splintering of collective experience, as increasingly heterogeneous and multigenerational experiences exist in the same spatial locales. Consequently, older forms of solidarity exist alongside the emergence of new cultural formations and while the future aspirations of young people display an adherence to traditional values, they also revealed a simultaneous desire to transcend the gender-specific routes to adulthood followed by older generations of Gypsies and Travellers. Elements of the values and practices of the parent culture influence perceptions of life chances and opportunities, and compete with social milieu and neighbourhood loyalties in shaping educational and occupational aspirations (Furlong et al, 1996). MacDonald and Marsh (2005) employ the notion of 'bounded agency' to capture the spatial aspects of young people's social landscapes and highlight how:

> local cultural knowledge and values bound individual choices and actions. It is at the local level that young people learn informally – particularly from friends and family and through their own lived experience – a 'sense of future possibilities'; the culturally sanctioned ways of being a young person and becoming an adult. (MacDonald and Marsh, 2005, pp 142–3)

Amongst our cohort, aspirations and attitudes towards other communities frequently challenged those of their elders in terms of gendered expectations and patterns of sociability and, as in other minority communities, were a potential cause of generational tensions (Epstein and Heizler, 2009). It has been noted that one consequence of modernisation has been to weaken the economic role of Gypsy women (Okely, 1983). Indeed the emphasis on the 'traditional' domestic role of women in Gypsy and Traveller culture is more likely a reinvention of tradition and assertion of patriarchal control since evidence indicates that for much of their history women have played an important economic role in nomadic cultures, with their roles generally involving greater interaction with outside society than that of men (Gmelch, 1986). There is significant evidence that the strongly gendered expectations placed on young women are instilled during socialisation, not least utilising methods of social control designed to minimise contact with the potentially corrupting influences of 'gorjer' society. These can include withdrawing girls from school at a young age, a response to concerns that they may be required to participate in sex education classes and become sexualised prior to marriage, reflecting relatively widespread concerns over possible liaisons with boys in mixed educational settings (Bhopal et al, 2000; Levinson and Sparkes, 2003). Regardless of these cultural norms, a number of young women who participated in the focus groups challenged the expectations and attitudes of their elders in terms of social mixing and employment ambitions, findings which embodied differing levels of receptivity to outside influences and mirrored those of youth from varied social groups (Epstein and Heizler, 2009). One young woman in the South West noted that:

"you know, sometimes we do get expected to get married
– and that's that really – it's arranged and then you're a wife
... and I wonder what it would be like to be something –
someone – different."

The impact of such 'traditional' patriarchal attitudes on female
aspirations for gender equality and a desire for a less constrained social
life mirrored comments from young women interviewed in London
and the South East for a study investigating attitudes to employment,
during which one female respondent remarked that "if you wanted
to go out to work you would need to marry a country boy [not an
Irish Traveller]. No Travelling man will be happy with his woman out
when he gets back" (Greenfields, 2007b, p 74). Frustration at the social
restrictions and limited options open to young women were voiced
in both regions where focus groups were undertaken. One young
Romany woman in the South East drew parallels between the position
of women in Gypsy/Traveller culture with those of other minority
groups, noting that "in the travelling community you are not allowed
to be anything but a housewife ... I'm not trying to be horrible but
it's the same as a Muslim, you can't work and you're not allowed to
look at another man". However, other women were clearly defying
the collective mores and assumptions of older generations based on a
'realization of potentialities' (Mannheim, 1936). An unmarried woman
in her early 20s who participated in a focus group in the South East
recalled how she had left home to live with a group of friends rather
than following gendered expectations that she would only set up home
following marriage. Even though she was still subject to communally
based forms of surveillance, having not moved far and living amongst,
and working on a part-time basis with, other Gypsies, as well as being
effectively chaperoned by an older woman, she experienced a significant
degree of criticism from older family members for her breach of
community norms:

"For instance my granny found out I was moving up here
and [when] she found out I was leaving my community
and family home she wasn't very happy and she was quite
ignorant with me, and whenever I saw her or phoned it
was as if like she was quite angry at me."

Whilst some young people – particularly females – identified some
degree of parental or community pressure to conform to 'Traveller
appropriate' behaviour and the preservation of traditional lifestyles

(especially with regard to employment or marital expectations) a number of young women in particular indicated that their mothers (especially where they had found themselves as lone parents following marital breakdown) encouraged them to consider alternative options to early marriage, albeit with some remaining cultural restrictions. One middle-aged woman in the South West observed how her own experiences had reoriented her aspirations for her daughters, due to wider changes in family structures that impacted on Gypsy and Traveller families:

> "look it's not common but it's happening more – travelling people are getting separated and divorced and that now – it happened to me – so I want my girls to learn something and stay in school so that they can get a job if they need to. You never think it will happen but it does for some people."

Despite a discernible shift in the attitudes and ambitions of many young women interviewed during the focus groups, the imposition of strict moral and behavioural codes continue to exert a considerable influence and is often experienced as a significant restriction on personal autonomy. Moreover, the progressive attitudes and desire for greater freedom expressed by some were balanced by the more conservative and traditional views of other young women, indicating a more basic and intra-generational schism in collective attitudes towards employment and marriage. These divisions are based upon observable differences in lifestyle and adherence to older notions of respectability. One woman recounted how she had ceased working after marriage to conform to cultural expectations, recalling that "I worked for two years then I got married and I've never had to work since, that is how it is with us – the husband looks after us". Another young woman highlighted the advantages of following customary gender roles in comparison to the vagaries of low income menial work arguing:

> "Look love why would you want to go out and work when you've got chavvies to look after and a nice husband bringing home the vonga [money]? It's my place to keep the home nice and that's what I'm proud to do."

The extent of local social ties with peers in a broadly similar socioeconomic position correlated with the desire for a life different from their parents, with those more immersed in neighbourhood-based networks more likely to express differing or more progressive attitudes.

This tendency also displayed ethnic variations and was more noticeable amongst young Romany women than Irish Traveller girls. Among the latter group there was a tendency to articulate more conservative views and a greater tendency to accept the status quo, contemplating early marriage and perhaps movement into a trailer with their new spouse, or travel to Ireland, with these young women often expressing sentiments that were qualitatively different from the Gypsy respondents. Indeed Irish Traveller respondents of all ages generally appeared to retain closer connections to a nomadic way of life than did Gypsies, who tended to have been settled for considerably longer periods of time. Given the shorter history of settlement amongst our Irish Traveller respondents and parental histories which frequently consisted of movement between housing and sites, it was perhaps unsurprising that a number of young women expressed no desire to adapt in order to adhere more closely to 'settled' norms. One young Irish Traveller girl interviewed as part of the employment study cited above (Greenfields, 2007b) noted:

> "... well, as part of our tradition we marry early on so you imagine we only have a certain amount of time to do well. I'm 19 and I only have a certain amount of time to have a job. I can't spend years and years training when I only earn the minimum wage. I have to do as much as I can before I get married."

Irish Traveller women (of all ages) were also less likely to report friendships outside of the travelling community, although occasionally Irish Traveller and Romany Gypsy girls formed social relationships and in some cases were connected through intercommunity marriages. In Chapters Seven and Eight it was posited that there were gendered differences in social and spatial practices, with housed males more likely to develop friendships (in school, work and through shared social activities such as football and boxing) with boys and young men from other communities, some of which continued into adulthood and were more likely to be geographically dispersed rather than (or as well as) being highly localised. With young women, social networks were more likely to be based in the immediate vicinity and there appeared to be a lessening of out-group contacts as they entered adulthood. Cassidy et al (2006) identified similar patterns in their study of the inter-ethnic friendships of second and third generation immigrant groups, with boys from minority ethnic communities tending to gain more friends from other ethnic and social groups as they became older and left school, whilst the opposite occurred for young women as following the transition to adulthood and marriage they withdrew more into their own community networks.

Nevertheless, it is difficult to generalise from our sample, since the composition of social networks and levels of intercommunity relations are shaped by various exogenous factors such as the proportion of the local housed Traveller population in specific neighbourhoods, the length of time which such communities have been established, and the historical and contemporary nature of relations with other social groups resident in the same locality (see Chapters Three and Seven). As discussed in greater detail below, many young people who have grown up in housing have formed distinctive age-segmented and locality-based groupings and cohorts, which often include relatively large numbers of 'mixed marriages' (Burrell, 2008; Duncan and Edwards, 1999). In such contexts hybridised identities emerge and become solidified, in the same way as clusters of friendship groups appear amongst young mothers in 'mixed race' partnerships or parenting relationships whose networks vary significantly in terms of ethnic heterogeneity from those of their parents' generations (Caballero, 2010; Okitikpi, 2009).

In contrast, young men expressed a higher degree of conservatism in their attitudes, which perhaps originates in the perceived advantages of living in what is still, by the standards of the wider society, a highly patriarchal community that retains a sharp division of gender roles. Certainly young men espoused a more explicit determination to return to an 'authentic' nomadic lifestyle and to affirm a way of life followed by their grandparents and parents. During the focus groups boys and young men expressed a stronger adherence to accustomed cultural practices than did the females, for example, attending cultural events was given a high priority, as one boy commented, "we go to the horse fairs a lot and that's where all the Travellers go – that's what I want to keep on doing". In Kornblum's (1975) study of Gypsy family life in a shanty town outside Paris he noted a lack of generational conflict, with adolescents taking pride in family solidarity and identifying their futures with those of their families. In our studies the sense of affinity with their cultural heritage and with the worldview bestowed on them by older generations was markedly more apparent in males, who in many cases envisioned their adult lives as marking a return to a 'traditional' nomadic life. One teenage boy in the South East who had spent most of his life on the same housing estate reported that "I'd love to live in a trailer – leave here [house] go travelling and live like a real Traveller on a site". Another expressed similar and widely held ambitions noting that "I'd like them [local authority] to build a Travellers site. Let us Travellers go driving when we're 16. So then we can go travelling when we're 16 and not wait till we're 18 and [we can] take our own trailer". Most also stressed a preference for continuing the types of work and employment practices of their fathers and uncles characterised by family-based self-employment. A teenage Irish Traveller male interviewed in the South East said:

> "Look, you just want to be out – leave schooling and be working with your family – that's what Traveller men – boys and fathers do – so like [working in] plastering for the boys and bricklaying and things like that."

Thus a strongly gendered split was apparent among young people in conceptualising Gypsy or Traveller identity, with boys elevating and reifying nomadism, caravan dwelling, traditional patterns of work and family relationship as markers of 'authentic' collective identity. Females by contrast were more likely to acknowledge that 'authenticity' does not necessarily mean that traditional practices and attitudes remain unchanged. The views of the following young woman, who has grown up in housing, suggests that gendered differences in the commitment to caravan dwelling and in corresponding notions of authenticity are informed by the daily realities that nomadism versus settlement offered her as a potential wife and a mother:

> "... it is changing – but that's not necessarily a bad thing – not that the old ones would agree with us on it – but I like my comforts, maybe travel a bit in the summer, house in the winter but I want some choice thank you – not married at 16, a baby a year and kept on moving on, no way to see the doctor, nothing but trouble – but it don't mean I'm not a Traveller."

Although young men were generally less likely than girls to challenge the status quo or indicate that there were certain aspects of 'traditional' culture which they found difficult to accept or which could limit their autonomy, one young man noted that:

> "... if you want to do something different – like say you said you wanted to be a gavver [police officer] like – well your Da' would just murder you – you'd be beat – like you couldn't do that and like I know people what aren't Travellers and they're not getting married and having a wife and babies when they're 19 – not that I'm saying it is wrong."

Indeed two young Gypsy men who took part in focus groups indicated the tension between older notions of masculinity that valorises traditional work and gender roles, stressing the collectivity over the individual, and their own personal ambitions not to remain uneducated and workless like many of their older relatives. One teenage boy in the South West noted: "I would prefer not to leave school really young as those that do won't be able to read or write and my uncle is a grown man and still can't read or write". This generation of young Gypsy men is the first to experience this dilemma as it would not have occurred amongst previous generations who lived more communal and inter-mutual lives, where family-based education combined with developing skill sets relevant to a nomadic life and seasonal working patterns were the norm. One focus group participant, a 15-year-old boy in the South East, remarked:

> "I think boys have more pressure than the girls ... well, some people say about going to school and some people laugh at that. Then I think the boys have more pressure 'cos they're not working with their dads [when there is no work] and then, that's it really – they think you're gay if you stay on – or there's work and you're supposed to get married and support a wife."

Nevertheless and despite the antipathy and suspicion of formal education expressed by many Gypsies and Travellers, far-reaching changes to labour markets, the formalisation of previously casual work relationships and the necessity of paper qualifications for most trades means that increasing numbers of Gypsy and Traveller parents are encouraging boys in particular to learn a trade or to obtain skilled tradesmen qualifications (Ryder and Greenfields, 2010). Parental attitudes to education and qualifications therefore encompass elements of cultural adaptation and conservatism. Education is viewed instrumentally in so far as it ensures individual and group survival, while emphasising practical over academic skills that allow for the continuation of self-employed family-based working patterns (Smith and Greenfields, 2012). Many studies of young Gypsies and Travellers report that young people are highly likely to leave school early, citing a lack of engagement with the curriculum, racism and/or family pressures as the primary reasons for early exit (Derrington and Kendall, 2004; Cemlyn et al, 2009). By contrast a number of housed young people emphasised a burgeoning ambition to attain qualifications and maximise their options in the sphere of employment. Despite the frequency of poor relations that exist between Gypsies/Travellers and educational establishments, if schools and colleges are culturally aware and instigate positive relationships with their Gypsy and Traveller students, attitudes to education are more positive. The following Romany male for example, who was attending a vocational training course at a local Further Education college at the time of interview, reported:

> "At the college I go to they're really amazing, they always talk to us about it [Gypsy culture] ... They aren't like – [some] people – but the ones at our college ... they accept us as us and talk to us as us – and that's alright – that's just normal."

Hybridisation and cultural identity

A high percentage of young people born into housing opted to identify themselves using the generic term 'Traveller', as a metonym for their cultural heritage, prior to confirming their 'ethnicity' as (for example) Romany Gypsy or Irish Traveller. Accordingly, for young people who differ little from their non-Gypsy peers, use of the term 'Traveller' has the dual function of grounding the speaker's status as a member of a 'non-sedentary' people whilst demarcating the speaker from 'the other' amongst whom they reside. By identifying themselves as a member of the Gypsy or Traveller community a young person in turn creates a series of expectations (amongst their elders, peers and outside agents) in relation to their behaviours, attitudes and adherence to specific sets of norms and values; albeit the generationally specific manner in which those attributes are interpreted and performed may lead to inter-generational tensions (Epstein and Heizler, 2009).

It was indicated above (and in Chapter Seven) that where young Gypsies and Travellers share social space and a similar framework of opportunities with youth from other social groups, commonalities in lived experience propagate a sense of solidarity that cuts across ethnic boundaries. It is clear that younger cohorts of housed Gypsies and Travellers were in the process of constructing a hybridised identity which displayed greater affiliation with youth culture and neighbourhood networks than did their parents' generation. As discussed in Chapter Six many older respondents, particularly those who moved from sites into housing, emphasised that residence in housing is 'unnatural' and equated nomadism with an inherited trait or as part of their 'nature'. One participant in the South East, for example, argued that "we're not meant for housing. We were born to roam the roads, it's our way", thus articulating a hierarchical concept of 'natural' behaviour that parallels models of scientific racism, upon which a similar archetypal image of the 'true Gypsy' was constructed (Gheorghe, 1997; Willems, 1997). For older participants who had 'settled' into housing and typically had less immediate access to the visible markers of cultural capital than their sited relatives, discourse around the central trope of 'travel' centred on the time frame since their last period of travelling, the extent of their travelling prior to movement into 'bricks and mortar' and of their own and relatives' history of residence in caravans. Moreover narratives of one's (or immediate relatives') birth 'on the road' were frequently utilised to buttress claims of 'authenticity' and to highlight the distress and traumatic impact at feeling trapped and "as though I'm in prison" in housing. Whilst there is no doubting the genuine distress and pain felt by individuals who had been forcibly settled, the extent of dislocation and the alien nature of life in housing also represent another marker of authenticity that contributes to a sense of collective difference from their non-Gypsy neighbours and facilitates processes of social closure.

To a certain extent the constituent elements of ethnic identity articulated by younger respondents' mirrored those of their elders, while also diverging from those understandings in certain important aspects. As discussed above, amongst younger people (particularly boys) the trope of nomadism and 'site life' remained a salient element of their identity, with discourse around experiences of travelling prominent as were aspirations to live in caravans when they reached adulthood and positioning of the self in relation to relatives who still live on sites or who travel for work or cultural reasons. One young man in the South West, for example, proudly announced that "we've got lots of family living on sites in the East counties – don't really see much of them and they don't travel much but they are on a site". Another, despite living in housing himself, made reference to his more 'authentic' relatives which in turn legitimised his own claims to Gypsy identity, "my aunt and uncle, they are the real thing, they have a wagon parked up in their garden – they live in a bungalow but they got the wagon alright and it comes out for the fairs". As such, many young people who had grown up in housing were confident in their ethnic identity drawing upon the trope of nomadism whilst still acknowledging the hybridity of their own situation.

Many of the younger participants were sensitive concerning discourses from within their own community, and also in the wider society, that de-legitimised the identity of housed Gypsies and Travellers. These youth were adamant that identity is not wholly dependent on nomadism or caravan dwelling but is situationally shaped. While travelling was recognised as an important element of cultural identity, focus group participants were more likely to prioritise ethnic origins, familial descent, adherence to core cultural values and norms and an awareness of changing community dynamics. One young woman for example noted: "I hate it when people say 'I was a Gypsy' [or] 'my nan was a Gypsy' [or] 'I am a Gypsy because I live in a trailer'". Another young man was equally critical of the association of 'real' Gypsies with an unchanging lifestyle consisting of nomadic caravan dwelling, while expressing a desire to live such a lifestyle himself:

> "What bugs me is [the assumption] that just because we live in a house and don't go travelling that you're not Travellers. It doesn't mean that at all – you're still Gypsies even though you don't go travelling. My nan always lived in wagons and when I get older I want to live in them and go travelling – I don't want to live in a house."

The issue of changing intercommunity relations over time was one which around a third of young people identified as significant in terms of sense of local identity. Despite the casual racism that most youngsters experienced, particularly at school, there was a general consensus that relations between young people on the estates where they lived were not especially problematic, in stark contrast to the largely negative encounters recounted by their older relatives (Chapters Seven and Eight). Such divergent experiences indicate differing multi-generational experiences of racism, marginalisation and social segregation within particular neighbourhoods. One young man for example, in contrast to the emphasis placed on the conflictual and antagonistic nature of intercommunity relations on his estate stressed by his parents' generation, noted:

> "No offence like but you don't want to listen to all the old people tell you – it's not so bad living here. People stay around here a long time, been born here. It's alright really if you don't go looking for trouble like what some people do."

Others noted the possibilities offered by the development of social ties and relations outside the Gypsy/Traveller community as wider 'bridging' ties yield new sources of information broadening cultural horizons through intercommunity exchange (Granovetter, 1973; Wellman and Wortley, 1990). One young woman who had entered into a relationship with a non–Gypsy, reflected on how this had both broadened her network of social relations and altered her perceptions. In spite of allowing this young woman to transcend the close-knit nature of her social ties prior to meeting her boyfriend and the exposure to a different social world that this had entailed, she also felt that it had diminished her status as a 'proper' Traveller as she no longer adhered so completely to cultural expectations and norms:

> "I reckon that in the last couple of years I've got out more and meeting friends that aren't Travellers. I used to be with my family all the time and used to be a proper Traveller. I used to sit down with them but over these last two years because I've been going out with a boy and he's not a Traveller I started to pick up their [gorjer] ways and started using posh words."

Another young Gypsy woman identified several advantages to socialising with non-Gypsies, in particular the seemingly more permissive climate and the greater degree of personal liberty granted to young 'gorjer' girls compared to the strict social and moral boundaries enforced by her own parents:

> "I quite like being with gorjers. There's not all the noise and the shouting and that and they're not so strict, like if I wanted to see a boy then his people would have to talk to my mum and dad because they'd want to know. But it's not so serious with gorjers you can talk to someone's brother at their house and it's not like – can't be in the same room as them."

In the more heterogeneous networks found among younger housed Gypsies and Travellers, local peer groups based on life-long social bonds were important reference groups. Shared formative experiences and focal concerns combined with a similarly marginalised social status generated a collective solidarity that transcended ethnic boundaries. Gilroy (2004) refers to 'boisterous everyday interactions' between young people from different ethnic groups in urban settings. Similarly, in the housing estates in our study areas, like Gilroy, we were able to identify a

> ... convivial culture where racial and ethnic differences have been rendered unremarkable ... they are able to become 'ordinary'. Instead of adding to the premium of race as political ontology and economic fate, people discover that

the things which really divide them [from their elders and other populations] are much more profound: taste; lifestyle; leisure preferences. (Gilroy, 2004, pp 39–40)

In such contexts, youth cultural formations can emerge through a hybridisation whereby aspects of style, linguistic codes and argot are appropriated by one group or exchanged and refashioned between groups to denote a collective identity in the public domain (Cotterell, 1996). The adoption of Gypsy lifestyles and characteristics by members of mainstream society has a long history which has frequently troubled the authorities (see further Chapter Three). Okely (1983, pp 3–4) notes that in 1562 the death penalty was extended not only to those in the company of 'Egyptians' (Gypsies) but also to those 'counterfeiting, transforming or disguising themselves by their Apparel, Speech or other Behaviour'. In *Capital*, Marx observed the appeal of 'the gipsy life' arguing that 'Coarse freedom, a noisy jollity and obscenest impudence give attractions to the gang' (cited by Bancroft, 2005, p 6) while the emergence of 'New' Travellers from the 1960s onwards represents the latest manifestation of this trend. Similar interactions among young people have been documented in both the UK and the US in relation to white working- and middle-class appropriation of black urban cultural behaviours and styles (Hebdidge, 1981; Reay et al, 2007). As far as we are aware, nobody has yet explored the 'Gypsy wannabe' identity. Thus in one focus group in the South West, a young woman who attended with a group of Romany Gypsies and who in her accent and intonation, style of dress and choice of jewellery could 'pass' as a member of the community, was pointed out during the discussion as being "gorjer – but she's got a Gypsy baby", whilst in relation to another young woman it was noted that "She's Irish [Traveller] behind you. But let me explain to you – her Mum's boyfriend's a Gypsy". When pressed to identify what the 'new' form of housed identity consisted of, there was a general opinion that in estates which had a large number of Gypsy and Traveller residents, this had left its mark (both sartorial and social) on the surrounding populations.

One young man perceptively observed that for 'wannabes', Gypsies are admired for retaining core elements resonant of 'traditional' working-class culture before the central pillars of family, work and community were eroded by large-scale social, industrial and labour market changes (Smith, 2005). He noted: "well, they [other young people] are quite jealous of us – we have family, we have community – and they want to be like us". Thus the emulation of Gypsy styles and community structures must be located in the context of a hegemonic middle-class disdain towards the working class as witnessed in the media presentation of white working-class people (Jones, 2011); the loss of many traditional 'blue-collar' forms of manual work; decline of the nuclear family unit and the fragmentation of working-class communities. In this sense such imitative and derivative forms of behaviour may symbolise a nostalgic and 'magical recovery of community' similar to that identified in Clarke's analysis of skinheads in late 1960s inner London (Clarke, 1993). Another participant argued that the security that results from membership of close-knit yet extensive networks and the violent stereotypes that are attributed to Gypsies and Travellers was actually a desirable form of cultural capital on deprived housing estates (see Chapter Seven), "they like it that we don't take no nonsense from nobody", while a young woman added, "and they want to be like us – to dress like us – to wear the jewellery".

The performers of such a 'wannabe' role, despite circulating in the same friendship circles, are not completely accepted by the group to which they aspire and they are recognised as inauthentic by some young people. Thus 'wannabes' were the subject of considerable mockery and contempt: "who do they think they are fooling? They want to be us, to be like us, to dress like us and talk like us, but they can't be us". Another participant detected an element of hypocrisy in 'gorjer' appropriation of Gypsy/ Traveller identity:

> "People say 'oh, they're Travellers that, Travellers this, Travellers the other' [said in a disparaging tone of voice], really deep down inside they'd love to be a Traveller 'cos they dress up like Travellers, they wear gold earrings, they talk like us."

Increasing convergence between Gypsy and non-Gypsy youth was also reported by a Romany community worker in the South West who observed that "the police, the council, sometimes they say 'can't you get your young people to do X or stop doing Y?' and we say 'Z isn't a Traveller, or they're gorjer boys' and they say 'it's hard to tell nowadays'". Similar complaints were echoed by several parents who reported that "wannabes are the ones I've got no time for – causing trouble around here so the gavvers thinks it's our lads". Our exploration to date, suggest that the 'wannabe' phenomenon is largely confined to young males rather than girls, whom (as in the case above), may to some extent gain membership of the Gypsy/Traveller community through marriage, or through having a 'Gypsy baby' and thus becoming part of the wider extended family network within an estate, as explored further in the next section.

Mixed families

That notable rates of exogamous marriage and partnering have occurred between Gypsies/Travellers and non-Gypsies, both historically and contemporaneously, has been remarked on previously (Chapters Three and Eight). In the focus groups, approximately 60 per cent of young participants in the South West area and half of those in the South East referred to relatives or close family members from outside the travelling community or 'half and half'. One young Gypsy woman (a lone parent with two children) who had grown up on a housing estate in our South West area reflected thoughtfully on the changing dynamics of inter-personal relations in her local area, noting that "there are various mixed marriages on the estate between gorjers and Travellers and I think it is quite healthy". The prevalence of generally favourable (or neutral) attitudes towards inter-ethnic marriage and partnering constituted a further source of inter-generational conflict as among many older people preference was expressed for endogamy, with intermarriage largely discouraged, "you should really marry your own breed"; "well, Travelling people only like to marry up with other Travellers". Indeed for many older interviewees, even when married to individuals from other communities themselves, there was a frequent implication that the relationship had either met with some disapproval from 'traditional' kin or that it remained a taboo topic and not to be discussed publicly.

Several young women indicated that there could be substantial advantages to inter-ethnic relationships, given the patriarchal attitudes of some of their male peers. One young woman in the South West pointed out, "we should really go out with our own breed but if you go out with someone who's not a Gypsy they might treat you better". Rather than submitting to traditional gender roles and domesticity, many young women were engaged in carving greater freedom and independence for themselves by eschewing the male's autocratic control over their households and seeking relationships outside their own community. Another young woman added that "Gypsy boys can take advantage because they expect you to be cleaning all the time and there when they get in". A more general realignment in family structures and a rise in lone parent households is occurring, which though less pronounced than amongst non-Gypsy/Traveller communities mirrored family trends in their neighbourhoods. As a result some young women (particularly where their parents had divorced) reported that their own mothers actively encouraged them to seek relationships outside the Gypsy/Traveller community (the corollary being that many parents express a preference for their sons to marry within the community). One young woman in the South East said that "my Mam says do not do it – do not get married to a travelling boy so my sister is on the lookout for a nice one [non-Gypsy/Traveller] with a car and that to marry".

Despite the length of settlement among family members and extensive intermarriage outside the Gypsy/Traveller community, overwhelmingly young people emphasised their Gypsy identity. During the course of the focus groups many participants of significantly mixed heritage, and whose families had been 'settled' for over 40 years, reiterated proudly that "I'm a Traveller, me" and their peer group – who were often also the children of inter-married, long-housed couples – similarly stressed their membership of and identification with the community, whilst simultaneously noting that "my dad's a gorjer" or "my sister's dad's mum's a Traveller and our mum is a Traveller so we are too" without seeing any contradiction in their foregrounding of one side of their heritage at the expense of another. Platt (2009) notes that one in ten children are now living in some form of 'mixed race' family at home and there are clear parallels between our findings and discourse around identity politics among children who are 'visibly' of dual-heritage or members of 'mixed race' families (Tizard and Pheonix, 2002; Song, 2003). Although Gypsies and Travellers are not explicitly referred to in any of the existing literature, findings from GTAAs indicate that young people from Gypsy and Traveller communities who live in housing are significantly more likely to live in a dual-heritage household (predominantly of 'white' gorjer/Traveller heritage) than the aggregate figure of 10 per cent cited by Platt.

In Caballero et al's (2008) study of parenting of young people of mixed heritage it was noted that family members could act both as a resource to strengthen a child or young adult's sense of identity or as a hindrance, disrupting connections with the 'other' side of their family. One woman in the South East highlighted the tensions inherent in 'mixed' marriages, which was especially pertinent given social attitudes towards Gypsies and Travellers and the latter's perceptions of non-Gypsy society:

> "I feel sorry for them to tell you the truth – like if there's family trouble then they got the one side of the family giving it 'Gypsies this, pikeys that' and the other side going 'bloody gorjers, you know what they're like' and they're

like caught in the middle – but they're all still family so you can't just walk away from it."

Despite the sometimes conflicting influences from family members, Caballero et al (2008) also note that even where parents did not share the same approach to cultural difference and identity issues, this did not mean that their children were necessarily in conflict. One young woman who had lived her entire life in housing commented on her enjoyment in engaging with both sides of her heritage: "when I was younger my Granny used to take me away on holiday and we used to stay in a caravan for maybe two weeks ... go travelling to the horse fairs and that". Indeed, in common with Caballero et al's findings, a number of young focus group participants identified the ways in which having parents or relatives from different communities enabled them to appreciate a more diverse set of experiences and explore different aspects of their identity:

> "when we lived on a site me and my sister we used to go and stay with my Gran who isn't a Traveller and she had a house and the stairs were funny to get used to but I loved having the taps to turn on and off and the bath to play in."

Neighbourhood attachment and inter-ethnic solidarities

The strength of neighbourhood ties for those young people should therefore not be underestimated, as the sharing of social space and similar experiences can act to transcend boundaries which might otherwise exist as communities develop collective strategies and responses to marginalisation. The significance of neighbourhood as a generator of community identity was considered by Earle and Phillips (2009) whose study of male prison inmates found that although race was a factor which featured in everyday discourse, there was a high degree of inter-ethnic social mixing as shared attachments to aspects of popular culture reached across ethnic boundaries. Indeed, they noted that primary identification tended to focus on the geographical area in which the young men had lived prior to being sentenced. Accordingly, they referred to inmates as expressing 'postcode pride' or 'neighbourhood nationalism' based around particular estates or streets often associated with sub-cultural gang membership, enabling young men to form networks and attain symbolic capital through their relationship to an area and community. Nevertheless this process, while facilitating greater levels of intercommunity relations, may also increase their collective exclusion when such interactions occur within spatially marginalised neighbourhoods among different social groups whose lives are characterised by a similar landscape of limited employment opportunities, government training schemes and unemployment. Under these conditions social networks may surmount ethnic boundaries but will remain spatially localised and age segmented, as traditional methods of social reproduction and the cultural supports that formerly provided young people with gender specific routes to adulthood have been progressively weakened (Strathdee, 2005).

In support of the contention that attachment to locality may over time prove a stronger 'social glue' than ethnic identity, based on intergenerational differences in socialisation, disparities in formative experiences and in the more heterogeneous social relations of younger generations of Gypsies and Travellers, over time a potential exists for diminished rates of intra-community cohesion. Increasing segmentation consists not only in relation to forms of accommodation (site or housing) but also the areas in which young people reside. Moreover, despite the aping of elements of Gypsy and Traveller culture by some disenfranchised working-class youth this is not a one-way process and some internalisation of the values and norms of the wider society is perhaps an inevitable outcome of living in housing with prolonged and close spatial proximity to non-Gypsies. One male Romany elder, resident on a housing estate, observed the manner in which the material aspirations of many younger Gypsies and Travellers differed from previous generations, accompanied by a depreciation of the inter-mutual solidarity that is the foundation of Gypsy and Traveller society:

> "You've got classes now … nowadays there is upper class Travellers, middle class Travellers and working class Travellers … what it all boils down to is this: when we was falsely settled, what happened is we try to imitate those in housing so now we've come into that modernist world where chavvies want flash motors they want to present themselves in a flash way but before we could only have what a horse could pull plus ourselves and our family … at the end of the day we're all the same breed."

A female participant of the same focus group added:

> "We're all Travellers, we're no different but some people are up their own gearbox. I don't know why. I have known

people who walk past me and never say hello – and I've known them for years."

However, as discussed in Chapter Seven, it is mistaken to posit the extinction of Gypsy culture based on a decline in nomadic lifestyles and an increasing convergence in terms of appearance and aspirations with working-class youth from a variety of ethnic groups. As demonstrated above, a sense of identification with Gypsy and Traveller culture and identity remains strong, even where young people have spent most or all of their lives in housing. This occurs because while the underlying cultural structure of life is shared, Gypsy culture is situationally shaped, producing many variations depending on the particular environment (Silverman, 1988, p 273). We conclude this section by highlighting one particularly telling exchange between two young women (aged 18 and 23). In their discussion the women illustrated the changing nature of Traveller identities across generations, which challenged the mistaken assumption of policy makers that settling Britain's nomadic peoples into housing will result in their ultimate assimilation and disappearance:

> "Don't you think things have changed from the old Travellers to our generation? Cos you knew most of them all your life, didn't you?"

> "Yes, I did – but what I think is happening is that because we have third, second and first generations on the estate, there is the culture, to use the term, is evolving, so where you had the original, its becoming its own culture on the estate, so you've got the Travellers of thirty, forty years ago that originally came onto the estate all those years back and now you've got the generations coming on and the culture is evolving."

Note
[1] See Chapter Four, Table 6 for details of this sample.

TEN

Conclusion

Social inclusion, diversity and cultural resilience

As outlined at the beginning of this book, the key objectives of this study were to highlight the main causes behind the settlement of Britain's travelling communities and to explore the individual and collective manifestations of this trend. We have discussed the ways in which longer-term processes of settlement and sedenterisation have occurred in tandem with wider processes of urbanisation and industrialisation. In this study we have made manifest the stark impact of the implementation of successive post-war government policies, transforming an entire culture through making nomadic lifestyles progressively untenable.

The enforced immobilisation of the majority of Britain's Gypsies and Travellers and their continuing marginalisation highlights a number of basic contradictions in what is purported to be a diverse yet socially inclusive nation while raising fundamental questions over the nature of inclusivity and 'tolerance'. Enforced settlement (which, as the empirical sections of the text testify, has been the majority experience for housed Gypsies and Travellers) has for many of our participants been a deeply dispiriting experience which has left a legacy of social exclusion, bewilderment and resentment mirroring the narratives of Aboriginal peoples in America, Australia and elsewhere (ALRC, 1986; Manson et al, 1996). The relentless drive to sedentarisation regardless of the human cost, begs the question of whether political support for 'choice', minority lifestyles and endorsements of equal rights is motivated primarily by political expedience, as a diversion from more deep-seated economic and class-based social divisions and a malaise in citizen engagement across the UK

McGhee (2005) suggests that 'intolerance of intolerance' represents more than political 'lip service' and is in fact part of a wider political project striving towards commonality in respect of the 'shared values and standards of an emergent citizenship for a multi-ethnic, multi-lingual and multi-faith Britain' (2005, p 12). Whilst on the surface this may seem laudable, it does raise the problematic spectre of a mono-cultural amorphous model which submerges class, culture and individual identities and practices. These policy goals are also continually frustrated both by subversive individuality and undermined, as Tam (2005) notes, by the spread of insecurity and social fragmentation engendered by economic forces and an increasing concentration of power. Striking a balance between commonality and diversity, Tam argues, requires more than policies aimed at building 'community cohesion' and encouraging civic engagement, since focusing policies on civil society and its associational networks neglects the economic and political context which shape divisions in civil society (Fine, 2001). This is ever more pertinent at the time of writing, when Britain (even more specifically England) is facing savage cuts in public services, reduction of available housing support and rapidly spiralling pressures not only on the most marginalised members of society but even those who had previously regarded themselves as relatively secure.

When considering collective and individual survival in times of crisis, we suggest that in some senses Gypsies and Travellers are better adapted than many other populations, a legacy of generations of resilience and access to strong family support networks. In such an environment many of the non-Gypsies amongst whom they live, to echo the words of a young respondent quoted in Chapter Nine, may indeed 'want to be us', and access some of the networks of reciprocity and loyalty which we have identified throughout this study. Herbert Gans (1962) amongst others has highlighted how external processes and threats can foster intergroup relations and a sense of neighbourhood identity that can transcend ethnic boundaries, even when this coexists with a degree of mutual avoidance, suspicion and mistrust between those groups. Increased intergroup relations as discussed, however, do little to advance collective interests when they occur between groups who are spatially separated into areas of concentrated deprivation and who remain similarly excluded socially, economically and politically. Instead, as witnessed during the widespread unrest across England in August 2011, it is more likely that communities may erupt if the context of their exclusion is theorised without listening to the narratives of those most affected (Power, 2011). Redressing exclusion and the attendant political and media scapegoating of residents of impoverished areas will thus not be addressed by strategies to foster greater sociability between inhabitants of poor areas (in moves frequently branded as outcomes of the 'Big Society', see Saba, 2011) but require a 'progressive solidarity' and a commitment to social justice and equality which includes all members of society.

The case for progressive solidarity is grounded on our experience of how socio-economic pressures, left unchecked, can weaken communal and democratic bonds so much that citizens are reduced to vulnerable individuals in the face of any challenge that comes their way. People must be empowered both by the government acting to limit and reduce the widening gaps between the powerful and the powerless, and through government-citizen partnerships to enable those with relatively little power to make their influence count. (Tam, 2005, p 22)

On virtually a global scale, Gypsies and Travellers represent the most extreme example of exclusion and discrimination in contemporary society and are the most disadvantaged group on many domains, representing, in the words of former Czech President Vaclav Havel, (paraphrasing Brearley, 1996, p 1) a 'litmus test not for democracy but for civil society' (*New York Times*, 1993). The sobering nature of Havel's statement forces consideration of the contemporary politics of inclusion and exclusion and the precise nature of equality of access afforded to particular groups. This begs the question of to whom influence in economic and decision-making spheres is extended and on what basis. Despite the exponential growth in interest in the circumstances of Europe's largest minority group, Gypsies, Roma and Travellers have clearly failed to benefit from the limited gains made by other ethnic minority groups in Britain recent years (Ryder et al, 2011). On mainland Europe meanwhile, the rise of anti-Gypsyism continues ever more virulently (Council of Europe, 2012).

While conflict between settled and nomadic people has been a constant theme in human history, in recent years these have reached new heights as a consequence of economic globalisation, an intensification of capitalist development and the intersection of states' and multinational corporations' interests (Chapter Two). These combined forces have put increasing pressure on the rights of nomadic peoples to use traditional itinerant territories (Gilbert, 2007). In Britain and other western nations these pressures have occurred alongside what Young (1999) presciently terms a shift from *inclusive* towards *exclusive* societies or 'from a society whose accent was on assimilation and incorporation towards one that separates and excludes' (1999, p 7). Exclusive societies, he asserts, are based on a *cordon sanitaire* – or a clear line – between a shrinking core of the population with relatively stable employment and biographical trajectories and a heterogeneous out-group who symbolise all of society's ills. The out-group, Young states, is spatially divided from the core group and herded into areas where they are regarded as:

> ... the social impurities of the late modern world ... victims of sanitizing and moralizing geographies reminiscent of the nineteenth century reformers. But unlike the reformers of the late nineteenth century up until the 1960s the goal is not to physically eliminate their areas and integrate their members into the body politics; it is to hold at bay and exclude. (Young, 1999, pp 19–20)

As demonstrated in this book, settlement into deprived and residualised areas of social and public housing has been the experience of the majority of Gypsies and Travellers relocated from sites or from the roadside. Whilst for many of our sample locality-based networks provide a vehicle for local solidarities and place-based identification, they also reinforce collective exclusion, a theme captured in W. J. Wilson's (1987) conceptual dyad of 'social concentration' (increasing spatial concentrations of poor and disadvantaged people) and 'social isolation' (from the wider society).

Although, within our sample, some respondents (largely owner occupiers) have made a successful transition into housing by refashioning traditional economic traits of flexibility, diversity and family-based self-employment to fit with a permanent residence and changing labour market demands, for many others, settlement on housing estates has led to concentrations of social exclusion. Many of the (particularly older) Gypsies and Travellers in our sample who are largely unqualified and under-skilled in conventional terms are virtually unemployable in an increasingly credential-based job market where qualifications, literacy and computer proficiency are required for the most menial of work (Smith and Greenfields, 2012). For these people, isolation from mainstream society may appear an almost insurmountable barrier – and one which many have no desire to cross. Institutional racism, the prevalence and toleration of negative stereotypes, the suppression of nomadism combined with insufficient site capacity and enforced settlement in housing thus lie at the heart of the intersectional disadvantages experienced by many members of this community. Cemlyn et al's (2009) comprehensive review for the Equalities and Human Rights Commission concludes that:

> The evidence of ... discrimination and a lack of equality for Gypsies and Travellers also reflects a lack of human

rights. Indeed, the review reveals the depth and extent of the denial of rights to Gypsies and Travellers throughout the domains explored and across civil/political, social/ economic, participatory and cultural rights … the lack of rights is mutually reinforcing: lack of a home undermines the right to family life and to freedom from degrading or unfair treatment and participation as citizens in economic, social and political life. (Cemlyn et al, 2009, pp 220–221)

Exploring the individual and collective outcomes of these trends involved delineating the distinctive gender and generational impacts of settlement and, for a group intrinsically defined in relation to nomadism, the implications of a more fixed residence on collective identity. In unpacking these complex threads of evolving identities we were repeatedly struck by the sophisticated and resourceful strategies utilised by individuals who frequently had little access to 'conventional' capitals yet who 'moved hell and high water' to keep their community structures, families and cultures intact; demonstrating yet again the skills of cultural bricolage and adaptability remarked upon by Acton (1974), Okely (1983) and others. A key element of this study consisted of consideration of the overlapping and frequently conflicting relations between our respondents and the white working-class communities whom they in many ways resemble closely, but from whom the older generation, in particular, sharply distinguished themselves.

As demonstrated in Chapter Three, though largely ignored in both historical and contemporary analyses of city life, there is a long history of house-dwelling Gypsies within certain urban neighbourhoods – partners in a process of symbiosis that has coloured the social, cultural and aesthetic fabric of those locales. Historic settlement patterns have been accompanied by an equally long process of encounter and exchange with the urban working classes and other marginal and peripatetic groups with whom an affinity in terms of certain 'focal concerns' exists (Miller, 1958). Thus the often porous nature of cultural boundaries while 'destabilizing existing cultures and cultural identities, [and] enabling us to recognise their complex and intertwined histories' (Hopper, 2007, p 146) has not led to absorption into the ranks of the urban poor, despite the prediction of 'cultural degeneration' and the 'extinction' of Gypsies and Travellers predicted so confidently by 19th- and early 20th-century contributors to the *Journal of the Gypsy Lore Society* and more recently by Arnold (1970) and Charlemagne (1984). As considered in Chapter Nine, increasing spatial proximity has, though, inevitably resulted in a process of hybridisation, particularly among younger generations of Gypsies and Travellers, a complicating turn which, as we discuss in our consideration of 'wannabes', has caused confusion amongst 'authorities' who claim to be unable to distinguish between 'gorjer' and Gypsy; and a sense of superiority amongst Travellers themselves who are complacent in the uniqueness of their culture.

However, regardless of the blurring of cultural boundaries and increasingly high levels of intermarriage between communities, for the vast majority of Gypsies and Travellers, a sense of collective identity has been consistently maintained and embodied in shared social practices and orientations to everyday life. While these demonstrate clear generational differences based in the divergence of lifecycle experiences between those who have been largely or wholly socialised in conventional housing, and an older generation whose formative years were spent on the road and/or on sites, participants across the life-course adhered to a core set of values that are mediated through spatially bounded networks. These act as conduits of information, collective knowledge and understandings through which an awareness of group difference is produced and which encompasses 'collective action through routines and conventions that frame, order and provide meaning within and between associated networks' (Southerton, 2002, p 191).

We suggest that the decline of customary lifestyles and economic practices is also apposite to questions surrounding the ability of social networks to devise culturally grounded strategies to offset such fundamental changes in modes of living. The concept of cultural resilience – the capacity to forge adaptive trajectories in the face of adversity – is of paramount importance in comprehending the processes which either assist newly housed Gypsy and Traveller communities to adapt, or alternatively to experience negative and intergenerational personal and community impacts. Resilience is context dependent and can be promoted, or otherwise, by cultural milieu and social practices (Theron et al, 2011). For participants, the ability to reformulate spatially bounded networks and kinship connections within housing significantly alleviate many of the difficulties of transition and adjustment we outlined in Chapter Six. Thus community structures are a vital source of support and solidarity while serving as a locus for reaffirming collective identity in a new and often unfamiliar physical environmental. Social networks and access to a body of collective knowledge and the strategies that are communicated through such channels also provide a means of resisting dispersal and assimilation by facilitating the development of co-resident enclaves of housed

Gypsies and Travellers and sustaining high levels of mobility even within housing (Chapter Eight). The strategies operationalised represent 'everyday' forms of cultural resistance (Duncombe, 2002) or 'low profile techniques' through which groups lacking in political and economic power are able to 'deny or mitigate claims made by appropriating classes' (Scott, 1985, p 302). Zatta (1988, p 58) notes that from the perspective of Gypsies the difference between themselves and non-Gypsy society is that the latter can be manipulated and exploited without social censure or stigma, whereas similar behaviours towards members of their own communities would be regarded as unacceptable. Indeed such acts of exploitation are more likely to have a symbolic rather than economic value, as noted by Gmelch (1977), who observed that many Travellers regard negotiation with settled society as a battle of wits, with the ability to outwit the 'gorjer' a source of pride and social status. Similarly, among many participants in our studies, the capacity to resist policies antithetical to their way of life and to thwart the dictates of local government bureaucrats have an important symbolic value in raising self-esteem and avoiding the corrosion of identity. As one young Gypsy male in the South East focus group remarked:

> "My house is in front of me wherever I go that's where I live. Where I stay is where I lay. If I go out this door at night and sleep at his place that's where I live and if I go back home I live there. The council won't build us a site and [they have] got us all in houses but it's no different in the end. They can't stop me moving – I travel with my grandfather. Wherever he goes I go with him and when I'm back here I'm still moving. It works for me – so how are they [council] going to stop me?"

Whilst this young man like many others has formulated his strategy of resistance, the empirical sections of the text have repeatedly demonstrated how the more destructive impacts of settlement have deep-rooted individual and social dimensions. In presenting the findings we have deliberately avoided imposing external or 'etic' understandings of the meanings and significance of settlement for people who have a history of nomadism by placing their own perceptions and experiences in the foreground of the analysis. However, we argue here that misunderstandings arising from the application of 'gorjer' frameworks and understandings have distinguished the history of relations between Gypsies and the wider society. To give one recent example of conflicting world-views, the well-publicised eviction of the Dale Farm site in

Basildon, Essex, was justified in the eyes of many sedentary people on the grounds that the residents of the site had breached planning legislation and been offered 'alternative accommodation' (such as bricks and mortar housing) which they willfully rejected (Home, 2012). The implication was that Basildon Council had done their best to re-accommodate the Dale Farm families and the recalcitrant Travellers were to blame for pushing the council into a corner where they had no choice but to forcibly evict them. The evidence in this book and other publications cited within it, suggests that the Dale Farm Travellers turned down conventional housing for good reason.

Despite the supposed European adherence to respect for diversity and equality of treatment for minority groups discussed at the beginning of this chapter, Laungani (2002) identifies a significant counter-tendency: the increasing disposition among politicians, policy makers, psychologists and social workers to offer universalistic explanations of culturally specific behaviours. When these trends persist they ossify into negative stereotypes, mutual incomprehension and a punitive approach towards groups who cannot, or will not, be moulded into dominant notions of what is rational, appropriate and in the group's 'best interests'. It is within this context that the political and media response to the Dale Farm Travellers and the incomprehension surrounding their refusal to enter housing should be viewed.

> To assign an accurate meaning to the event one needs to be either an integral part of that cultural group, or to have acquired a close and intimate knowledge of the culture in question. Otherwise one is likely to fall into the trap of offering 'etic' (universal) explanations of an event which is uniquely 'emic' (culture-specific) in its construction. (Laungani, 2002, p 138)

Erikson (1995) notes that trauma has both centripetal and centrifugal forces simultaneously fragmenting people – as was apparent in our study in the cultural domain where clear tensions exist between cultural mores and precepts held by older community members and the evolving culture of younger Gypsies and Travellers raised on housing estates. Under such conditions:

> Because of old cultural inertia the legacy of earlier, and already obsolete culture survives the system for which it was functionally adequate, and for some time it coexists with the new culture thus becoming functionally inadequate for the

new system. The condition of cultural split or ambivalence provides a conducive background that can engender fully fledged cultural trauma. (Sztompka, 2000, p 463).

Despite the potential for intra-community schisms and polarisation highlighted by Sztompka, Erikson notes that traumatic events can also unite people by serving as 'a source of communality in the same way that common languages and common backgrounds can' (1995, p 186). This, he suggests, is not because communal trauma strengthens community bonds (on the contrary it more frequently weakens them), but because the shared experiences become the source of a common culture and sense of kinship, as we found when analysing discourse on eviction and accommodation trauma, coupled with almost mythologised memories of life 'on the road'. Subsequently, he continues, the shared experiences and a legacy of collective memories alter people's worldviews, engendering feelings of vulnerability, fatalism, vigilance and a heightened sense of impending disaster amongst those who have survived earlier dramatic shifts in fortune and cultural dislocation (Erikson, 1995, pp 190–5). One Gypsy woman in the South East, for example, expressed this collective mood poignantly during a focus group with her observation that:

> "All Gypsies in this country seem to be picking up, we don't know what it is and we're all getting together, we're all talking, we're on the phone to each other all over this country, something bad is going to happen to us. We're all picking it up … I was like it this morning and I said I need to tell you something we know there is something bad there … So we're waiting for the next concentration camp, who's going to build it, who's going to put us in it, who's going to exterminate us. We all know something is going to happen to us, we're just waiting for it."

Sztompka (2000, p 464) identifies two potential outcomes of such elemental and potentially detrimental changes in cultural practice – one is the *vicious cycle of cultural decline* and the other a *virtuous cycle of cultural reconstruction* (represented for example in the UK in the flourishing Gypsy, Traveller arts and music scene which has gone from strength to strength since the turn of the 21st century). Under the former scenario an obsolete culture is maintained through a retrospective preoccupation with the past, often coupled with self-destructive behaviours such as increased rates of substance misuse to dull the pain of cultural loss and social exclusion. Under the latter scenario, trauma is ameliorated through coping strategies and the eventual disappearance of the older cultural order through generational turnover. The purposeful, active and innovative strategies employed to resist sedentarisation and incorporation into 'gorjer' society utilised by participants in the studies reported here, along with the reformulation of Gypsy and Traveller identity articulated by younger community members, suggests the second outcome is occurring, at least amongst those individuals who have access to supportive, resilient community networks. We are witnessing a community in transition, with those members in housing both developing an evolving culture and dynamic of their own (and one, moreover, which operates in a circumstance of dialectic tension with the surrounding working-class community), and their peers resident on sites operating in different yet overlapping fields of experience where cultures will share similarities yet may ultimately become distinct, in a manner similar to that found amongst transnational diasporic communities and their relatives 'back home' (Vertovec, 2004). In contrast, for those individuals, more isolated, perhaps older, poorer or experiencing a number of personal traumas which impact on their resilience, the situation may be more bleak. As Breakwell (1986) suggests, individuals in those sets of circumstances experience a:

> ... threat to identity when the processes of identity, assimilation–accommodation and evaluation are, for some reason, unable to comply with the principles of continuity, distinctiveness and self-esteem which habitually guide their operation. (Breakwell, 1986, p 47)

Policy responses and recommendations

Accordingly, we suggest that a clear policy response is required to engage with the challenges inherent in allowing a community (however well developed in devising situationally specific adaptive and flexible responses to external pressures) to free-fall into unknown space. At the heart of the problem lies the failure of policy discourse and those agencies engaged with issues of ethnicity to recognise both the size and distinctiveness of housed Gypsy and Traveller communities given the tendency for these populations (in the eyes of local authorities) to be merged into the amorphous 'white' category and consigned to the hinterlands of poorly resourced, public housing. Where resistance to such labelling occurs, or Gypsies and Traveller seek to differentiate themselves from the communities within which they live, respondents frequently reported a general disinterest or incomprehension from public officials. It was reported that those officials often failed to understand how someone who appeared 'white', English speaking and British born and who lived in a house could be *unlike* their neighbours, and repeatedly misunderstood that conflicts which occurred (whether with 'authorities' or other residents) were frequently the outcomes of culture clashes (or even overt racism) rather than deliberate anti-social behaviour on the behalf of Traveller households.

Whilst, in some circumstances respondents reported that the concerns which brought them into contact with bureaucratic actors were taken into account, and local authorities and other agencies operated within a clear set of protocols, we were struck (even in localities with large, long-established Gypsy and Traveller populations) by the general lack of cultural awareness amongst both officials and other local residents. Blatant hostility from local government officials and other public service employees was commonly reported and sympathetic responses or explanations, appeared frequently to be the practice of individual officers or community workers who were either of the Gypsy/ Traveller population themselves or who had a close familiarity with the community. Thus 'street level bureaucrats' could either engage with housed Gypsies and Travellers in a manner which was perceived of as smoothing pathways (with the added bonus of aiding community cohesion) or be coded as 'racist' or obstructive, creating an additional negative feedback loop in terms of perceptions of gorjer society.

We have therefore compiled the following list of recommendations which we propose may act as a starting point for local authorities, health agencies and other practitioners seeking to penetrate societal stereotypes and engage with these 'hidden populations' more effectively.

- Service providers should ensure that Gypsies and Travellers are included in ethnic monitoring systems and local authorities should seek to develop partnerships with other registered social landlords known to accommodate members of the communities. Potentially, specialist cultural advice, mediation services and support could be offered to private landlords where disputes arise to which Gypsy or Traveller tenants are a party.
- Homelessness strategies need to be reviewed regularly to see how they address the issues faced by Gypsies and Travellers. A wide range of accommodation should be considered and provided for members of these communities (for example, group housing, the development of mixed tenure sites and provision of small-scale sites embedded within areas of social housing (such as are found in London). See

Cemlyn et al (2009) for a more in-depth discussion of policy recommendations per accommodation requirements.

- The current focus and approach to 'mainstreaming' of services should to some extent be reconsidered in relation to marginalised Gypsy and Traveller communities, given the poor outcomes in terms of education, health and employment common to these populations (Cemlyn et al, 2009).

- Outreach and support agencies (where possible staffed at least in part by Gypsies and Travellers) should continue to actively engage with Gypsies and Travellers who move into housing – preferably through providing outreach multi-agency services in localities known to have high Gypsy and Traveller populations. Wherever possible, multi-agency working should be encouraged, including through Children's Centres, or utilising existing community facilities to provide drop-in advice sessions for both housed and sited community members.

- Local authorities, registered social landlords, police, race equality councils and community fora should formally monitor all incidents of racist abuse against Gypsies and Travellers resident in housing (and on local sites), and ensure that appropriate and accessible publicity materials (for example in cartoon and DVD format) exist to encourage reporting of incidents by Gypsies and Travellers.

- We would recommend continued local-level support of activities undertaken in Gypsy Roma Traveller History month to aid the broadening of the knowledge base of the wider community and to promote neighbourliness whilst reducing discrimination and combating isolation for some individuals and households.

- The active promotion of Choice Based Lettings systems and/or assistance with bidding processes should be provided, where possible, to aid in strengthening and developing communities in areas near to established sites and/or communities of housed Gypsies and Travellers.

Further research

Inevitably, we have identified the need for further research to be undertaken. Not least because we are aware that a deficit in this study is the lack of alternative perspectives which would provide information on the experiences of non-Gypsies living in areas where there are significant Gypsy and Traveller populations and who, for example, live next to, or in close proximity to a family that may be perceived as overly disruptive, noisy and boisterous. Further information is also required on how great is the understanding between communities, enabling us to question whether the 'wannabes' are consciously imitating Gypsy and Traveller culture or if the two groups are converging around shared focal concerns, linguistic patterns, argot and fashions through a process of hybridisation and cross-fertilisation – which is what the historical and contemporary evidence appears to suggest – rather than a one-way process of emulation.

These and many other questions still remain to be answered, not least, the need to know more about housed communities of Gypsies and Travellers in wider areas of the UK, and the relations which pertain between themselves and new migrant groups. We have identified too, the need to explore the perceptions of 'gorjers' about Gypsies and Travellers; how this is mediated by social class, gender and locality; and how young people in school and community settings relate to their Gypsy and Traveller peers. For the moment, however, whilst we may only have presented one side of the story of a community which frequently perceives of itself as in internal diasporic exile, we are aware that this will be a developing, dynamic narrative for generations to come regardless of whether the majority of this population live in caravans, on permanent sites or in housing. As one young lady remarked during a focus group in the South West:

> "It will never disappear, because my kids and all these little kids and their kids – there'll still be Gypsy generations even 20 years down the line. When mine grow up they'll say 'my mum was a Gypsy'."

APPENDIX A

Methodologies

This project has entailed use of a variety of qualitative methodologies as a result of the mixed data sources mined for information on the subject of housed Gypsies and Travellers.

Literature review

A combination of desk-top and manual library searches was undertaken to gather information on the presence of Gypsies and Travellers in areas relevant to the study. Whilst the authors possess a considerable number of the relevant texts cited, further research was undertaken in the University of Liverpool library (Gypsy Lore Society collection); the University of Cambridge library and the British Library, London. Internet searches utilising search terms such as 'housed', 'Traveller' and 'Gypsy' were made. The Merton Historical Society was a useful source of information on the Gypsy connection to south London. In addition, sweeps of specialist collections such as the Old Bailey on-line search engine, archives of local history held in public libraries and generalised searches for references to Gypsies and Travellers in specific areas of London, the South East and South West were undertaken.

Secondary analysis of Gypsy Traveller Accommodation Assessment (GTAA) data

As the authors have, in partnership and individually, undertaken a considerable number of GTAAs across the study areas we were privileged to have access to full data sets for the wider areas within which our focused studies took place (other than London).

The process by which we undertook calculations of the numbers of Gypsies and Travellers and the general methodology entailed in undertaking GTAAs is explained in depth in Chapter Four. Having access to primary data sources meant that we were able to carry out detailed analysis of core themes of interest in this text – drawing on occasion on qualitative quotations gathered for the purposes of relevant GTAAs.

Focus group data

Within the GTAAs which we have been responsible for, or worked on, we have evolved a practice of embedding focus groups into our research design to enable us to explore key themes (both with professionals and community members) in greater depth. The transcripts of focus groups carried out with Gypsy and Traveller participants resident in housing were data-washed and sorted to enable selection of housed participants, then subjected to in-depth secondary analysis utilising 'Framework' processes (Ritchie and Spencer, 1994). The same practice was carried out to review the relevance of findings and at times select from previously unused data stored from other studies on which we had worked in the core research locales (for example, health and employment need assessments and community cohesion studies).

In addition (see Chapter Four) we convened a number of specialist focus groups for the purposes of this project. Full analysis (after transcription) was undertaken of these new materials using a combination of 'Framework' and triangulation of thematic analysis via (for data collected at a later stage in the research series) the NVivo software package.

Questionnaires and individual interviews

As part of the targeted research designed to explicitly engage with housed Gypsies and Travellers we undertook a small-scale mixed-methodology survey (quantitative and qualitative elements, predominantly administered by community interviewers) and a number of individual depth interviews with housed respondents.

Data from the purposive sample was entered into an Excel spreadsheet for quantitative analysis (for example duration of residence in housing, number of moves, and so on) with qualitative elements being subjected to Framework/NVivo analysis as above to enable the identification of key themes.

APPENDIX B

Glossary of words and terms

Authorised site (also known as a 'licensed site')
A site which has planning permission for use as a Gypsy and Traveller site.

Cant/Gammon/Shelta
Cant is technically a form of Celtic language group which includes Gammon and Shelta languages used respectively by Irish and Scottish Travellers. Irish Travellers will often use the term 'Cant' interchangeably with 'Gammon', the specific language spoken within their community.

Caravan
Mobile accommodation consisting of kitchen area and bedrooms. Referred to as a trailer by many Gypsies and Travellers. (New Travellers may often live in converted trucks/buses/vans or other forms of living vehicles which fulfil the same function as a caravan.)

Chalet
Term used by Gypsies and Travellers, usually referring to a mobile home on a site, specifically a form of mobile home which resembles a bungalow.

Chavvy/chavvies
Romani word for 'child/children'.

Cushti/cushy/ kushti
Romani for 'good'/something positive.

Divvy
Mad ("my cousin can be right divvy ..."). Romani term.

Dukkering
Romani word for fortune-telling.

Fairs, or specifically named events such as 'Appleby' or 'Stow'
Horse Fairs and associated cultural events dating back centuries attended by large numbers of Gypsies and Travellers to trade animals, meet friends and relatives; buy and sell and meet potential marriage partners. Of huge cultural significance, and for many sedentarised Gypsies and Travellers the only times in the year when they 'travel' or live in a trailer.

Family site
A private caravan site owned and occupied by an (extended) family. Broadly equivalent to owner-occupation in mainstream housing.

Gavver
Romany word used by Gypsies/Travellers to refer to the police.

Gorje/Gorgio/Gorge/Gaujo/ Gadje/Gaje – 'Settled community'/Country People/ Flatties
'Gorjer' (spelt in a variety of different ways) is a Romani term used by Gypsies to describe all non-Gypsies and Travellers.
'Settled community' is a term used by Gypsies and Travellers to describe people who are not Gypsy or Traveller by ethnicity or culture and who live in bricks and mortar housing.
'Country People'/'Flatties' are the Irish Traveller equivalents of the 'gorjer' and refer to non-Travellers resident in housing.

Gypsies/Travellers (statutory definition – 2004 Housing Act)
The Housing (Assessment of Accommodation Needs) (Meaning of Gypsies and Travellers) (England) Regulations 2006 (Statutory Instrument 3190/2006) were implemented in order to resolve the definition of Gypsies and Travellers in relation to the duties under the Housing Act 2004.

> For the purposes of section 225 of the Housing Act 2004 (duties of local housing authorities: accommodation needs of gypsies and travellers), 'gypsies and travellers' means:
>
> (a) persons with a cultural tradition of nomadism or of living in a caravan; and
> (b) all other persons of a nomadic habit of life, whatever their race or origin, including:
> (i) such persons who, on grounds only of their own or their family's or dependant's educational or health

needs or old age, have ceased to travel temporarily or permanently; and

(ii) members of an organised group of travelling showpeople or circus people (whether or not travelling together as such).

The term 'Gypsies and Travellers' is sometimes used to encompass a wide range of different groups and cultures. Working within the guidance from government, the following groups tend to be specifically included as categories for respondents to 'self-define' in GTAA surveys:

• Romany Gypsies;
• Irish Travellers;
• New Travellers;
• Welsh Travellers;
• Scottish Travellers; and
• Travelling Showpeople (as defined in Circular 22/91).

Gypsy (or English Gypsy)
Member of the largest group of nomadic (and formerly nomadic) groups of Gypsies and Travellers in Britain. Romany Gypsies trace their ethnic origin back to migrations, probably from India, taking place at intervals over many centuries. They have been known to be in the UK since the 15th century. Gypsies were recognised as an ethnic group in 1989.

Gypsy and Traveller
In this study, we use this term to include all ethnic Gypsies and Irish Travellers, plus other Travellers who adopt a nomadic or semi-nomadic way of life, although on the few occasions when we speak of New Travellers we identify their origins.

Gypsy Traveller Accommodation Assessment (GTAA)
A statutory assessment of the extent of site provision and housing need for Gypsies and Travellers in a given area. Carried out under the Housing Act 2004. Typically a sample of Gypsies and Travellers are interviewed and a survey carried out of household size, health and education-related accommodation needs and related issues to ascertain the extent of local authority provision. Such surveys provide the most comprehensive general information source about Gypsies and Travellers available to date.

Irish Traveller

Member of one of the main groups of Gypsies and Travellers in Britain. Irish Travellers have a distinct indigenous origin in Ireland although they have been known to be resident in the UK for at least two centuries, and were recognised as an ethnic group in England in 2000.

Kerrer/Kennet

Derogatory Romani word for a housed Gypsy who is perceived of as 'losing their culture' through residence in 'bricks and mortar'. From the term for 'house' (Ker or Ken).

Ladged

Romani word for 'embarrassed'. ("You would be ladged to death if one of your family did that.")

Mobile home/static

Legally a caravan, but not usually capable of being moved by towing. Residential mobile homes are usually of a large size and may resemble either static holiday caravans or chalets.

Muller(ed)

Killed/Dead (may be used in a 'semi-serious' manner, "I'll muller that chavvie if I get my hands on him"). Romani word.

New Traveller

Term used here to refer to members of the settled community who have adopted a nomadic or semi-nomadic lifestyle living in moveable dwellings. There are now second and third generation 'New' Travellers in England. Some New Travellers prefer the more neutral term 'Traveller'. In general Romany Gypsies and Irish Travellers are not particularly enthusiastic about New Travellers, regarding them as having appropriated their culture and often being mistaken for 'ethnic' Travellers.

Pitch/plot

Area of a Gypsy/Traveller site where a single household live in their caravans (trailers). Pitch sizes may vary between large enough for one residential trailer (or mobile home) and one touring (small) trailer to spacious enough to hold one or two large mobile homes and several 'tourers' as well as working vehicles. On public (socially provided) sites rented pitches tend to be smaller and are easily delineated by fencing.

On private family sites where several related households may own the site it may be less easy to identify separate pitches/plots. A large household with a number of children may require more than one pitch if living on a public (or private rented) site with limited pitch size.

Private site
May be an owner-occupied site or one where a Gypsy/Traveller rents a pitch from the owner.

Registered Social Landlords (RSL)
Not-for-profit housing organisation such as a local authority which may provide housing or run Gypsy and Traveller sites (for example, residential and transit sites).

Residential site/pitch
A site/pitch intended for long-stay/often permanent use by residents – might be owner-occupied or owned by an RSL.

Roadside/unauthorised site/encampment
A piece of land where Gypsies and Travellers reside in vehicles or 'bender' tents without permission. The land is not owned by the residents and is often located on the edge of roads/carparks or in other unsafe and unsuitable environments which present hazards for residents (particularly the frail, elderly or children) and which are often a cause of conflict with 'settled' local people.

Rocker
Romani word for 'talk' ("Does he rocker Romanes?"; as in: can he speak/understand Romani?)

Romani Jib/Romani
The Indic origin language used by Romany Gypsies.

Site
Generic terms to describe an area of land laid out and used for Gypsy and Traveller caravans. Sites vary in type and size and can range from one-caravan private family sites on Gypsies' and Travellers' own land (with or without planning permission), through to large local authority sites.

Socially rented site (often known as a 'council site')

A Gypsy and Traveller caravan site owned by a council or registered social landlord.

Static

See under 'Mobile home'.

Tent (Bender)

Tent-like structure constructed by using a mesh of poles and tarpaulins. Used historically (up until the early 20th century) as accommodation by Gypsies and Travellers who required greater living space than a Vardo/ Wagon could afford. Some New Travellers still travel with and live in Benders, which can be very warm and cosy inside if appropriately constructed and waterproofed.

Tolerated

An unauthorised development or encampment may be 'tolerated' for a period of time during which no enforcement action is taken.

Tourer

Caravan which can be towed behind a car or vehicle – typically used for shorter-term travel (such as when attending 'Fairs') by site dwellers and housed families, or by 'roadsiders' who do not have access to a pitch or are unable to site a 'static'. Where possible the majority of housed Gypsies and Travellers retain the use of a 'tourer' as both a culturally suitable accommodation alternative and to allow themselves freedom to 'travel' when possible.

Travel

The act of nomadising (whether on a long-term basis, for example where a household does not have access to a secure site and thus are 'roadsiders'; or when travelling to attend cultural events such as Horse Fairs, often utilising 'tourers' or even horse-drawn 'wagons' when attending these greatly valued annual community reunions.)

Trailer

Gypsies and Travellers generally use the term 'trailer' for caravans.

Vardo (also known as a Wagon)

The term typically used by Gypsies and Travellers to refer to horse-drawn 'traditional' living caravans, commonly used by families in earlier centuries and much prized as cultural objects, lovingly restored and brought out for festive occasions such as Appleby Fair.

Vonga
Romani word for money/earnings

Further information on the above subjects (particularly those relating to Horse Fairs or more about the Romani and Cant languages) can be easily found by undertaking an internet search or visiting the websites of Gypsy and Traveller community organisations such as: The Gypsy Council; Friends, Families and Travellers; Irish Traveller Movement (Britain) or Derbyshire Gypsy Liaison Group. For information relating to the Romani language and linguistics, see the 'Romani Project' at the University of Manchester at http://romani.humanities.manchester.ac.uk/.

References

Acton, T. (1974) *Gypsy politics and social change: the development of ethnic identity and pressure politics among British Gypsies from Victorian reformism to Romany nationalism,* London: Routledge and Kegan Paul.

Alba, R. (1990) *Ethnic identity: the transformation of white America,* USA: Yale University Press.

Alexander, J. C. (2004) 'Towards a theory of cultural trauma' in J. C. Alexander et al *Cultural trauma and colective identity,* Berkely, CA: University of California Press.

Anglia Ruskin University, Law School (2006) *Dorset Traveller Needs Assessment,* available at www.dorsetforyou.com/media.jsp?mediaid =129873&filetype=pdf, accessed 3 August 2011.

Anthias, F. (2001) 'The material and the symbolic in theorizing social stratification: issues of gender, ethnicity and class', *British Journal of Sociology,* vol 52, no 3, pp 367–90.

Arnold, H. A. (1970) 'On the assimilation of Gypsy population and speech in Central Europe', *Journal of the Gypsy Lore Society,* Series 3, pt 2, pp 61–64.

Ashkam, J. (1975) *Fertility and deprivation: a study of differential fertility amongst working class families in Aberdeen,* New York: Cambridge University Press.

Australian Law Reform Commission (1986) *Recognition of Aboriginal Customary Laws (ALRC Report 31)* [specifically see Chapter 3: Aboriginal Societies: The Experience of Contact] available at http://www.alrc.gov.au/publications/3.%20Aboriginal%20 Societies%3A%20The%20Experience%20of%20Contact/impacts-settlement-aboriginal-people, accessed 13 October 2012.

Bailey, N., Kearns, A., and Livingston, M. (2012) 'Place attachment in deprived neighbourhoods: The impacts of population turnover and social mix', *Housing Studies,* vol 27, no 2, pp 208–31.

Baker, P. (2002) *Polari: The lost language of gay men,* London: Routledge.

Bancroft, A. (2000) 'No interest in land: legal and spatial enclosure of Gypsy-Travellers in Britain', *Space and Polity,* vol 4, no 1, pp 41–56.

Bancroft, A. (2005) *Roma and Gypsy-Travellers in Europe: modernity, race, space and exclusion,* Gateshead: Athenaeum Press.

Barker, J. (2012) 'Negative cultural capital and homeless young people', *Journal of Youth Studies,* vol 15, no 6, pp 730–43.

Barth, F. (1969) *Ethnic groups and boundaries: the social organization of culture difference,* Boston: Little, Brown and Co.

Bath, C., Smart, H. and Crofton, T. (1875) *The dialect of the English Gypsies*, London: Asher and Co.

Becker, H. (1963) *Outsiders: studies in sociology of deviance*, New York: Free Press.

Behlmer, G.K. (1985) 'The Gypsy problem in Victorian England', *Victorian Studies*, vol 28, no 2, Winter, pp 231–53.

Beider, H. (2011) *Community cohesion: the views of white working-class communities*, York: JRF.

Beier, A. L. (1974) 'Vagrants and the social order in Elizabethan England', *Past and Present*, no 64, August, pp 3–29.

Beier, A. L. (1985) *Masterless men: the vagrancy problem in England 1560–1640*, New York: Methuen.

Belton, B. A. (2005) *Gypsy and Traveller ethnicity: the social generation of an ethnic phenomenon*, London: Routledge.

Bennett, J. M. (1998) 'Transition shock: Putting culture shock in perspective', in J. M. Bennett (ed) *Basic Concepts of Intercultural Communication: Selected Readings*, USA: Intercultural Press.

Berger, J. (1979) *Pig earth*, London: Writers and Readers Publishing Cooperative.

Berlin, J. (2012) *Housing-related problems of Roma in Finland and Gypsies and Travellers in England*, Salford: SPARC 10 Conference Proceedings

Besant, W. B. (1912) *London: South of the Thames (The survey of London)*, London: The Macmillan Co.

Bexley News Shopper (2011) 'Andy Scott gipsy cob horse sculpture installed at Belvedere Roundabout', 16 February.

Bhreatnach C. and Bhreatnach, A. (eds) (2006) *Portraying Irish Travellers: histories and representations*, Newcastle upon Tyne: Cambridge Scholars Publishing.

Bird, C. E. and Rieker, P. (1999) 'Gender matters: an integrated model for understanding men's and women's health', *Social Science and Medicine*, 48, pp 745–55.

Birmingham Post (1919) 'The Clapham Gipsies', 9 September.

Bhopal, K. et al (2000). *Working towards inclusive education for Gypsy Traveller pupils* (RR 238), London: DfEE.

Bloul, R. (1999) 'Beyond ethnic identity: Resisting exclusionary identification', *Social Identities: Journal for the Study of Race, Nation and Culture*, vol 5, no 1, pp 7–30.

Bond, L. et al (2012) 'Exploring the relationships between housing, neighbourhoods and mental wellbeing for residents of deprived areas', *BMC Public Health*, vol 12, no 48, pp 1–14.

Booth, C. (1902) *Life and labour of the people in London, Volume III*, Booth Manuscripts held at the London School of Economics.

Borgois, P. (1996) *In search of respect: selling crack in El Barrio*, Cambridge: Cambridge University Press.

Borrow, G. (2001) *Romano Lavo Lil: word-book of the Romany, or English Gypsy language,* e-books, Globusz online Publishing.

Bott, E. (1957) *Family and social networks: roles, norms and external relationships in ordinary urban families*, London: Tavistock Publications.

Bottero, W. and Irwin, S. (2003) 'Locating difference: class, "race" and gender, and the shaping of social inequalities', *The Sociological Review*, vol 51, no 4, pp 463–483.

Bourdieu, P. (1984) *Distinction: a social critique of the judgment of taste*, Harvard: Harvard University Press.

Bourdieu, P. (1985) *Outline of a theory of practice*, Cambridge: Cambridge University Press.

Bourdieu, P. (1986) 'The forms of capital', in J. G. Richardson (ed) *Handbook of theory and research for the sociology of education*, New York: Greenwood Press.

Bowen, P. (2004) 'The schooling of Gypsy Children in Surrey 1906–1933', *Journal of Educational Administration and History*, vol 36, no 1, April, pp 57–67.

Bowes, A. and Sim, D. (2002) 'Patterns of residential settlement among black and minority ethnic groups', in P. Somerville and A. Steele (eds) *'Race', housing and social exclusion*, London and Philadelphia: Jessica Kingsley Publishers.

Boyle, P. and Halfacree, K. (1998) *Migration into rural areas: theories and issues*, University of Michigan: Wiley.

Brah, A. (1996) *Cartographies of diaspora: contesting identities* London: Routledge.

Breakwell, G. (1986) *Coping with threatened identities*, London: Methuen.

Brearley, M. (1996) *The Roma/Gypsies of Europe: a persecuted people*, London: JPR.

Burgess, P. (2000) 'Discovering hidden histories: the identity of place and time', *Journal of Urban History*, 26, pp 645–58.

Burnett, C. (2009) 'Travellers leave Mitcham Common', *Wimbledon Guardian*, 13 August.

Burnett, J. (1986) *A Social History of Housing 1815–1985* (2nd edn), London: Methuen.

Burney, E. (1999) *Crime and banishment: nuisance and exclusion in social housing*, London: Routledge.

Burney, E. (2009) *Making people behave: anti-social behaviour, politics and policy*, Cullompton: Willan Publishing.

Burrell, I. (2008) 'Race and identity in 21st century Britain', *The Independent*, 18 November.

Byrne, D. (2005) *Social exclusion* (2nd edn), Maidenhead: Open University Press.

Caballero, C. (2010) *Lone mothers of children from mixed racial and ethnic backgrounds: a case study*, Bristol: SPAN.

Caballero, C., et al (2008) *Parenting 'mixed' children: negotiating difference and belonging in mixed race, ethnicity and faith families*, London: Joseph Rowntree Foundation.

Cantle, T. (2005) *Community cohesion: a new framework for race and diversity*, Basingstoke: Palgrave Macmillan.

Cassidy, C., O'Connor, R. and Dorner, N. (2006) *A comparison of how young people from different ethnic groups experience leaving school*, York: Joseph Rowntree Foundation.

Cemlyn, S. (2000a) 'Assimilation control, mediation or advocacy? Social work dilemmas in providing anti-oppressive services for Traveller children and families', *Child and Family Social Work*, vol 5, no 4, pp 327–41.

Cemlyn, S. (2000b) 'From neglect to partnership? Challenges for social service in promoting the welfare of Traveller children', *Child Abuse Review*, vol 9, no 5, pp 349–63.

Cemlyn, S., Greenfields, M., Burnett, S., Matthews, Z., and Whitewell, C. (2009) *Inequalities experienced by Gypsy and Traveller communities: a review*, Manchester: Equalities and Human Rights Commission.

Charlemagne, J. (1984) 'Bridging the cultural gap', *Unesco Courier*, October, pp 15–17.

Chattoe, E. and Gilbert, N. (1999) 'Talking about budgets: time and uncertainty in household decision making', *Sociology*, vol 33, no 1, pp 85–103.

Clapham, D., et al (2012) *Housing options and solutions for young people in 2020*, York: JRF.

Clark, C. (2006) 'Defining Ethnicity in a cultural and socio-legal context: the case of Scottish Gypsy-Travellers', *Scottish Affairs*, vol 54, pp 39–67.

Clark, C. and Greenfields, M. (2006) *Here to stay: the Gypsies and Travellers of Britain*, Hatfield: University of Hertfordshire Press.

Clark, J. (2009) 'On the road to change: dealing with domestic violence in Gypsy and Traveller groups', *The Guardian*, 14 August.

Clarke, J. (1993) 'Skinheads and the magical recovery of community', in S. Hall and T. Jefferson (eds) *Resistance through rituals: youth subcultures in postwar Britain*, London: Routledge.

Clarke, J., et al (1993) 'Subcultures, culture and class', in S. Hall and T. Jefferson (eds) *Resistance through rituals: youth subcultures in postwar Britain*, London: Routledge.

Clements, L. and Campbell, S. (1999) 'The Criminal Justice and Public Order Act and its implications for Travellers', in T. Acton (ed) *Gypsy politics and Traveller identity*, Hatfield: University of Hertfordshire Press.

Clifford, J. (1992) 'Travelling cultures', in L. Grossberg, C. Nelson, and P. A. Treichler (eds) *Cultural studies*, London and New York: Routledge.

Cloke, P. and Little, J. (eds) (1997) *Contested countryside cultures*, London: Routledge.

Collins, E. (1976) 'Migrant labour in british agriculture in the nineteenth century', *The Economic History Review*, vol 29, no 1, February, pp 38–59.

Commission for Racial Equality (CRE) (2004) *Press Release: 'Gypsies and Travellers: A strategy for the CRE, 2004–2007'* Friday 2 April 2004, http://www.grtleeds.co.uk/information/CRE.html, accessed 30 September 2012.

Commission for Racial Equality (CRE) (2006) *Common ground: Equality, good race relations and sites for Gypsies and Irish Travellers*, London: CRE.

Commission for Rural Communities (CRC) (2006) *Calculating housing need in rural England*, London: CRC.

Commission for Rural Communities (CRC) (2007) *A8 migrant workers in rural areas*, London: CRC.

Communities and Local Government (CLG) (2007) *Gypsy and Traveller Accommodation Needs Assessments*, London: Department for Communities and Local Government.

Cotterell, J. (1996) *Social networks and social influence in adolescence*, London: Routledge.

Council of Europe (2012) *Declaration of the Committee of Ministers on the Rise of Anti-Gypsyism and Racist Violence against Roma in Europe*, available online at https://wcd.coe.int/ViewDoc.jsp?id=1902151&Site=CM.

Crawley, H. (2004) *Moving forward: the provision of accommodation for Travellers and Gypsies*, London: Institute for Public Policy Research.

Croasman, J. (2006) 'Found: generations later the struggle to regain identity wages on', *Ancestry*, vol 24, no 5, pp 41–4.

Dabbler, The (2011) *Plotlands*, available at http://thedabbler.co.uk/2011/06/plotlands/, accessed 18 July 2012.

Dahya, B. (1974) 'The nature of Pakistani ethnicity in industrial cities in Britain', in A. Cohen (ed) *Urban Ethnicity*, London: Tavistock.

Daily Chronicle (1909) 'Gipsy nuisance', 19 January.

Davies, E. (1987) *Gypsies and housing: the results of a survey*, London: Department of the Environment.

Dawkins, C. (2006) 'Are social networks the ties that bind families to neighbourhoods?', *Housing Studies*, vol 21, no 6, pp 867–81.

Dawson, R. (2005) *A Romany in the family: aspects of Romany genealogy*, Derby: Robert Dawson.

David Couttie Associates (2006) *North Kent Gypsy and Traveller Study* http://www.swale.gov.uk/assets/Planning-Forms-and-Leaflets/ Local-Development-Framework/Gypsy-and-Travellers/North-Kent-GTAA.pdf, accessed 3 August 2011.

Davis, M. (1990) *City of quartz: excavating the future in Los Angeles*, London: Verso.

Dearling, A. (1997) 'Rebels with a cause? Travellers, protestors and the DiY culture', *Criminal Justice Matters*, vol 28, no 2, available at http://www.enablerpublications.co.uk/pages/rebels.htm, accessed 30 September 2012.

Dearling, A. (1998) *No boundaries: new Travellers on the road (outside of England)*, Lyme Regis: Enabler Publications.

De Andrade, L. L. (2000) 'Negotiating from the inside: constructing racial and ethnic identity in qualitative research', *Journal of Contemporary Ethnography*, vol 29, no 3, pp 268–90.

Dench, G., Gavron, K., and Young, M. (2006) *The new East End: kinship, race and conflict* London: Profile Books.

Department of Communities and Local Government (DCLG) (2007) *Preparing Regional Spatial Strategy reviews on Gypsies and Travellers by regional planning bodies*, London: The Queen's Printers & HMSO.

Department of Communities and Local Government (DCLG) (2012) *Count of Gypsy and Traveller caravans – January 2012*, available at http://www.communities.gov.uk/publications/corporate/statistics/ caravancountjan2012, accessed 12 July 2012.

Department for the Environment and Local Government (Ireland) (DELG) (2012) *Guidance for Group Housing for Travellers*, Dublin: DELG.

Derrington, C. (2007) 'Fight, flight and playing white: an examination of coping strategies adopted by Gypsy Traveller adolescents in English secondary schools', *International Journal of Educational Research*, vol 46, no 6, pp 357–67.

Derrington, C. and Kendall, S. (2004) *Gypsy Traveller students in secondary schools: culture, identity and achievement*, Stoke-on-Trent: Trentham Books Ltd.

Deutsch, N. L. (2008) *Pride in the projects: teens building identity in urban contexts*, New York: New York University Press.

Dorman, P. (1996) *Markets and mortality: economics, dangerous work and the value of human life*, Cambridge: Cambridge University Press.

Doyal, L. and Gough, I. (1991) *A theory of human need*, London: Macmillan.

Draper, N. (2004) 'Across the bridges: representations of Victorian South London', *The London Journal*, vol 29, no 1, pp 25–43.

Duncan, S. and Edwards, R. (1999) *Lone mothers, paid work and gendered moral rationalities*, London: Macmillan.

Duncombe, S. (ed) **(2002)** *Cultural resistance reader*, New York: Verso.

Durkheim, E. (1933) *The division of labor in society*, New York: Free Press.

Earle, F. et al (1994) *A time to travel: an introduction to Britain's newer Travellers*, Lyme Regis: Enabler Publications.

Earle, R. and Phillips, C. (2009) '"Con-viviality" and beyond: identity dynamics in a young men's prison' in M. Wetherell (ed) *Identity in the 21st century: new trends in changing times*, Basingstoke: Palgrave Macmillan.

East, J. (1980) 'When teapots went half and oysters were 3d a dozen', *Surrey Yesterdays*, no 1, pp 20–26.

Eastmond, M. (2007) 'Stories as lived experience: narratives in forced migration research', *Journal of Refugee Studies*, vol 20, no 2, pp 248–64.

Echo, The (1879) 'Gypsies in the Metropolis', 21 February.

Edmunds, J. and Turner, B. S. (2002) *Generations, culture and society*, Buckingham and Philadelphia PA: Open University Press.

Elias, N. and Scotson, J. (1994) *The established and the outsider: a sociological enquiry into community problems*, London: Sage.

Emerson, A. and Brodie, A. (2001) *Housed Irish Travellers in North London*, London: Gypsy and Traveller Unit Publication.

Epstein, G.S. and Heizler, O. (2009) *Network formations among immigrants and natives*, IZA Discussion Paper No 4234, Bonn: Institute for the Study of Labour.

Erikson, K. (1995) 'Notes on trauma and community', in C. Caruth (ed) *Trauma: explorations in memory*, Baltimore and London: John Hopkins Press.

Evans, S. (2004) *Stopping places: a Gypsy history of South London and Kent*, Hertford: University of Hertford Press.

Evening Standard (1935) 'Gipsy town within 12 miles of Charing Cross: there are dark eyes and ready tongues in this caravan colony', 3 January.

Eyerman, R. (2004) 'The past in the present: culture and the transmission of memory', *Acta Sociologica*, vol 47, no 2, June, pp 159–69.

Fenton, A. (2010) 'How will changes to Local Housing allowance affect low-income tenants in private rented housing?', Cambridge Centre for Housing and Planning Research, available at http://england. shelter.org.uk/professional_resources/policy_and_research/policy_ library/policy_library_folder/how_will_changes_to_local_housing_ allowance_affect_low-income_tenants_in_private_rented_housing, accessed 12 November 2012.

Ferlander, S. (2007) 'The importance of different forms of social capital for health', *Acta Sociologica*, vol 50, no 2 June, pp 115–28.

Fernandez Kelly, M. P. (1994) 'Towanda's triumph: social and cultural capital in the transition to adulthood in the urban ghetto', *International Journal of Urban and Regional Research*, vol 18, no 1, pp 88–111.

Finch, J. (1989) *Family obligations and social change*, Cambridge: Polity Press.

Finch, J. and Mason, J. (1993) *Negotiating family responsibilities*, London; Routledge.

Fine, B. (2001) *Social capital versus social theory: political economy and social science at the turn of the millennium*, London: Routledge.

Fletcher, D. (2009) 'Social tenants, attachment to place and work in the post-industrial labour market: underlining the limits of housing-based explanations of labour immobility?', *Housing Studies*, vol 24, no 6, pp 775–791.

Fordham Research (2008) *London Boroughs' Gypsy and Traveller Accommodation Needs Assessment,* available at http://legacy.london. gov.uk/mayor/housing/gtana/index.jsp; http://www.kingston.gov. uk/london_gypsy_and_traveller_neesds_assessment.pdf. **[[author to locate]]**

Fordham Research (2009) *Research into the needs of Gypsies and Travellers in bricks & mortar housing,* West London Housing Partnership: Fordham Research.

Formoso, B. and Burrell, J. (2000) 'Economic habitus and management of needs: the example of Gypsies', *Diogenes*, vol 48, no 50, pp 58–73.

Fortier, J. (2009) *Kings of the forest: the cultural resilience of Himalayan hunter gatherers*, Honolulu: University of Hawaii Press.

Fraser, A. (1995) *The Gypsies: the peoples of Europe*, Oxford: Blackwell Publishing.

Furlong, A., Biggart, A., and Cartmel, F. (1996) 'Neighbourhoods, opportunity structures and occupational aspirations', *Sociology*, vol 30, no 3, pp 551–65.

Gans, H. J. (1962) *The urban villagers: group and class in the life of Italian-Americans*, New York: Free Press.

Garland, D. (2001) *The culture of control: crime and social order in contemporary society*, Oxford: Oxford University Press.

Garner, S. (2007) *Whiteness: an introduction*, London: Routledge.

Geremek, B. (1991) *Poverty: a history*, Oxford: Blackwell Publications.

Gheorghe, N. (1997) 'The social construction of Romani identity', in T. Acton (ed) *Gypsy politics and Traveller identity*, Hatfield: University of Hertfordshire Press.

Giddens, A. (1991a) *Modernity and self identity*, Cambridge: Polity Press.

Giddens, A. (1991b) *The Consequences of Modernity*, California: Stanford University Press.

Gidley, B. and Rooke, A. (2008) *Learning from the local: the Newtown neighbourhood project Final Report*, London: Centre for Urban and Community Research Goldsmiths College, University of London/West Kent Extra/Housing Corporation.

Gilbert, A. and Varley, A. (1991) *Landlord and tenant: housing the poor in urban Mexico*, London: Routledge.

Gilbert, J. (1999) *Discographies: dance music, culture and the politics of sound*, London: Routledge.

Gilbert, J. (2007) 'Nomadic territories: a human rights approach to nomadic peoples' land rights', *Human Rights Law Review*, vol 7, no 4, pp 681–716.

Gilchrist, A. and Kyprianou, P. (2011) *Social networks, poverty and ethnicity*, York: Joseph Rowntree Foundation.

Gill, N. and Bialski, P. (2011) 'New friends in new places: network formation during the migration process among Poles in the UK', *Geoforum*, vol 42, no 2, pp 241–9.

Gilroy, P. (2004) *After Empire: multiculture or postcolonial melancholia*, London: Routledge.

Glasgow, D. (1980) *The Black underclass: poverty, entrapment and entrapment of Ghetto youth*, San Francisco: CA: Jossey-Bass Publishers.

Gmelch, G. (1977) *The Irish tinkers: the urbanization of an itinerant people*, California: Cummins Publishing Co. Ltd.

Gmelch, S. B. (1986a) 'Groups that don't want in: Gypsies and other artisan, trader and entertainment minorities', *Annual Review of Anthropology*, vol 15, pp 307–30.

Gmelch, S.B. (1986b) *Nan the life of an Irish Travelling woman*, New York: W. W. Norton.

Gmelch, G. and Gmelch, S. B (1976) 'The emergence of an ethnic group: the Irish tinkers', *Anthropological Quarterly*, vol 49, no 4, pp 225–38.

Gmelch, G. and Gmelch, S. B. (1985) 'The Cross-Channel migration of Irish Travellers', in *The Economic and Social Review*, vol 16, no 4, pp 287–96.

Gmelch, S. and Gmelch, G. (1974) 'The itinerant settlement movement: its policies and effects on Irish Travellers', *Studies: an Irish quarterly of letters*, Spring, pp 1–16.

Goffman, E. (1981) *Stigma: notes on the management of spoiled identity*, Great Britain: Penguin Books.

Goffman, E. (1982) *The presentation of self in everyday life*, Great Britain: Penguin Books.

Goodall, L. (2011) 'The Dale Farm eviction is the ugly side of localism', *The New Statesman*, 2 September.

Grand'Maison, J. and Lefebvre, S. (1996) 'A new historical context', in J. Grand'Maison and S. Lefebvre, *Sharing the blessings: the role of seniors in today's society*, Montreal: Fides.

Granovetter, M. (1973) 'The strength of weak ties', *American Journal of Sociology*, vol 78, no 6, pp 1360–79.

Greenfields, M. (1999) *Travelling light: the impact on family relationships of 'going on the road'*. Unpublished MSc Thesis, University of Bath.

Greenfields, M. (2006) 'Bricks and mortar accommodation: Travellers in houses', in C. Clark and M. Greenfields, *Here to stay: the Gypsies and Travellers of Britain*, Hatfield: University of Hertfordshire Press.

Greenfields M. (2007a) 'Accommodation needs of Gypsies/Travellers: new approaches to policy in England', *Social Policy & Society*, vol 7, no 1, pp 73–89.

Greenfields, M. (2007b) *A good job for a Traveller? Exploring Gypsy and Travellers' perceptions of health and social care careers: barriers and solutions to recruitment training and retention of social care students*, Aim Higher South East: Bucks New University.

Greenfields, M. (2008) *Gypsies, Travellers and accommodation: Better Housing Briefing 10*, London, Race Equality Foundation.

Greenfields, M. (2010) 'Romany Roots: Gypsies and Travellers in Britain: sustaining belonging and identity over 600 Years of nomadising', in L. DePretto et al (eds) *Diasporas: Revisiting and Discovering*, Oxford: Inter-Disciplinary Press (e-book); available at: https://www.interdisciplinarypress.net/online-store/ebooks/diversity-and-recognition/diasporas-revisiting-and-discovering.

Greenfields, M. and Home, R. (2008) 'Women Travellers and the paradox of the settled nomad', in A. Bottomley and H. Lim (eds) *Feminist Perspectives on Land Law*, Abingdon: Routledge-Cavendish.

Greenfields, M. and Smith, D. (2010) 'Housed Gypsy Travellers, social segregation and the reconstruction of communities, *Housing Studies*, vol 25, no 3, May, pp 397–412.

Greenfields, M. and Smith, D. (2011) 'A question of identity: the social exclusion of housed Gypsies and Travellers' *Research, Policy and Planning*, vol 28, no 3, pp 65–78.

Greenfields, M., Home, R., Cemlyn, S., Bloxham, J. and Lishman, R. (2007) 'West of England Gypsy & Traveller accommodation assessment (August 2007)', Report for Bristol, South Gloucestershire and North Somerset and Bath and North East Somerset Councils, High Wycombe: BNU.

Griffin, C. (2002a) 'The religion and social organisation of Irish Travellers on a London caravan site (Part 1)' *Nomadic Peoples*, vol 6, no 1, pp 45–68.

Griffin, C. (2002b) 'The religion and social organisations of Irish Travellers (part 2): cleanliness and dirt, bodies and borders', *Nomadic Peoples*, vol 6, no 2, pp 110–29.

Griffin, C. (2008) *Nomads under the Westway: Irish Travellers, Gypsies and other traders in west London*, Hatfield: University of Hertfordshire Press.

Gropper, R. C. (1975) *Gypsies in the city: culture patterns and survival*, Princeton, New Jersey: The Darwin Press.

Hancock, I. (2002) *We are the Romani people: ame sam e Rromane džene*, Hatfield: Hertfordshire University Press.

Hancock, I. (2007) 'The "Gypsy" stereotype and the sexualization of Romani women', in V. Glajar (ed) *Gypsies in literature and culture*, Basingstoke: Palgrave-Macmillan.

Hanley, T. (2011) *Globalisation, UK poverty and communities*, York: JRF.

Hannerz, U. (1980) *Exploring the city: inquiries toward an urban anthropology*, USA: Columbia University Press.

Hardy, D. and Ward, C. (1984) *Arcadia for all: the legacy of a makeshift landscape*, Nottingham: Five Leaves.

Harris, J. (2007) 'So now we've finally got our own "white trash"', *The Guardian*, 3 June.

Harrison, M. (2003) 'Housing black and minority ethnic communities: diversity and constraint', in D. Mason (ed) *Explaining ethnic differences: changing patterns of disadvantage in Britain*, Bristol: Policy Press.

Hastings, A. (2004) 'Stigma and housing estates: beyond pathological explanations', *Journal of Housing and the Built Environment*, vol 19, no 3, pp 233–54.

Haug, S. (2008) 'Migration networks and migration decision-making', *Journal of Ethnic and Migration Studies*, vol 34, no 4, pp 585–605.

Hawes, D. and Perez, B. (1995) *The Gypsy and the State: the ethnic cleansing of British Society*, Bristol: SAUS Publications.

Hayes, M. (2006) 'Indigenous otherness: some aspects of Irish Traveller social history' in *Éire-Ireland*, vol 41, nos 3 and 4, pp 133–61.

Hebdidge, d. (1981) *Subculture: the meaning of style*, London: Metheun and Co Ltd.

Helleiner, J. (2001) *Irish Travellers: racism and the politics of culture*, Toronto: Toronto University Press.

Henman, P. and Marston, G. (2008) 'The social division of welfare surveillance', *Journal of Social Policy*, vol 37, part 2, April, pp 186–205.

Hewstone, M., et al (2007) 'Prejudice, intergroup contact and identity: do neighbourhoods matter?', in M. Weatherell, M. Lafleche, and R. Berkeley (eds) *Identity, ethnic diversity and community cohesion*, London: Sage Publications.

Hickman, M., Crowley, H. and Mai, N. (2008) *Immigration and social cohesion in the UK: the rhythms and realities of everyday life,* York: Joseph Rowntree Foundation.

Hill, A. (2010) 'Gypsies prepare to fight government housing policy', *The Guardian Society*, 8 June.

Hinsliff, G. (2008) 'Ethnic middle classes join the "white flight"', *The Observer*, 20 April.

Hobbes, D. (1989) *Doing the business: entrepeneurship, the working class, and detectives in the East End of London*, Oxford: Oxford University Press.

Hollander, J. A. and Einwhoner, R. L. (2004) 'Conceptualizing resistance', *Sociological Forum*, vol 19, no 4, pp 533–54.

Holloway, S. L. (2005) 'Articulating otherness? White rural residents talk about Gypsy-Travellers', *Transactions: The Institute of British Geographers*, vol 30, pp 351–67.

Home, R. (2006) 'The planning system and accommodation needs of Gypsies', in C. Clark and M. Greenfields, *Here to stay: the Gypsies and Travellers of Britain*, Hatfield: University of Hertfordshire Press.

Home, R. (2012) 'Forced eviction and planning enforcement: the Dale Farm Gypsies', in *International Journal of Law in the Built Environment*, vol 4, no 3, pp 178–88.

Home, R. and Greenfields, M. (2006) *Cambridge Sub-Region Traveller Needs Assessment*, Cambridge: Cambridgeshire County Council.

Home, R. and Greenfields, M. (2007) *Dorset Gypsy-Traveller Needs Assessment*, Chelmsford: Anglia Ruskin University.

Home Office, (2001) *Building cohesive communities: a report of the ministerial group on public order and community cohesion*, London: HMSO.

Hopper, P. (2007) *Understanding cultural globalisation*, Cambridge: Polity Press.

Hough, J. (2011) 'DNA study: Travellers a distinct ethnicity' in *The Irish Examiner*, 31 May 2011, available at http://www.irishexaminer.com/ireland/dna-study-travellers-a-distinct-ethnicity-156324.html, accessed 5 December 2012.

Hudson, M., et al, (2007) *Social cohesion in diverse communities*, York: Joseph Rowntree Foundation.

Iddenden, R. S., Porter, M., Alabady, K., Greene, T. and Taylor, A. (2008) *Hull's Gypsy and Traveller health and lifestyle survey 2007*, Hull: Hull NHS.

Irish Times (2012) 'Irish Traveller numbers increase by 32%', news report 29 March 2012, available at http://www.irishtimes.com/newspaper/breaking/2012/0329/breaking46.html, accessed 14 December 2012.

Irish Traveller Movement Britain (2010) *Irish Travellers: can Europe help?* London: ITMB available at http://irishtraveller.org.uk/wp-content/uploads/2011/09/ITMB-european-briefinmg-paper-11.101.pdf, accessed 8 December 2012.

Jameson, F. (1989) 'Marxism and postmodernism', *New Left Review*, vol 177, pp 53–92.

Jayaweera, H. and Choudhury, T. (2008) *Immigration, faith and cohesion*, York: Joseph Rowntree Foundation.

Jenkins, R. (2002) *Pierre Bourdieu* (revised edition), London: Routledge.

Johnson, C. and Willers, M. (2007) *Gypsy and Traveller law* (2nd edn), London: Legal Action Group.

Jones, O. (2011) *Chavs: the demonization of the working class*, London: Verso.

Kabachnik, P. (2007) *The place of the nomad: situating Gypsy and Traveller mobility in contemporary Britain*, Ann Arbor MI: ProQuest LLC.

Kabachnik, P. (2009) 'To choose, fix or ignore culture? The cultural politics of Gypsy and Traveller mobility in England', Social and Cultural Geography, vol 10, no 4, pp 461–79.

Kendall, S. (1997) 'Sites of resistance: places on the margin – the Traveller "homeplace"', in T. Acton and G. Munday (eds) *Gypsy politics and Traveller identity*, Hatfield: University of Hertfordshire Press.

Kenrick, D. (2004) *Gypsies: from the Ganges to the Thames*, Hatfield: University of Hertfordshire Press.

Kenrick, D. and Clark, C. (1999) *Moving on: the Gypsies and Travellers of Britain*, Hatfield: University of Hertfordshire Press.

Kenrick, D. and Puxon, G. (1972) *The destiny of Europe's Gypsies*, New York: Basic Books.

Khazanov A. (1994) *Nomads and the outside world*, Cambridge: Cambridge University Press.

Kim, U. (1995) Individualism and collectivism: a psychological, cultural and ecological analysis, Copenhagen: NIAS report series, No 21.

King, P. (2008b) *In dwelling: implacability, exclusion and acceptance*, Aldershot: Ashgate Publishing.

King, P. (2008a) 'No choice: reforming social housing in England', *Economic Affairs*, vol 28, no 2, pp 37–41.

Konstantinov, Y., Kressel, G. M., and Thuen, T. (1998) 'Outclassed by former outcasts: petty trading in Varna', American Ethnologist, vol 25, no 4, pp 729–45.

Kornblum, W. (1975) 'Boyash Gypsies: shantytown ethnicity', in F. Rehfisch (ed) Gypsies, tinkers and other travellers, London: Academic Press.

Kornblum, W. and Lichter, P. (1972) 'Urban Gypsies and the culture of poverty', Urban Life and Culture, vol 1, no 3, pp 239–57.

Lau, A and Ridge, M. (2011) 'Addressing the impact of social exclusion on mental health in Gypsy, Roma and Traveller communities', *Mental Health and Social Inclusion*, vol 15, no 3, pp 129–37.

Laungani, P. (2002) 'Stress, trauma and coping strategies: cross-cultural variations', *International Journal of Group Tensions*, vol 31, no 2, pp 127–54.

Leach, N. (2009) 'Setting up a GP Enhanced Service for Travellers' Annex 3 in *Primary Care Service Framework, Gypsy and Traveller Communities*, London: NHS, Primary Care Contracting.

Leeds Mercury, The (1896) 'Gipsy movements', 4 November.

Letki, N. (2008) 'Does diversity erode social cohesion? Social capital and race in British neighbourhoods', *Political Studies*, vol 56, issue 1, pp 99–126.

Levinson, M., and Sparkes, A. (2003) 'Gypsy masculinities and the school-home interface: exploring contradictions and tensions', *British Journal of Sociology of Education*, vol 24, no 5, pp 587–603.

Lewis, O. (1968) *A study of slum culture: background for La Vida*, New York: Random House.

Link, B. and Phelan, J. (2001) 'Conceptualizing stigma', *Annual Review of Sociology*, vol 27, pp 363–85.

Little Folks (1884) 'Little toilers of the night', London, 1 November.

Local Government Chronicle (1879) 'Wandsworth Gypsies', 4 January.

Local Dialogue for London Borough of Bexley (2009) *Bexley Gypsy and Travellers Accommodation Needs Assessment*, Local Dialogues: London Borough of Bexley.

London Borough of Bromley (2008) *Gypsy Traveller Health and Education Needs Assessment*, London: LBB.

London Borough of Merton (2004) *Ethnic Minority Communities Research Report 2004–2006,* London: LBM.

Lucassen, L., Wilems, W., and Cottaar, A. (1998) *Gypsies and other itinerant groups: a socio-historical approach*, New York: St Martins Press.

MacDonald, R. and Marsh, C. (2005) *Disconnected youth? Growing up in Britain's poor neighbourhoods*, Basingstoke: Palgrave.

MacGabhann, C. (2011) *Voices unheard: a study of Irish Travellers in prison*, London: Irish Chaplaincy in Britain.

MacLaughlin, J. (1998) 'The political geography of anti-Traveller racism in Ireland: the politics of exclusion and the geography of closure', in *Political Geography*, vol 17, no 4, pp 417–35.

McAusland, R. (2008) 'Indigenous trauma, grief and loss', in A. Day et al (eds) *Anger and indigenous men*, Sydney: The Federation Press.

McCann, M., O'Siochain, S., and Ruane, J. (eds) (1994) *Irish Travellers: culture and ethnicity* Belfast: Institute of Irish Studies.

McCulloch, A. (2007) 'The changing structure of ethnic diversity and segregation in England 1991–2001', *Environment and Planning A*, vol 39, pp 909–27.

McGhee, D. (2005) *Intolerant Britain: hate, citizenship & difference*, Berkshire: Open University Press.

McKinley, R. (2011) *Gypsy girl*, London: Hodder & Stoughton.

McPherson, M., Smith-Lovin, L., and Cook, J. M. (2001) 'Birds of a feather: homophily in social networks', *Annual Review of Sociology*, vol 27, pp 415–44.

McVeigh, R. (1997) 'Theorising sedentarism: the roots of anti-nomadism', in T. Acton (ed) *Gypsy politics and Traveller identity*, Hertford: University of Hertfordshire Press.

McVeigh, R. (2008). 'The 'final solution': reformism, ethnicity denial and the politics of antitravellerism in Ireland', *Social Policy and Society*, 7, pp 91–102.

Manley, D. and van Ham, M. (2011) 'Choice-based letting, ethnicity and segregation in England', *Urban Studies*, 48, pp 1–19.

Mannheim, K. (1936) *Ideology and utopia*, London: Routledge.

Manson S., Beals J., and O'Neil, T. (1996) 'Wounded spirits, ailing hearts: PTSD and related disorders among American Indians', in A. Marsella et al (eds) *Ethnocultural aspects of post-traumatic stress disorders: issues, research and clinical applications*, Washington: American Psychological Association.

Marmot, M. (2004) *Social status: how your social standing directly affects your health and life expectancy*, London: Bloomsbury.

Matras, Y. (2010) *Romani in Britain: the afterlife of a language*, Edinburgh: Edinburgh University Press.

Mayall, D. (1988) *Gypsy-travellers in nineteenth-century society*, Cambridge: Cambridge University Press.

Mayall, D. (1995) *English Gypsies and state policies: Interface Collection*, Hatfield: University of Hertfordshire Press.

Mayall, D. (2004) *Gypsy Identities 1500–2000: From Egyptians and Moon-men to the ethnic Romany*, London: Routledge.

Mayhew, H. (1985) *London labour and the London poor*, London: Penguin.

Mencher, S. (1967) *Poor Law to Poverty Program: economic security policy in Britain and the United States*, USA: University of Pittsburgh Press.

Merton Council (2010) *Gypsy and Traveller Sites*, available at http://www.merton.gov.uk/housing/housing-policy-performance/gypsy-traveller-sites.htm, accessed 13 February 2012.

Milbourne, P. (ed) (1997) *Revealing rural 'others': representation, power and identity in the British countryside*, London: Pinter.

Miller, W. (1958) 'Lower-class culture as a generating milieu of gang delinquency', *Journal of Social Issues*, vol 14, pp 5–19.

Missing Link Magazine, The (1856) *Bible work at home and abroad*, London: Butler and Tanner.

Montague, E. N. (2006) *Phipps Bridge: Mitcham histories 8*, Wimbledon: Merton Historical Society.

Mulcahy, A. (2012) '"Alright in their own place": policing and the spatial regulation of Irish Travellers', *Criminology and Criminal Justice*, vol 12, no 3, pp 307–27.

Musterd, S. (2008) 'Residents' views on social mix: social mix, social networks and social stigmatisation in post-war housing estates in Europe', *Urban Studies*, vol 45, no 4, pp 897–915.

Nadel, J. H. (1984) 'Stigma and separation: pariah status and community persistence in a Scottish fishing village', *Ethnology*, vol 23, no 2, pp 101–15.

Naficy, H. (2003) 'Phobic spaces and liminal panics: independent transnational film genre', in E. Shohat and R. Stam (eds) *Multiculturalism Postcolonialism and Transnational Media*, USA: Rutgers University Press.

Nayak, A. (2006) 'Displaced masculinities: chavs, youth and class in the post-industrial city', *Sociology*, vol 40, no 5, pp 813–31.

Netto, G. (2006) 'Vulnerability to homelessness, use of homelessness prevention in black and minority ethnic communities', *Housing Studies*, vol 21, no 4, pp 581–601.

Netzloff, M. (2001) '"Counterfeit Egyptians" and imagined borders: Jonson's The Gypsies metamorphosed', *English Literary History*, vol 68, no 4, pp 763–93.

New York Times (1993) 'Havel calls the Gypsy "Litmus Test"', 10 December, available at http://www.nytimes.com/1993/12/10/world/havel-calls-the-gypsies-litmus-test.html?pagewanted=2&src=pm, accessed 13 October 2012.

Niner, P. (2003) *Local authority Gypsy/Traveller sites in England*, London: Office of the Deputy Prime Minister.

Niner, P. (2004) *Counting Gypsies and Travellers: a review of the Gypsy caravan count system*, London: Office of the Deputy Prime Minister.

Ni Shuinear, S. (1994) 'Irish Travellers, ethnicity and the origins question', in M. McCann et al (eds) *Irish Travellers: Culture and Ethnicity*, Belfast: Institute of Irish Studies.

Ni Shuinear, S. (1997) 'Why do Gaujos hate Gypsies so much anyway? A case study', in T. Acton (ed) *Gypsy politics and Traveller identity*, Hatfield: University of Hertfordshire Press.

Noonan, P. (1998) 'Pathologisation and resistance: Travellers, nomadism and the state', in Hainsworth, P. (ed) *Divided society: ethnic minorities and racism in Northern Ireland*, London: Pluto Press.

Norris, M and Winston, N (2005) 'Housing and accommodation of Irish Travellers: from assimilationism to multiculturalism and back again', *Social Policy & Administration*, vol 39, no 7, pp 802–821.

Obadina, D. (1998) 'Judicial review and Gypsy site provision', in T. Buck (ed) *Judicial review and social welfare*, London: Pinter.

Ober, C. et al (2000) 'Debriefing in different cultural frameworks: responding to acute trauma in Australian Aboriginal contexts', in B. Raphael and J. P. Wilson (eds) *Psychological debriefing: theory, practice and evidence*, Cambridge: Cambridge University Press.

O'Dwyer, M. (1997) *Irish Travellers Health Access Project Draft Report*, BIAS Irish Travellers Project and NHS Ethnic Health Unit.

Office for National Statistics (ONS) (2011) 'Statistical Bulletin: Families and Households 2001 to 2011', available at http://www.ons.gov.uk/ons/rel/family-demography/families-and-households/2011/stb-families-households.html, accessed 12 September 2012.

Okely, T. (1983) *The Traveller-Gypsies*, Cambridge: University of Cambridge Press.

Okitikpi, T. (2009) *Understanding interracial relationships*, Lyme Regis: Russell House Publishing.

O'Neill, G. (1990) *Pull no more bines: hop picking – memories of a vanished way of life,* London: The Women's Press.

O'Nions, H. (1995) 'The marginalisation of Gypsies', *Web Journal of Current Legal Issues*, 3 http://webjcli.ncl.ac.uk/articles3/onions3.html, accessed 12 January 2012.

O'Riain, G (ed) (1997) *Travellers: nomads of Ireland*, Dublin: Pavee Point Publications.

Ormston, R., et al (2011) *Scottish Social Attitudes survey 2010: Attitudes to discrimination and positive action*, Edinburgh: SCSR, available at http://www.scotland.gov.uk/Resource/Doc/355763/0120175.pdf, accessed 27 September 2012.

Parkin, F. (1979) *Marxism and class theory: a bourgeois critique*, London: Tavistock Publications.

Parry, G. et al (2004) *The health status of Gypsies and Travellers in England*, Sheffield: University of Sheffield.

Parvin, P. (2011) 'Localism and the left: the need for strong local government', *Renewal*, vol 19, no 2, pp 37–49.

Peach, C. (1998) 'South Asian and Caribbean ethnic minority housing choice in Britain', *Urban Studies*, vol 35, no 10, pp 1657–80.

Peoples Journal (1911) 'Gipsy Barons in Silk and gold: splendid queen sways rich and luxurious London camp', 2 September.

Peters, K. (2011) *Living together in multi-ethnic neighbourhoods: The meaning of public spaces for issues of social integration*, Netherlands: Wageningen Publishers.

Phillips, D. (1998) 'Black minority ethnic concentration, segregation and dispersal in Britain', in *Urban Studies*, vol 35, no 10, pp 1681–702.

Phillips, D. (2007) 'Ethnic and racial segregation: a critical perspective', in *Geography Compass*, 1, pp 1138–59.

Phillips, D. and Harrison, M. (2010), 'Constructing an integrated society: historical lessons for tackling black and minority ethnic housing segregation in Britain', *Housing Studies,* vol 25, no 2, pp 221–35.

Pillai, R., Kyambi, S., Nowacka, K., and Sriskandarajah, D. (2007) *The reception and integration of new migrant communities*, London: IPPR.

Platt, L. (2009) *Ethnicity and family*, Colchester: Institute for Social and Economic Research.

Polk, K. (1999) 'Males and honor contest violence', *Homicide Studies*, vol 3, no 6, pp 6–29.

Porter, M. and Taylor, B. (2010) 'Gypsies and Travellers', in P. Thane (ed) *Unequal Britain: inequalities in Britain since 1945*, Cornwall: MPG Books Ltd.

Powell, C. (2008) 'Understanding the stigmatization of Gypsies: power and the dialectics of (dis) identification', *Housing, Theory and Society*, vol 25, no 2, pp 87–109.

Powell, R. (2007) 'Civilising offences and ambivalence: the case of British Gypsies', *People, Place and Policy Online*, vol 1, no 3, pp 112–23.

Power, C. (2004) *Room to roam: England's Irish Travellers*, London: The Community Fund.

Power, N. (2011) 'There is a context to London's riots that can't be ignored', *The Guardian* (article), 8 August, available at http://www.guardian.co.uk/commentisfree/2011/aug/08/context-london-riots, accessed 13 October 2012.

Prior, D. (2009) 'Policy, power and the potential for counter agency', in M. Barnes and D. Prior (eds) *Subversive citizens: power, agency and resistance in public services*, Bristol: Policy Press.

Prior, D. and Barnes, M. (2011) 'Subverting social policy on the front line: agencies of resistance in the delivery of services', *Social Policy and Administration*, vol 45, no 3, pp 264-79.

Propper C., et al (2007) 'The impact of neighbourhood on the income and mental health of British social renters', *Urban Studies*, vol 44, no 2, pp 393–415.

Putnam, R. (2000) *Bowling alone: the collapse and revival of American community*, New York: Simon and Schuster.

Radical Islington (2012) *The demolition of social housing? The state attack on tenants and tenancies*, London: Radical Islington Collective

Ratcliffe, P. (2000) 'Race, ethnicity and housing decisions: rational choice theory and the choice-constraints debate', in M. S. Archer and J. Q. Tritter (eds) *Rational choice theory: resisting colonization*, London: Routledge.

Ratcliffe, P. (2002) 'Theorising ethnic and 'racial' exclusion in housing', in P. Somerville and A Steele (eds) *'Race', housing and social exclusion*, London and Philadelphia: Jessica Kingsley Publishers.

Ray, L. and Reed, K. (2005) 'Community, mobility and racism in a semi-rural area: Comparing minority experience in East Kent', *Ethnic and Racial Studies*, vol 28, no 2, pp 212–34.

Reay, D., et al (2007) '"A darker shade of pale?" whiteness, the middle classes and multi-ethnic inner city schooling', *Sociology*, vol 41, no 6, pp 1041–60.

Rex, J. and Moore, R. (1967) *Race, community and conflict: a study of Sparkbrook*, Oxford: Oxford University Press.

Richardson, J. (2006) *The Gypsy debate: can discourse control?*, Exeter: Imprint Academic.

Richardson, J. (2007a) *Providing Gypsy and Traveller sites: contentious spaces*, York: Joseph Rowntree Foundation. Richardson, J. (2007b) 'Policing Gypsies and Travellers', in M. Hayes and T. Acton (eds) *Travellers, Gypsies, Roma: the demonisation of difference*, Newcastle: Cambridge Scholars Publishing.

Richardson, J., Bloxham, J. and Greenfields, M. (2007) *East Kent Gypsy Traveller Accommodation Report 2007–2012*, Leicester: De Montfort University.

Rickard, G. (1995) *Vagrants, Gypsies and 'Travellers' in Kent 1572–1948*, Canterbury: Mickle Print Ltd.

Ritchie, J. and Spencer, L. (1994). 'Qualitative data analysis for applied policy research', in A. Bryman and R. G. Burgess (eds), *Analyzing qualitative data*, 1994, pp 173–94.

Robinson, D. and Reeve, K. (2006), *Neighbourhood experiences of new immigration: reflections from the evidence base*, York: Joseph Rowntree Foundation.

Rooke, A. and Gidley, B. (2010) 'Asdatown: the intersections of classed places and identities', in unspecified, (ed) *Classed Intersections: spaces, selves, knowledges*, Goldsmiths Research Online, available at http://eprints.gold.ac.uk/5614/, accessed 16 July 2012.

Rosaldo, M. and Lampshere, L. (eds) (1974) *Women, culture and society*, Stanford CA: Stanford University Press.

Rutter, J. and Latorre, M. (2009) *Social housing allocation and immigrant communities*, London: EHRC.

Ryder, A. and Greenfields, M. (2010) *Roads to success: routes to economic and social inclusion for Gypsies and Travellers*, London: Irish Traveller Movement.

Ryder, A., et al (2011) *A big or a divided society? Interim recommendations and report of the panel review into the impact of the Localism Bill and Coalition Government policy on Gypsies and Travellers*, Travellers Aid Trust: Joseph Rowntree Charitable Fund.

Saba, S (2011) 'Is Cameron's 'big society' reserved for the rich?', *The Guardian* (discussion piece), 18 May, available at: www.guardian.co.uk/society/2011/may/18/camerons-big-society-rich-surrey

Samuel, R. (1973) 'Comers and goers', in H. G. Dyos and M. Wolff (eds) *The Victorian City: images and realities Vol. 1*, London: Routledge.

Sanders, J. M. (2002), 'Ethnic boundaries and identity in plural societies', *Annual Review of Sociology*, vol 28, pp 327–57.

Sandford, J. (2000) *Rokkering to the Gorjios*, Hatfield: University of Hertfordshire Press.

Sarre, P. (1986) 'Choice and constraint in ethnic minority housing: a structurationist view' *Housing Studies*, vol 1, no 2, pp 71–86.

Sarre, P., Phillips, D., and Skellington, R. (1989) *Ethnic minority housing: explanations and policies*. Aldershot: Avebury.

Saugeres, L. (2000) 'Of tidy gardens and clean houses: housing officers as agents of social control', *Geoforum, vol* 31, pp 587–99.

School Government Chronicle (1910) 'Surrey: Gypsy Children', 10 June.

Schopflin, G. (2000) *Nations, identity, power. The new politics of Europe*, London: Hurst and Company.

Scott, J. C. (1985) *Weapons of the weak: everyday forms of peasant resistance*, New Haven: Yale University Press.

Sedgemore, F. (2011) 'Dale Farm – the Final Battle', available at http://sedgemore.com/2011/10/dale-farm-the-final-battle.

Seymour, J. (2011) 'On not going home at the end of the day: spatialized discourses of family life in single location home/workplaces', in L. Holt (ed) *Geographies of children, youth and families: an international perspective*, London: Routledge.

Shelter (2004) 'The black and minority housing crisis', available at http://england.shelter.org.uk/__data/assets/pdf_file/0009/48555/The_Black_and_Ethnic_Minority_Housing_Crisis_Sep_2004.pdf, accessed 7 January 2011.

Shelter (2007) *Good practice briefing: working with housed Gypsies and Travellers*, London: Shelter.

Shelter (2010a) 'Which neighbourhoods in London will be affordable for housing benefit claimants 2010–16 as the Government's reforms take effect?', available online at http://www.shelter.org.uk/__data/assets/pdf_file/0018/300906/Summary_of_London_housing_benefit_affordability_map.pdf, accessed 16 May 2011.

Shelter (2010b) 'Who Gets Social Housing?', available online at http://england.shelter.org.uk/housing_issues/Improving_social_housing/who_gets_social_housing#_ednref4, accessed 7 January 2011.

Shenk, P. P. (2007) 'I'm Mexican remember? Constructing ethnic identities via authenticating discourse', *Journal of Sociolinguistics*, vol 11, no 2, pp 194–220.

Shimoni, B. (2006) 'Cultural Borders, hybridization and a sense of boundaries in Thailand, Mexico and Israel', *Journal of Anthropological Research*, vol 62, no 2, pp 217–34.

Shoard, M. (1987) *This land is our land. The struggle for Britain's countryside*, London: Paladin.

Sibley, D. (1981) *Outsiders in urban society*, New York: St Martins Press.

Sibley, D. (1995) *Geographies of exclusion: society and difference in the West*, London: Routledge.

Sigona, N. and Trehan, N. (eds) (2009) *Romani politics in contemporary Europe: poverty, ethnic mobilisation and the neoliberal order*, London: Palgrave MacMillan.

Silverman, C. (1988) 'Negotiating "Gypsiness": strategy in context', *The Journal of American Folklore*, vol 101, no 401, July–September, pp 261–75.

Silverstein, P. and Tetreault, C. (2006) *Postcolonial urban apartheid: civil unrest in the French Suburbs*, New York: Social Science Research Council, available at: http://riotsfrance.ssrc.org/Silverstein_Tetreault/, accessed 14 September 2011.

Simmel, G. (1971) 'The stranger', in D. Levine (ed) *Georg Simmel: on individuality and social forms*, Chicago: University of Chicago Press.

Smelser, N. (2004) 'Psychological and cultural trauma', in J. C. Alexander et al *Cultural Trauma and Collective Identity*, Berkely, CA: University of California Press.

Smith, D. (2005) *On the margins of inclusion: changing labour markets and social exclusion in London*, Bristol: Policy Press.

Smith, D. (2008) *Sittingbourne Gypsy and Traveller survey*, Canterbury, Amacus Housing: CCCU.

Smith, D. and Greenfields, M. (2012) 'Housed Gypsies and Travellers in the UK: work, exclusion and adaptation', *Race and Class*, vol 53, no 3, pp 48–65.

Somerville, P. and Steele, A. (eds) (2002) *'Race', housing and social exclusion*, London: Jessica Kingsley.

Song, M. (2003) *Choosing ethnic identity*, Cambridge: Polity Press.

Southerton, D. (2002) 'Boundaries of 'us' and 'them': class, mobility and identification in a new town', *Sociology*, vol 36, no 1, pp 171–93.

Spectator, The (1935) 'The slum Gypsies', 29 March.

Stanley, B. (2002) *Memories of the marsh: a Traveller life in Kent*, South Chailey: R&TFHS.

Stedman Jones, G. (1974) 'Working-class culture and working-class politics in London 1870–1900: notes on the remaking of a working class', *Journal of Social History*, vol 7, no 4, pp 460–508.

Stedman Jones, G. (2002) *Outcast London: a study in the relations between classes in Victorian society*, Milton Keynes: Open University.

Stonewall (2003) *Profiles of prejudice: detailed summary of findings*, London: Stonewall.

Strathdee, R. (2005) *Social exclusion and the remaking of social networks*, Aldershot: Ashgate.

Suedfeld, P. (1997) 'Reactions to societal trauma: distress and/or eustress', *Political Psychology*, vol 18, no 4, December, pp 849–61.

Sutherland, A. (1975) *Gypsies: the hidden Americans*, Illinois: Waveland Press Inc.

Suttles, G. D. (1968) *The social order of the slum: ethnicity and territory in the inner city*, Chicago: University of Chicago Press.

Sztompka, P. (2000) 'Cultural trauma: the other face of social change', *European Journal of Social Theory*, vol 3, no 4, pp 449–66.

Sztompka, P. (2004) 'The trauma of social change', in J. C. Alexander et al *Cultural trauma and collective identity*, Berkely, CA: University of California Press.

Tam, H. (2005) 'The case for progressive solidarity', in M. Wetherell, M. Lafleche, and M. Berkely (eds) *Identity, ethnic diversity and community cohesion*, London: Sage.

Tatz, C. (2004) 'Aboriginal, Maori and Inuit youth suicide: avenues to alleviation?', *Australian Aboriginal Studies*, issue 2, pp 15–25.

Taylor, B. (2008) *A minority and the state: Travellers in Britain in the twentieth century*, Manchester: Manchester University Press.

Taylor, J. (2012) 'Plans to house London's poor in Stoke attacked as "social cleansing"', *The Independent*, 25 April.

Temple, B., et al (2005) *Learning to live together: developing communities with dispersed people seeking asylum*, York: Joseph Rowntree Foundation

Theron, L., et al (2011) 'A "day in the lives" of four resilient youths: cultural roots of resilience', *Youth and Society*, vol 43, no 3, pp 799–818.

Thomas, P.A. and Campbell, S. (1992) *Housing Gypsies*, Cardiff: Traveller Law Research Unit.

Thompson, E. P. (1968) *The making of the English working class*, London: Penguin.

Thomson, J. and Smith, A. (1877) *Street life in London*, London, Sampson Low, Searle and Rivington.

Tilly, C. (2005) 'The economic environment of housing: income inequality and insecurity', available at http://www.uml.edu/centers/cic/Research/Tilly_Research/Housing-Tilly%20chapter-GRBT106-2299G-01-020-037.pdf, accessed 2 July 2012.

Titley, G. (2008) *The politics of diversity in Europe*, Strasbourg: Council of Europe Publishing.

Tizard, B. and Phoenix, A. (2002) *Black, white or mixed race? Race and racism in the lives of young people of mixed parentage*, London: Routledge.

Valentine, C. A. (1968) *Culture and poverty: critique and counter proposals*, Chicago: University of Chicago Press.

Van Bochove, M. and Burgers, J. (2010) 'Disciplining the drifter: the domestication of Travellers in the Netherlands', *British Journal of Criminology*, vol 50, no 2, pp 206–21.

Van Cleemput, P. (2008) 'Health impact of Gypsy sites policy in the UK', *Social Policy and Society*, vol 7, part 1, January, pp 103–18.

Van den Berghe, P. L. (1981) *The ethnic phenomenon*, Connecticut: Greenwood Press.

Vermeesch, P. (2007) *The Romani movement: minority politics and ethnic mobilization in contemporary Central Europe*, USA: Berghahn Books.

Vertovec, S. (2004) 'Migrant transnationalism and modes of transformation', *International Migration Review*, vol 38, no 3, pp 970–1001.

Vesey-Fitzgerald, B. (1973) *Gypsies of Britain* (2nd edn), Newton Abbot: David and Charles.

Wacquant, L. (2008) *Urban outcasts: a comparative sociology of advanced marginality*, Cambridge: Polity.

Walsh, M. (2011) *Gypsy boy on the run*, London: Hodder & Stoughton Ltd.

Walter, B. (2001) *Outsiders inside: whiteness, place and Irish women*, London: Routledge.

Wangler, A. (2012) *Rethinking history, reframing identity: memory, generations and the dynamics of national identity in Poland*, Heidelberg: Springer VS.

Ward, C. (2002) *Cotters and squatters: housing's hidden history*, Nottingham: Five Leaves Publishing.

Warrington, C (2006) 'Gypsy and Traveller children ought to be engaged more by mainstream services', *Community Care*, 14 September.

Warwick, A. R. (1972) *The Pheonix suburb: a South London social history*, London: Blue Boar Press.

Waterson, M. (1997) 'I want more than green leaves for my children. Some developments in Gypsy/Traveller education 1970–1996', in T. Acton and G. Munday (eds) *Romani culture and Gypsy identity*, Hatfield: University of Hertfordshire Press.

Watt, P. (2008) 'Moving to a better place? Geographies of aspiration and anxiety in the Thames Gateway', in P. Cohen and M. J. Rustin (eds) *London's turning: the making of Thames Gateway*, Aldershot: Ashgate.

Watt, P. (2009) 'Living in an oasis: middle-class disaffiliation and selective belonging in an English suburb', *Environment and Planning*, vol 41, pp 2974–892.

Webster, C. (2007) *Understanding race and crime*, Buckinghamshire, Open University Press.

Webster, C. (2008) 'Marginalized white ethnicity, race and crime', *Theoretical Criminology*, vol 12, no 3, pp 293–312.

Wellman, B. and Wortley, S. (1990) 'Different strokes for different folks: community ties and social support', *The American Journal of Sociology*, vol 96, no 3, pp 558–88.

Weston, P. (2002) *South London odyssey*, Devon: Arthur H Stockwell Ltd.

White, J. (1986) *Campbell Bunk: the worst street in North London between the wars*, London: Routledge and Keegan Paul.

White, J. (2008) *London in the 19th century*, London: Vintage Books.

Willems, W. (1997) *In search of the true Gypsy: from enlightenment to final solution*, London: Frank Cass.

Willers, M. et al (2010) 'Facilitating the Gypsy and Traveller way of life in England and Wales through the courts'. Paper presented at *Romani mobilities in Europe: multidisciplinary perspectives*, Oxford University, 14 January.

Wilson, W. J. (1987) *The truly disadvantaged: the inner city, the underclass and public policy*, Chicago: University of Chicago Press.

Winstedt, E. O. (1913) 'The Gypsy coppersmiths invasion of 1911–1913', *Journal of the Gypsy Lore Society*, vol VI, pt 4, pp 244–302.

Winstedt, E. O. (1916) 'The Norwood Gypsies and their vocabulary', *Journal of the Gypsy Lore Society*, vol 9, pts 3–4, pp 129–64.

Wordie, J. R. (1983) 'The chronology of English inclosure', *The Economic History Review*, vol 36, no 4, pp 483–505.

Young, J. (1999) *The exclusive society*, London: Sage Publications.

Young, M. and Willmott, P. (1957) *Family and kinship in East London*, London: Penguin Books.

Zafirovski, M. (2007) *Liberal modernity and its adversaries: freedom, liberalism and anti-liberalism in the 21st century*, Leiden, Netherlands: Brill NV.

Zatta, J. D. (1988) 'Oral tradition and social context: language and cognitive structure among the Roma', in M. T. Salo (ed) *100 Years of Gypsy Studies: Publication No. 5*, Cheverley, MD: The Gypsy Lore Society.

Index